THE FAME MACHINE

THE
FAME MACHINE

*Book Reviewing
and Eighteenth-Century
Literary Careers*

FRANK DONOGHUE

Stanford University Press, Stanford, California
1996

Stanford University Press
Stanford, California
© 1996 by the Board of Trustees of the
Leland Stanford Junior University
Printed in the United States of America

CIP data are at the end of the book

Stanford University Press publications are
distributed exclusively by Stanford University Press
within the United States, Canada, Mexico, and
Central America; they are distributed exclusively
by Cambridge University Press throughout
the rest of the world.

To My Mother and the Memory of My Father

Acknowledgments

Part of Chapter 1 appeared under the title "Colonizing Readers: Review Criticism and the Formation of a Reading Public" in Ann Bermingham and John Brewer, eds., *The Consumption of Culture* (Routledge, 1995, pp. 53–73). Part of Chapter 2 appeared under the title "Laurence Sterne and the Fantasy of Individual Patronage" in *Biography* 18 (Spring 1995): 97–116. Part of Chapter 3 appeared as "'He Never Gives Us Nothing That's *Low*': Goldsmith's Plays and the Reviewers" in *ELH* 55 (Fall 1988): 665–84.

The idea for this book evolved out of graduate seminars with Leo Braudy and Jerome McGann, and it is to them that I owe my greatest intellectual debts. Ronald Paulson and Jerome Christensen inherited the project and supervised its progress as my dissertation. John Bender, W. B. Carnochan, and John Richetti offered valuable support at a later stage, and James Battersby helped me bring the book to completion. From the beginning until nearly the end, no one was a greater source of encouragement or a more insightful reader than Laura Levine. And though the lessons I have learned from them are not fully represented here, Stanley Fish, Allen Grossman, and especially Susan Staves have all influenced my thinking about literary studies in important ways.

Others who have read all or parts of the manuscript and who have offered valuable advice include Ann Bermingham, Elizabeth Bohls, John Brewer, Terry Lovell, Deidre Lynch, Elizabeth Renker, David Riede, Laura Rigal, William Walker, and Linda Zionkowski.

Before her untimely death, Carol Virginia Pohli did extraordinary work as my research assistant, and Chapters 1 and 5 were greatly enriched through her efforts. I regret that she will not see this book in print.

Finally, writing a book about the effects of book reviewers on authors encumbered me with a special set of oddly self-reflexive anxieties. Melanie Blackburn helped me keep all of them in perspective, and I am deeply grateful for her support.

Lowell, Massachusetts   F.D.
May 1994

I fancied myself placed in the yard of a large inn, in which there were an infinite number of waggons and stage-coaches. . . . Each vehicle had its inscription, shewing the place of its destination. On one I could read, *The pleasure stage-coach*; on another, *The waggon of industry*; on a third, *The vanity of whim*; and on a fourth, *The landau of riches*. I had some inclination to step into each of these, one after another; but I know not by what means I passed them by, and at last fixed my eye upon a small carriage, Berlin fashion, which seemed the most convenient vehicle at a distance in the world; and, upon my nearer approach, found it to be *The fame machine*.

—Oliver Goldsmith, *The Bee*,
no. 5 (November 1759)

Introduction

This study takes as its starting point the premise, by now common-place, that literary production in the eighteenth century existed in a kind of limbo, between an age of substantial aristocratic support and the fully developed literary market of the nineteenth century. Direct sponsorship of literary figures by the ~~nobility~~ failed to keep pace with a mushrooming population of writers, and this pattern reduced individual patronage to an insignificant fraction of literary sponsorship. Its place was taken by a variety of other more broadly based and indirect forms of patronage, such as publication by subscription and the open market. The exact date of the death of aristocratic patronage has been widely disputed. Various candidates are Johnson's triumphant pronouncement to Boswell in 1773, "We have done with patronage"; Johnson's earlier, famous letter to Chesterfield in 1755, in which Johnson berates the lord for his failure to support the *Dictionary*; or Pope's enterprising subscription project for his translation of the *Iliad* (1714), which freed him for life from the need of patrons. Peter Lindenbaum has recently suggested Milton as "an example of someone who began his career within the aristocratic patronage system and worked his way free of it."[1]

Even if one acknowledges the continued though much less important presence of aristocratic patronage, as time passed, the book trade increasingly transformed readers into the social group capable of conferring fame upon authors. Whereas the patron was, in theory at least, a known entity whose expectations as a reader were predictable, the expectations of the consuming public of the eighteenth century rapidly became too extensive and varied to comprehend or characterize easily. The expansion of the reading public made it very difficult for authors to determine whether they were successful, except in a purely material sense. By midcentury, readers could no longer be enumerated, either as people receiving a privately circulated manuscript or as names on a subscription list. Their large numbers and the volume of copies that reached them made specific assessments of their constitution and interests impossible. The most urgent question for the eighteenth-century book trade became how to identify and cater to the tastes of this increasing plurality of readers.[2]

My argument operates on the assumption that this transformation of the conditions of literary production precipitated a crisis among aspiring authors. By midcentury they had neither a clear index of literary fame (such as affiliation with a patron had once bestowed) nor a way to specify the relationship of one piece of their writing to the next (since market demands so greatly influenced what they chose to write). The most forceful steps toward making sense of these transformed conditions were taken not by individual authors but rather by the periodical culture that increasingly came to dominate the literary scene in ways that are still not fully appreciated. Excluding newspapers, there were more than 30 different periodicals published in London in 1745. By 1755, that number had increased to more than 50, and by 1765 to more than 75.[3]

Thus, by midcentury or shortly after, periodicals as a collective were a central cultural presence, one uniquely suited to the vagaries of the open market in which they, along with nearly all other literary productions, were situated. For, whatever their particular agendas, periodicals necessarily lead a different "social life" than do books.[4] They can be responsive both to changing public events and circumstances and to the needs and desires of their readers. Individual issues are ephemeral, yet periodicals that last long enough are not only preserved as bound volumes, but take on the status of institutions to an extent that is unavailable to books. Because they are less expensive than books, periodicals can potentially reach a broader and more diverse audience than any other literary productions. To cite a representative example: the sale of 6,500 copies of *Joseph Andrews* (1742) in three editions was rightly celebrated as an unprecedented success for a novel. But England's most popular periodical of the time, the *Gentleman's Magazine,* issued 3,500 copies every month.

My observations build on a long history of valuable scholarship that describes English periodical culture, but it is not my intention to duplicate those descriptions here. Rather, I am interested in the relationship between periodicals, the quintessential market-driven literary phenomena, and authorship, the changing conception of which was chiefly a function of that market as well. Accordingly, I have limited the scope of my account of periodicals to popular criticism and, for the most part, have chosen to focus on the two successful midcentury journals, the *Monthly Review* and the *Critical Review,* which dedicated themselves exclusively to reviewing new publications. Though I have drawn what are in a sense narrow boundaries for my inquiry, I do not underestimate the importance of the many kinds of periodicals, including newspapers, that I do not directly treat. Each magazine represents a different voice, each interpellates and tries to energize a different audience in an extensive and influential popular conversation, and each individual magazine's voice is strengthened by the prominence of periodical culture as a whole.

In my examination of the politics of the emergent literary marketplace, I argue that authorship became increasingly defined in popular criticism, and that from 1750 onward, literary careers were chiefly described, and indeed made possible, by reviewers. The *Monthly,* founded in 1749, and the *Critical,* founded in 1756, projected themselves as sole arbiters of literary production. They claimed to represent the interest of the elite among the English reading public and to articulate those interests in their review articles. From this privileged position, they supplied the plots for a variety of literary careers.

Though it is usual to think of a career as a natural phenomenon or as a simple function of capitalism, I have sought to emphasize instead the ways in which careers are a product of interpretation. In contrast to sociologists who have tended to see careers as largely self-determined by the professionals who live them out, I assert that a career is a narrative that cannot be authored entirely by its own subject.⁵ Indeed, careers are worked out against a variety of powerful and often oppressive institutional constraints. In the cases of Sterne, Goldsmith, and Smollett, these constraints were tangible: all three turned to writing after other career paths became untenable. Sterne constantly felt pressure from his various audiences to produce novelty after novelty. Smollett and Goldsmith labored against, respectively, anti-Scottish and anti-Irish prejudice on the London cultural scene.⁶ Other writers faced other kinds of resistance. Indeed, the late eighteenth century is replete with examples of the struggle between writer and reviewer for the authority to describe the shape of the writer's efforts. Out of this very struggle, which is also, paradoxically, an uneasy collaboration, emerge the literary history, literary biography, and established canons that are the hallmarks of later-eighteenth-century letters.

In Chapter 1 I describe what I will call the institution of critical reading. Following Raymond Williams's discussion of the word "institution" in *Keywords*, I examine the range of rhetorical strategies by which the two major Reviews turned the process of critical reading into "something apparently objective and systematic."⁷ The audience for this rhetoric consisted, obviously, of authors and readers, but in practice these groups clearly overlapped: readers were sometimes authors, all authors were readers. The Reviews' polemical purposes were best advanced by artificially separating them, since the phantom of the English reading public was an ever present but always silent variable in the discourses of author and reviewer alike, and each used a partisan representation of the "public in general" as its chief warrant for claims to supremacy. Both authors and reviewers feared that their position in the literary world might be seriously jeopardized if that public turned out to be either an enemy or an uncontrollable mob, or if it appropriated books in a way that lay beyond the control of authorial intention or critical authority. I explore, in other words, the variety of polemical purposes to which this public is available for both authors and critics, as well as the less tangible ways in which the public seemed to assert a will of its own. The pages of the *Monthly* and the *Critical* were an important battleground on which the war to determine refined taste in a consumer society was waged.

In the context of this account of the politics of mid-eighteenth-century letters in which conflict is exploited by reviewers and authors, I examine the careers of three very different major writers. Laurence Sterne's first literary work was published (in 1760) when he was 46 years old. A latecomer to the professional literary scene, Sterne had to learn all of its conventions by trial and error. During the course of his career, he displayed the full range of authorial attitudes toward the Reviews, from happy ignorance of their importance, to denial of their influence, to a complex concession to their power to determine the course of his writing.

Oliver Goldsmith offers a case in which the Reviews ultimately took their cue from an experienced professional author. Against the backdrop of his sophisticated critique of cultural authority (worked out in several texts during the 1760s), Goldsmith waged a self-conscious battle with critics to decide the terms in which his two plays (his last major works) would be discussed. By means of the preface to *The Good-Natur'd Man* (1768), the "Comparison Between Laughing and Sentimental Comedy," and *She Stoops to Conquer* (1773) itself, Goldsmith implicitly urged critics to adopt *his* terms in their reviews of contemporary comedy. He succeeded: both supporters and detractors of *She Stoops to Conquer* took positions that Goldsmith himself had characterized, and the entire critical controversy aided the success of the play. Goldsmith's career aptly illustrates both the dialectical nature of the author-reviewer relationship and the ways in which that relationship could be worked out to the advantage of an author rather than a critic.

Tobias Smollett, as both an author of fiction and the editor of the *Critical Review*, occupied a unique position in the relationship between the institutions of writer and reviewer. Smollett's anxieties as an author arise from his first literary venture, a nine-year-long unsuccessful struggle to have his tragedy, *The Regicide*, produced on the London stage. After abandoning this attempt in the mid-1740s, he turned to novel writing where, I argue, he articulated his ordeal as a playwright in a series of plots about naïfs (Roderick Random, Peregrine Pickle, Ferdinand Count Fathom) who strive to gain admission to powerful elite social circles, such as the London theatrical establishment had been for Smollett. But after he became editor of the *Critical* in 1756, his interests as novelist changed drastically. Once he established himself in a position of great influence in the literary world, his narratives—*Launcelot Greaves* (1760), *Travels through France and Italy* (1766), and *Humphry Clinker* (1771)—begin to deal with the various ways of maintaining a social power that is now conceived of as internal. Smollett became deeply interested, particularly after he left the *Critical* in 1763, in the ways in which power could be conserved through the manipulation of conventions of writing.

My final chapter addresses, as a distinct issue, the problem of literary careers for women. Impediments to women's professional achievement were compounded in the literary world, where women authors had to defend constantly the unladylike decision to write for publication. I do not intend to rewrite the history of women's participation in literary culture, important aspects of which have been insightfully addressed in recent studies by Nancy Armstrong, Terry Lovell, and Kathryn Shevelow.[8] I wish, instead, to underscore the particular difficulty women experienced not only in writing professionally, but in having a professional life story analogous to those of successful male writers. The major Reviews simply evaluated women's writing by a different, less demanding standard, and they thereby deprived female authors of the same fame they purported to confer upon men. I explore various strategies (none of them entirely successful) employed by women authors to overcome these problems, and I culminate my discussion by examining Frances Burney's rhetorically ingenious dedication of her first novel to "the Authors of the *Monthly* and *Critical Review*."

All of these cases illustrate a great deal theoretically about possible relations between author and critic, and about the process by which authors acquire their credentials. As each of them makes clear, not only is the model for authorship at midcentury dynamic, but the relations between authors and the critics who in effect predict their careers are highly volatile as well, liable to be resolved in favor of author as well as critic. This vitally unstable state of affairs is the consequence of a comprehensive professionalization of literary production and reception, and is one signal of the beginnings of a consumer culture.

I have, of necessity, told only part of the story of the professionalization of eighteenth-century letters. I have excluded poets and philosophers as specialists whose relationships with the literary market in general and with the Reviews in particular unfolded along their own distinctive lines. Perhaps more controversially, I have excluded Samuel Johnson. Though I would hardly contest his importance as a literary figure, those scholars who make him the centerpiece and title character (the "Age of Johnson") of their studies run the risk of leaving the impression that he was somehow typical of professional writers at the time. One cannot help being mesmerized, as are all of his biographers, by Johnson's ability to overcome repeatedly the limiting conditions of professional authorship. Retelling the anecdotes that attest to the curious blend of idiosyncrasy and heroism that enabled Johnson to succeed is an irresistible urge. But to dwell on Johnson as a hero can lead one to forget how unique a figure he was, and can thereby skew a literary history of his time. Johnson's life of writing began before the founding of the *Monthly* and the *Critical*, and he quickly reached so prominent a place on the literary scene of his day that he did not need their validation of his work. Moreover, his three most significant projects, the *Dictionary*, the edition of Shakespeare, and the *Prefaces, Biographical and Critical, to the Works of the English Poets*, all adopt a transcendent perspective on literary culture. So, for the purposes of this study, I have somewhat reluctantly set Johnson aside in order to concentrate on three authors who led more ordinary professional lives.

Finally, I have excluded the first half of the eighteenth century, a period that is perhaps equally important to the development of the literary career as the one I consider here. The notion of a literary career defines a vastly different public identity in the seventeenth and early eighteenth century than during the lifetimes of Sterne, Goldsmith, and Smollett. The Renaissance ideal of the laureate, so skillfully described by Richard Helgerson in *Self-Crowned Laureates: Spenser, Johnson, Milton and the Literary System*, entailed a cultural version of the Roman *cursus honorum*, a static pattern of preordained literary accomplishments that culminated in the composition of an epic poem.[9] The predominance of aristocratic or state patronage exempted authors from the demands of an open market. In theory at least, an author wrote only for one reader (Elizabeth, for example, in Spenser's case). The successful author in the seventeenth century could, again in theory at least, imagine all of his literary productions as fully integrated in advance. There were no careers at all in the nineteenth-century sense of career as narrative; there were only composites of a lifetime's accomplishment that were either complete or incomplete.[10]

As the influence of aristocratic patronage began to wane toward the end of the seventeenth century, the ideal of the laureate was atomized under the pressure of an expanding literary economy, and the possibility of organizing one's literary productions along the classical patterns supplied by Virgil and Horace disappeared. There ensued a period of curious instability, during which Alexander Pope, struggling to recreate the now obsolete cultural *cursus honorum*, coexisted with the likes of Daniel Defoe, who wrote whatever he could sell. During the first decades of the eighteenth century, the emergent formal division between "serious" and other kinds of writing is strikingly illustrated by trends such as the increasing popularity of prose fiction (and other narratives we might classify as prenovelistic—criminal biography, for example).[11] It is also apparent from the enormous gap that separated Pope and Swift, the conservators of the old traditions, from Defoe and others like him who made no secret of being authors cum entrepreneurs. Swift mentions Defoe and John Tutchin, author of the *Observator*, as "two illiterate scribblers, both of them fanatics by profession."[12] Pope places Defoe in the *Dunciad*: "Earless on high, stood un-abash'd Defoe."[13]

Both comments are ironized by Swift's status as Defoe's chief rival propagandist and Pope's consummate skill in marketing his own work. Swift and Pope disguise their own connections with booksellers and associate Defoe with the vulgarity and dangers of promiscuous publication. And indeed, Defoe had been pilloried in 1703 for a piece of hired writing, *The Shortest Way with Dissenters*. Defoe, in turn, worked completely unself-consciously, with no aspirations to a literary career. In effect, he had no conception of authorship, but was, as Pope correctly described, unabashedly driven by market demand. The incongruous coexistence of these two kinds of literary practice, each standing in a different relation to increasingly powerful market influences, became clarified as the century progressed, helped in part by the relationship between professional authors and the *Monthly* and the *Critical*. That relationship contributed, as I will argue, to the realization of a new kind of literary career.

I envision this study as contributing to two broader fields of inquiry, one currently receiving considerable attention, the other not yet sufficiently explored. First, I hope to challenge the reigning understanding of print and the expanding print culture of the eighteenth century. In a trenchant critique of the dominant assumptions about the history of print, Michael Warner makes the following observation:

Most of the historians who work in the burgeoning field of the history of the book, and most people who speculate on the place of print in history . . . suppose printing to be a nonsymbolic form of material reality. Printing, in this view, is naturally distinct from rhetoric . . . and from forms of subjectivity. . . . It is mere technology, a medium itself unmediated. There are two main advantages to this set of premises: first, it guarantees that there will be a single object of study, despite vast and frequent changes in the world of culture; and second, it allows one to trace the effects of print within culture by bracketing cultural history itself, since it guarantees that the effects of printing will have a progressive teleology.[14]

As Warner goes on to demonstrate, this account fails to recognize that the development of print culture does not offer an answer but rather invites a host of questions, all following from the problem of why such a change should occur. The book trade did not expand because printing technology made books accessible to thousands of readers. It expanded in response to a demand for a variety of books other than those that had long been universally accessible (the Bible, *Pilgrim's Progress*, or Richard Baxter's religious tracts, for example). In part, this study attempts to describe the nuances of that demand, though it can only be traced imperfectly by the popularity of what was published. It is safe to say, though, that the vaguely discernible desires of the bookbuying public terrified authors and reviewers alike.

The second "advantage" Warner ascribes to the dominant theories about print is especially seductive because of its compatibility with progressive (Whig) notions of political history. The prevalent theory about the literature of the eighteenth century perceives the expansion of the book trade as a kind of pure progress, a simple democratization of reading. It marks for many a key step in the homogenization of English social and cultural classes. I argue that this picture is inaccurate. The very presence of the Reviews suggests that the growing reading public was perceived by many as a serious threat to social stability. The reviewers attempted to police the relations between that new variety of readers, the books they were buying, and the authors of those books. The extreme version of this role, as captured by an early-nineteenth-century American journalist, was the self-image of "the reviewer as executioner," in which "the office of reviewer . . . in the republic of letters" is described "as beneficial and necessary, though as odious and unpleasant, as that of an executioner in the civil state."[15]

The conflict between a cultural elite and the masses does not disappear at all; indeed, during the period I examine the battle lines between them are redrawn for a more urgent struggle. This issue is still relevant today, and one could easily pursue it in its present popular manifestations: "cultural literacy" can only be defined in relation to some kind of philistinism, refined taste only in relation to vulgar taste, high culture only in relation to popular culture. These are, significantly, always political discriminations, and this book tries to show who made them and how.

Second, I would like to contribute to the more slowly growing debate about the relationship of biography and criticism.[16] My aims in this study are broadly biographical, in that I give relatively little space to thematic analysis of texts and instead devote most of my efforts to analyzing the processes by which these three writers came to have their lives as public figures written for them. To argue this as convincingly as possible, I have moved in my discussion from what I consider one major phase of each author's life to the next (as a biographer would), and have included as much factual detail as I needed to make my claims understandable. Yet were this study to be examined according to the traditional standards by which the scholarly community evaluates biography, it would be found sadly wanting. It presents no original factual information—not surprising, since I did not do the kind of research that makes up the biographer's daily work.

Though they move chronologically, these chapters do so in a hap-hazard way, spending a great deal of time exploring some key moments and texts in the lives of these three authors, yet leaving many unexcused gaps as well: none of these case studies is complete in the way one would expect from a biography. Finally, and perhaps most heretically, I have not made my subjects, Sterne, Goldsmith, and Smollett, the heroes of my narratives, but instead have made it the goal of my narratives to show how these subjects are assembled.

One of my hopes is that this study will illumine the institutional boundaries that have for recent generations increasingly separated biography from literary studies. Those two disciplines now have a strikingly different set of values, emphases, and methods. This in-compatibility is especially, and ironically, troubling in eighteenth-century studies because biography forms the foundation of literary criticism as it emerged during that period. Biography and criticism are crucially interdependent in Johnson's *Lives of the Poets* (1784). These introductions, which cemented in place the literary canon of the previous century, rarely deviate from the pattern of a biographical sketch, followed by a critical survey of the author's work. In all of the major lives, there is considerable interconnection between the two, a characteristic that, far from troubling Johnson, served as his chief principle of composition.

But beginning with Boswell's *Life of Johnson*, published just seven years later, in 1791, we can witness a shift in priority, the de-velopment of a new aim of presenting the facts of the author's life as accurately and completely as possible. In Boswell's case there is an urge to make his subject's life even *more* complete than it otherwise might have been—take, for example, his successful staging of a meeting between Johnson and John Wilkes, so that the archconservative could have a conversation with his radical nemesis. And though the eccentricity of the *Life of Johnson* makes it an anomaly, ostensibly unrelated to the literary biographies that followed, Boswell's fanat-ical drive for factual accuracy pointed the way toward what biography would eventually become.[17]

The enormous influence of Boswell's *Life* as a model or at least an inspiration for life writing, combined with the development of literary studies as a discipline in our own century, has conspired to turn the genre of biography into the last bastion of positivism. This depreciation owes a great deal, it seems to me, to New Criticism, which, as a movement that pervaded literary studies, rendered biography an unnecessary or even, in the most extreme applications, an undesirable element in the interpretation of literary texts.[18] As biography and criticism began to drift apart, appearing to operate independently of each other, biographers and critics developed very different standards of excellence. The aims of criticism in the American academy evolved from humanistic appreciation to intellectually rigorous and nuanced analysis. Biography has aimed since the heyday of New Criticism at a different kind of rigor, that of factual accuracy. While never relinquishing the nineteenth-century ideal of capturing the essence of an important person and through that person, the spirit of an age (shared by Hazlitt, Macaulay, Carlyle, and Emerson), biographers from the mid–twentieth century to the present adopted a relentless "just the facts" approach that tended to yield a curious kind of book: virtually unreadable as a narrative, yet virtually indispensable as a reference.

To put the problem in another way: "facts," "accuracy," and "completeness" are highly problematic in academic literary criticism because they are the very grounds of contention. Indeed, the critic's modus vivendi is to challenge the accuracy and completeness of everyone else's treatment of whatever subject he or she has chosen to consider. The effect is an environment where interpretation is preeminent, and "the facts" are precisely what are always in question. In contrast to criticism's relentless skepticism, biography is necessarily epistemologically naive—in order to proceed, the biographer must presuppose a subject whose identity is continuous and who lives in a historical world, the details of which are unproblematically specifiable. Traditional biography cannot discuss its hero's subjectivity as ambiguous, cannot engage in any kind of speculative historiography, cannot do anything that might disrupt the fiction of a stable identity existing without complication in time. To do so would be to unravel the very account that the biographer attempts to put together.

The turn toward historicism in literary studies during the 1980s, the foundation for which is the work of Michel Foucault, has predictably, if ironically, deepened rather than closed the chasm between criticism and biography. For the advocates of historical criticism in our time, the facts of history that had once been conceived as the grounds of interpretation are now perceived as themselves the products of interpretation. But biography has continued all the while to be informed by the same positivist assumptions about history that had directed the older historicism. One might imagine that this sharp difference of opinion about the status of history would receive a great deal of attention, particularly since it plays into the more volatile debate about the place of critical theory in literary studies today. But in fact this has not been the case, and nowhere is the silence more apparent than in the response to the publication, during the 1980s, of several biographies of major eighteenth-century authors: Maynard Mack's *Alexander Pope: A Life* (1986), Arthur Cash's *Laurence Sterne: The Later Years* (1987), James Winn's *John Dryden and His World* (1987), Margaret Doody's *Frances Burney: The Life in the Works* (1988), Paula Backscheider's *Daniel Defoe: His Life* (1989), and Martin Battestin's *Henry Fielding* (1989). Each of these is generally recognized as a magisterial effort by a major figure in the field. Each has been privately chided for its old-fashioned critical methods by the very scholars who will rely upon these biographies any time they write as thematic critics about Sterne or Pope or Dryden or Defoe.

This uneasy coexistence continues because, as almost every academic critic would assent, literary biographies are necessary aids to their own work. Biographers establish the canons of authors whose works critics then scrupulously and self-consciously interpret; these critical revaluations in turn find their way into the next generation of biographies, and so on. But if it is difficult to imagine a radical separation between these seemingly incompatible disciplines, it has also proved extremely difficult to combine them in the same scholarly work. Perhaps the most ambitious attempt to forge a relationship between thematic criticism and biography yet to appear, Jerome Christensen's *Practicing Enlightenment: Hume and the Formation of a Literary Career* (1987), mortified those whose methodologies might be aligned with traditional biography, and mystified many of those scholars who might have been expected to welcome it. Even Christensen's daring move into the no-man's-land between traditional biography and criticism is prefaced by the humble qualification that without Ernest Mossner's standard biography of Hume, his own study "would have been unwritten, indeed, unthought."[19]

In the face of this crucial yet unstable and usually unstated relationship, I have tried in this book to forge one possible path for a new biography that might enable traditional biographers and critics to recognize the institutional nature of their mutual alienation and to see at least some of the shared features of their inquiries. My study is underwritten throughout by broad questions about how literary biography, the account of authors' public lives, comes into being and develops. Because I wish to make the important case studies that I consider as persuasive as possible, and because I do not proceed into the nineteenth century, my answers are necessarily incomplete. Who writes literary biography and with what motives? How are the criteria by which the biographer delineates his subject established? Most importantly, what determines the way a biographer defines the relationship between the author and his or her work? These questions go a long way toward determining our own understanding of authorship, and in doing so, largely determine how we organize our reading and teaching of literature. I have chosen to address them at the earliest possible stage of the modern period. Rather than considering the genre of literary biography as it emerged in the late eighteenth and nineteenth centuries, by which time the conventions for describing authors' lives had become formalized, I examine instead the process by which those conventions were invented and deployed in the periodical criticism of the mid–eighteenth century.

Literary biography and the literary career are interdependent. As Magali Larson says, "While biography is looking backward on one's life, an after the fact search for order and meaning, career is looking forward, with a sense of order to come." That is, careers often supply the paradigms upon which biographies are eventually written. This book suggests a way to describe the present, so to speak, in this subtle relationship between future and past through which author's professional lives enter history. No one during this period captures the mystery of this (distinctly modern) process better than Goldsmith, in the image of the fame machine that supplies me with my title. The image suggests that during this period the nature of literary fame was re-conceived in significant ways: it was, in Goldsmith's terms, deper-sonalized and mechanized; as Larson says in general of the emergent category of the professional, careers became "crucially dependent on the stability of institutions."[20]

The "Resverie," in which Goldsmith describes the fame machine, relates the story of a coach ride that includes several stops at which several authors, ranging in prominence from the hyperprolific John Hill to Samuel Johnson, come aboard (Smollett is among them). Goldsmith promised a conclusion to the narrative, the first half of which appeared in the fifth issue of *The Bee*, a weekly journal of six-teen octavo pages written almost entirely by Goldsmith himself. But *The Bee* lasted for only three more numbers, and thus the passengers on the fame machine never reached their unspecified destinations. The suspended narrative, appearing as it does in one of many mid-eighteenth-century journals that failed, is a fitting reminder of the kind of celebrity this book tries to describe, one that is imbricated in periodical culture, vulnerable to market demand, and extremely tenuous.

Review Criticism and Reading

1749–75

The act of consulting the *Monthly* and *Critical Reviews* is a commonplace of mid- and later-eighteenth-century literary biography,
memoirs, and letters:

This morning the *Critical Review* on our *Letters between the Hon. Erskine
and James Boswell* came out, and in great form did we read it. They did not
use us with candour, but they were less abusive than we imagined they might
be. (James Boswell, 1763)

Pray send to Sheffield for the last *Monthly Review*; there is a deal of stuff
about us and Mr. Colman. (Letter from Thomas Gray to William Mason,
1760)

My first publication, "Village Memoirs," (1761) was praised by the *Critical*
and *Monthly* Reviewers, who were unwilling, perhaps, to discourage a
young beginner. (Joseph Craddock)[1]

The popularity of these two journals was so considerable that many
authors would routinely check them whenever they or someone they
knew had just published a book. This custom developed over a remarkably short period of time. Before 1749, when the *Monthly* was
founded, consulting reviews was not a common recourse: the significance and consequences of a reviewer's opinion (if he even offered
one) were impossible to gauge. Henry Fielding, in *Tom Jones*, could
claim with impunity in 1749 that he was a better judge of his work
than "any pitiful critic whatever," and could warn "all those critics
to mind their own business, and not to intermeddle with affairs

or works, which no ways concern them: for till they produce the authority by which they are constituted judges, I shall plead their jurisdiction."[2]

But by 1767 the *Monthly* and the *Critical* were significant enough to merit discussion in the famous interview between Samuel Johnson and George III.[3] In 1778 Frances Burney dedicated her first novel, *Evelina*, to the editors of the *Monthly* and the *Critical*. And by 1812, Lord Byron, anxiously awaiting news of the reception of the first two cantos of *Childe Harold's Pilgrimage*, referred to the editors of the influential Reviews of his day, the *Edinburgh* and the *Quarterly*, as the "monarch-makers in poetry and prose."[4] A period, then, of a little more than 70 years witnessed the appearance of Reviews on the cultural landscape, authors' initial resistance to them, and a rapid ascendency that placed such journals, in Byron's perhaps exaggerated metaphor, at the top of the literary hierarchy, reputedly determining whether authors succeed or fail.

The obvious question, of course, is how did this happen? This chapter examines the foundations and consequences of the cultural authority that the Reviews acquired during the second half of the eighteenth century: how, in other words, they helped transform critical reading from a process or practice into an institution. It is a given that the increasing commercialization of literary production makes eighteenth-century literary culture fundamentally different from that of earlier periods, but all of the differences have yet to be explored adequately.[5] One of my general premises is that the expansion of book production and what one might call the reading trade created a complementary market for uniform standards, norms, guidelines—in short, for a means of discerning order in what was perceived to be an overwhelming proliferation of printed matter. This process took place amid, and itself fostered a diffusion of power in, the cultural field. Eighteenth-century literature increasingly became the scene of many competing claims to cultural authority. Authors sought to redefine their practice as a profession rather than a trade; readers, an expanding consumer market, indirectly exerted considerable influence on the shape of the literary commerce; and reviewers sought to police both the production and consumption of literature.

No sooner were the Reviews founded than they immediately entered into this general debate over the most pressing questions that followed from the mass production of literature and the expansion of the reading public that constituted a crucial part of what John Brewer, Neil McKendrick, and J. H. Plumb have called the "consumer revolution."[6] First, could there be a single standard of taste in an increasingly pluralistic class of readers? Who, if anyone, could presume the authority to identify and enforce it? Where would such authority be grounded—in some essentialist aesthetic? In popular opinion? Second, what value is to be placed on originality in an age in which reproducibility has become an economic imperative?[7] Third, how is one to conceive of the author-reader relationship once it has clearly outgrown the Renaissance model of a one-to-one correspondence?

When an author no longer thinks of himself as writing for a patron, for the members of a coterie, or for those on a subscription list, he may be paralyzed by an uncertainty about his audience's expectations and desires. Or, he may feel that he knows those expectations too well, and despair that they all but dictate his task. The increasingly numbing similarity in the plot lines of a great many popular novels illustrates this point. These questions had become urgent and confusing by midcentury, both contributing to and issuing from a vacuum of cultural authority in the field of literature. This chapter charts the Reviews' attempts to step in and exercise decisive authority in ways that quickly became accepted in literary culture as part of the status quo.[8]

Scholarship about the Reviews has thus far moved in a different direction, tending toward either identifying the reviewers or identifying the journals' organizing critical principles. Scholars working along these lines have brought to light valuable information, but their work runs the risk of misrepresenting the nature of eighteenth-century popular criticism. B. C. Nangle's *Indexes of Contributors to the Monthly* operates on the assumption that Reviews are primarily valuable to us as the work of individual writers. By identifying as many of these contributors as possible, one can begin to reconstruct a kind of specialized literary community. But by concentrating on this dimension of review criticism, one can easily lose sight of the institutional character of the *Monthly* and the *Critical*, of their capacity to take on identities independent of those contributors. This capacity, and much of the influence wielded by the Reviews, derives from their policy of anonymity, from the fact that their judgments did not issue from individuals, but rather came directly and impersonally from the journals themselves. The effect of the practice of anonymous reviews cannot be underestimated and is a prominent complaint in many attacks on the journals. Recovery of the authors of the reviews is important, but can easily mislead us about the dynamics of the author-reviewer relationships.

Attempts to describe the critical principles of the early Reviews arise, it seems to me, out of a commendable desire to demonstrate the consistency and intelligence of the criticism in the *Monthly* and the *Critical*. These scholars often wish to bring reviewing into line with more familiar eighteenth-century critical practice. In doing so, they help lay to rest the unflattering myths about the Reviews that originate in contemporary attacks and that continue to inform scholarship and literary biography throughout the nineteenth and much of the twentieth century—that the reviewers were unscrupulous, untrained hacks, who wrote in the service of booksellers, puffed their own work and that of their friends, used the Reviews as a forum for secret attacks on their enemies, and so on. In the process of rehabilitating the Reviews as serious intellectual projects, however, scholars who search for unifying principles are mistakenly treating the journals as homogeneous text, almost as if the *Monthly* or the *Critical* constituted a single book. Thus they also tend to overlook the institutional and professional characteristics that made the Reviews flexible, adaptable, and responsive to developments in literary society.[9]

In my effort to situate eighteenth-century literary careers in the important material context of review criticism, I will not attempt to rewrite the history of the *Monthly* and the *Critical*. Rather, I will focus in this chapter on the dynamic relationships among reviewers, authors, and readers that came to the forefront once the Reviews entered the literary scene. For the *Monthly* and the *Critical* constantly sought to define each other, and to specify the protocols for writing and reading for the mid-eighteenth century. I will look in particular at the ideologies of reading that underlay each Review, at the rhetoric by which the reviewers legitimated their practices as a profession, at the capacity of readers to undermine the authority of the reviewers as self-appointed arbiters of taste, and finally at the thematics of authors' attacks on Reviews. In each of these areas, I will not aim (as the Reviews themselves did) for comprehensiveness, but rather will examine representative issues and problems in these journals, so that their crucial role in the careers of Sterne, Goldsmith, and Smollett can be more easily understood.

I

A traditional history of review criticism would very likely trace the ancestry of the *Monthly* and the *Critical* to the abstract journals (both in England and France) of the seventeenth century, which surveyed contemporary publications for the benefit of intellectuals, and the essays of Addison and Steele, which in part sought to shape or create the cultural tastes of their readers.[10] To say, however, that the midcentury reviewing mode may in some general way have been a hybrid of the styles and aims of periodicals such as the *Journal des Sçavans* and the *Spectator* does not account for the success of the *Monthly* and the *Critical*. Nor, indeed, does the history of book reviewing in England during the first half of the century. The Reviews published between 1700 and 1749 were all short-lived, a fact usually taken as a sign of a weak and precarious demand for books. The bookseller Michael de La Roche started three abstract journals, none of which ran for more than four years: *Memoirs of Literature* (1710–14), *New Memoirs of Literature* (1725–27), and *The Literary Journal*, a quarterly publication that ran for only a few issues in 1730–31. Perhaps the most successful of these early Reviews was *The Present State of the Republic of Letters*, edited by Andrew Reid, which ran from 1728 to 1736. Though it chiefly treated classic authors, it did review Thomson's *Spring* in May 1728.[11]

Just before midcentury, however, a flurry of reviewing activity and planning of Review journals occurred, marking a vital turning point in the English literary trade's perception of its public. A chronology of this activity suggests a remarkable similarity among the projects being undertaken:

December 1748: Several members of a literary club gathered around Edward Cave, editor of the *Gentleman's Magazine*, began planning a journal that would "give an impartial account of *every* work published, in a 12d. monthly pamphlet" to be called the *Monthly Review*.[12] The journal never materialized.

February 1749: A group of professional writers under the direction of the bookseller Ralph Griffiths (and completely unconnected with Cave) produced the first issue of their journal, also titled the *Monthly Review*, the first English periodical devoted exclusively to reviewing.

March 1751: The *Gentleman's Magazine*, which had, since its inception in 1731, simply listed in each issue books published during the previous month, began to include descriptive commentary in that list, a move that was most likely a compromise on Cave's original plan for an independent Review. Since the *Gentleman's* had the largest circulation of any English magazine (roughly 3,000 copies a month were sold in 1746), this change reached a great many readers.[13]

December 1755: Within one week of each other, advertisements appeared for two more journals devoted solely to reviewing—the *Critical Review*, founded by Tobias Smollett, and the *Literary Magazine*, founded by Samuel Johnson. Smollett's Review went on to become the foremost competitor of the *Monthly*, while Johnson's, compiled entirely by himself, failed in 1758.

January 1762: The *London Magazine*, chief competitor of the *Gentleman's*, began offering brief reviews in its own monthly register of newly published books. It too had previously only listed them.

Of these, the *Monthly* and the *Critical* had the most significant, lasting impact on literary culture. Although the *Gentleman's* and the *London* continued to offer a monthly selection of reviews, the *Monthly* and the *Critical* were referred to simply as "the two Reviews." As Antonia Forster observes, "The judgments delivered elsewhere were not important. Indeed, one could read thirty attacks on reviewers from this period [1749–75] and not even discover the existence of reviewing in any other journals than the leading ones."[14]

It is not an exaggeration to say that this sweeping reconception of the practice of reviewing affected virtually everyone in the English reading public: these were the most popular magazines of the time, printed in very large numbers with each copy reaching several readers. Although a few scholars have recognized the suddenness and scope of this transformation, no one has adequately explained its significance. Rather, it has been subsumed by critics from A. S. Collins in *Authorship in the Days of Doctor Johnson* (1927) to Alvin Kernan in *Printing Technology, Letters, and Samuel Johnson* (1987) into the standard story of the democratization of reading.[15] That story, in short, is that Review journals and magazines that began reviewing books were answering a fast-developing need in the literary marketplace. By midcentury, so the argument goes, even the most literate readers could no longer keep up with the profusion of printed matter available to them. They were drowning in a newly born but rapidly growing information culture. More inexperienced readers, by the same token, were thrown into a situation in which they could not possibly make intelligent choices—there was simply too much from which to choose. A passage from Samuel Johnson's private notebooks epitomizes this need. Boswell relates the following: "In one of his little memorandum-books I find the following hints for his intended Review or Literary Journal: '*The Annals of Literature, foreign as well as domestick*. Imitate LeClerk—Bayle—Barbeyrac. Infelicity of Journals in England. Works of the Learned. We cannot take in all.' "[16]

The assumptions underlying this standard story need to be brought to light and evaluated, since they have spawned several examples of what Henry Knight Miller has called the Whig interpretation of literary history.[17] There is, it must be noted, some validity to Johnson's anxieties and the story that Kernan and others have constructed around them. There *was* an enormous increase in the volume of printed matter during the second half of the eighteenth century. Kernan cites studies that point out the increase in the number of printing presses in London from 65 in 1668 (licensed and strictly controlled by the state) to 625 in 1818.[18] He finds corroboration for his argument as well in C. J. Mitchell's study of eighteenth-century printing, which records 7,605 books printed in London during the decade 1741–50, and 16,243 for the decade 1791–1800.[19] Lance Bertelsen's account of paper wars during the 1750s and 1760s also conveys the impression that the London reading public was overwhelmed by the printed word.[20]

But "Whig literary history," of which Kernan is the most recent and most influential proponent, presents the expansion of the reading public in the eighteenth century as an inevitable, "natural" process, uninformed by ideological concerns and undaunted by conservative opposition. As far as the Reviews are concerned, the myth of the democratization of print entails a functionalist argument in that it grants explanatory power to the fact that the *Monthly* and the *Critical* seem so perfectly suited to the moment at which they appeared. Its persuasiveness hinges, though, on the conception of reading as an ideologically neutral practice. But nothing could be further from the truth. The pages of the Reviews reveal that the act of reading at mid–eighteenth century was (as it always is) ideologically conflicted and highly changeable. Any attempt to explain the place of popular criticism in this period will necessarily begin and end with the problem of what it means to read.[21]

One starting point in addressing this problem is to look at the very different ideologies of reading espoused by the two Reviews, and to recognize that those differences are closely tied to their respective origins and initial missions.[22] Ralph Griffiths, the founder and editor of the *Monthly* until his death at the age of 83 in 1803, was a Presbyterian who apprenticed for his vocation as a reviewer by working for the publisher Jacob Robinson. Robinson himself founded *The History of the Works of the Learned*, an ambitious abstract journal that lasted from 1737 until 1743.[23] A former watchmaker, and a bookseller by trade, Griffiths founded the *Monthly* as a business venture and ran it like a shop, tending to hire a large number of personal acquaintances, and closely supervising the contents of each issue.[24]

Perhaps most importantly, Griffiths did not diverge much from the traditional aims of an abstract journal, except that he sought an audience broader than just the learned. In practice, in the early years of the *Monthly*, this meant that Griffiths saw his journal primarily as something that would "be serviceable to such as would choose to have some idea of a book before they lay out their money or time on it" (*Monthly Review* 1 [May 1749]: "Advertisement"), a goal he

planned to reach by providing a "compendious account" of new publications. This premise was later more or less abandoned, I will argue,
as competitive pressure from the *Critical Review* (beginning in 1756)
pushed the *Monthly* into more and more opinionated articles, but it
was nevertheless initially underwritten by assumptions about the social function of reading gathered from the "genre," so to speak, of the
abstract journal.

Along with expectations about the genre of the Review journal,
Griffiths also brought to the *Monthly* a conception of reading, born
of what N. H. Keeble has called the "literary culture of nonconformity," and dating back to the beginning of the Puritan movement and
after it the English Civil War. As Keeble points out, the influence of
the dissenting or nonconformist tradition on English literary culture
has long been underestimated. Throughout the seventeenth century,
dissenting authors such as John Bunyan and Richard Baxter suited
their evangelism perfectly to a newly expanding print medium. They
endorsed reading for everyone as a means to conversion, and they
published their work in unprecedented volume: for example, 20,000
copies of Baxter's *Call to the Unconverted* were printed in the year
it was published, 1658. It had reached a twenty-third edition by
1685, the later editions accounting for an additional 25,000 copies.[25]
These authors minimized the value of formal doctrine, the classical
tradition, and traditional programs of study, and espoused instead
the pursuit of a kind of pure learning. As Bunyan claimed: "I have
not writ out of a venture, nor borrowed my Doctrine from Libraries.
I depend upon the sayings of no man: I found it in the Scriptures of
Truth, among the true sayings of God."[26] Baxter sums up this process
in one of his *Dying Thoughts*: "We must go on to learn as long as we
live."[27]

This nonconformist ideology of reading persisted into the eighteenth century, where its most colorful advocate was not Griffiths but
his fellow bookseller and literary entrepreneur James Lackington.
Lackington, "ex-shoemaker, random amorist, and converted Meth-
odist," broke ranks with the London bookselling establishment by
buying large numbers of books at auction and then selling them at
half or even a quarter of their retail prices.[28] His bookshop, The Tem-
ple of the Muses, as it was called, opened in 1774 and turned annual

profits of £4,000 by 1791. It remains unclear from Lackington's highly digressive memoirs whether he conceived of his radical marketing strategies primarily as a business venture or as a religious mission. He reflects with pride: "I could almost be vain enough to assert, that I have . . . been highly instrumental in diffusing that general desire for READING, now so prevalent among the inferior orders of society."[29] Profits aside, Lackington's Methodism incorporates nonconformist attitudes toward reading that Keeble describes and that find their way into the *Monthly* as well.

The *Critical* had an entirely different beginning. It was originally envisioned by its founders, Tobias Smollett and his friend Archibald Hamilton, as part of a learned society (so too was Johnson's *Literary Magazine*). Smollett seemed to perceive such a society as a kind of institutional community of the cultural elite and aimed in his journal to police the boundaries between classes. Most importantly, the Review committed itself to what it envisioned as the systematic exercise of critical judgment. Its writers promised, in an early preface, "to exert their best endeavours for the regulation of taste and the honour of criticism" (*Critical Review* 11 [January 1761]: "Preface"). The notions that there is an intrinsic, aristocratic merit to criticism ("honour") and that their task involved correcting or civilizing the tastes of the reading public combine to epitomize the *Critical*'s sense of its purpose, a purpose very different from the *Monthly*'s initially more modest aims.

Smollett seems to have believed as well that the "honour of criticism" would be jeopardized by any open association between his Review and the publishing industry: a central feature of his many attacks on the *Monthly* was the claim that Griffiths's dual role as bookseller and reviewer presented an insoluble conflict of interest. Indeed, James Basker has detected a pattern of partiality in the *Monthly*'s reviews of books published by Griffiths. The *Critical*, by contrast, was almost belligerently disinterested, routinely condemning books issued by the journal's own publisher, Robert Baldwin.[30] This emphasis on independent judgment was no doubt bolstered by the ethnic composition of the self-proclaimed "society of gentlemen," Smollett's staff: Smollett, his managing editor Hamilton, Patrick Murdoch, and John Armstrong were all Scottish, and Samuel Derrick was

Irish. Only Thomas Francklin, who joined the Review in its second month, was English. Smollett, at least, was keenly aware of his place as an interloper in London literary society.

Underlying the rhetoric of the *Critical* was a conception of reading as an activity that clarifies social hierarchy, and that perceived the spread of reading as a potential threat to social stability that needed to be aggressively contained. In the theories of social entropy that circulated throughout the century (but reached a fever pitch in the 1750s), reading could be seen as an agency of refinement, a process that would correct and sustain the cultural disposition of gentlemen "of candour and taste." This ideology of reading often found a place in conservative attacks on luxury and the degeneration of English values, treatises that addressed the threat to traditional class divisions posed by "the moneyed men" (the phrase is from Bolingbroke's *Idea of a Patriot King* [1749]) and the increasing possibilities for upward social mobility. Perhaps the most celebrated spokesman for this position was John Brown, whose background and social agenda contrast neatly with that of Lackington. A depressive minor Anglican curate, Brown won fame with the enormously popular *Estimate of the Manners and Principles of the Times* (1757), an attack on luxury and effeminacy. He also published attacks on licentiousness and gambling and was engaged in a project to civilize Russia through educational reform when he committed suicide at the age of 51 by cutting his throat.

This delineation of the respective "reading formations" of the *Monthly* and the *Critical* requires a couple of important qualifications.[31] First, because of the sheer number of voices contributing to both Reviews, it is difficult to make a compelling case for the firmness of the ideological differences I have described. That both Smollett and Goldsmith, to name two prominent examples, contributed at one time or another to both Reviews illustrates the problem. Nor do I mean to claim a cause-and-effect relationship between a dissenting ideology and the *Monthly*, or a conservative ideology and the *Critical*. These political predispositions obviously predate the Reviews, as does the perceived need for review criticism and the "genre" of the review article. Second, and more importantly, the *Monthly*'s conception of reviewing, after its rival was founded, became less clear. After

1756, that is, more opinion found its way into *Monthly* articles, and *Monthly* reviewers began speaking directly (and critically) to authors and readers.

In its first years of operation, the editors of the *Monthly* were extremely cautious about imposing their judgments on their readers and corrected against their possible influence by characterizing the extracts that they reproduced as a means of allowing the readers to make up their own minds. The typical formulation of this attempt to maintain a neutral balance was to say, for example, "That our readers may not think we have passed too severe and unjust a censure upon this work, we shall present them with a few extracts . . ." (*Monthly* 5 [June 1751]: 65), or "but that we may not be said to have anticipated the opinions of our readers, we shall lay before them . . . some extracts, whereby they may be enabled to form a judgment" of their own (*Monthly* 10 [January 1754]: 31), or "But herein we shall not, in the language of critics pretend to describe . . . the beauties and imperfections . . . of the production before us. No, but we shall take, what we believe our readers will think a much more agreeable and useful method; we shall extract from the work itself a few of such passages as we shall judge people to give a tolerably adequate idea of the whole" (*Monthly* 1 [May 1749]: 66–67).[32]

This concern that their reviews might somehow encroach upon their readers' attempts to form independent opinions followed from the *Monthly*'s original aim as stated in several early articles and is epitomized in the journal's comments on Richardson's *Sir Charles Grandison*. Stating that "the intention of this Review is *information* rather than *decision*," the reviewer declines to intervene in the popular discussion of the novel (*Monthly* 10 [January 1754]: 70–71).

Not long after the founding of the *Critical*, however, the *Monthly*'s general tone changed distinctly. Slipping into many of their reviews are the new assumptions that bad writing is an aspect of more widespread social ills, and that it is the Review's duty to resist this decline by, in effect, telling its audience what it should and should not read. There are, for example, disdainful references to "the Genius of Romance . . . drooping among us," (*Monthly* 24 [June 1761]: 415) "a nation absorbed in luxury," (*Monthly* 21 [April 1761]: 260), and perhaps most tellingly, "these novel-scrawling times, when footmen and servant-maids are the authors, as well as, occasionally, the heroes and heroines of their own most elegant memoirs" (*Monthly* 21 [November 1758]: 441). This attitude, steeped in distinctions based on social class, which the *Critical* had adopted from its outset, derides a large part of either Review's readers, a move that the *Monthly* was so reluctant to make before the founding of the *Critical*.

More significantly, *Monthly* articles after 1756 began to discriminate among reading practices, creating hierarchies among its audience by assessing the habits and tastes of different kinds of readers. A review of a posthumously published collection of poems by Thomas Parnell (that the reviewer believes are spurious) draws an opposition between "the hasty Reader," who will accept the poems as authentic, and "those who are curious and critical" and hence will not be fooled (*Monthly* 19 [October 1758]: 380). A broader and more elaborate distinction occurs in a notice about George Colman's *The Jealous Wife*, in which the writer tries to justify a negative review of the very popular play: "When Pliny was dissatisfied with the Judgment of his Critical Friends, to whom he submitted his compositions, he used to say, *Ad Populum provoco*. In all cases, whatever, the last resort is undoubtedly to the people, from whose decree no appeal can be made to any superior tribunal. Nevertheless, there are instances in which we may venture to appeal from the people to themselves" (*Monthly* 24 [March 1761]: 181–82).

The reviewer resorts to casuistry in an effort to overcome anxieties that follow from the *Monthly*'s original conception of itself. He delivers an unmistakably antipopulist review of the play, but does not want to admit it. The inconceivable notion of appealing "from the people to themselves" is hardly convincing, but is representative of the ambivalence often found in *Monthly* articles as that journal's rhetoric became absorbed into that of the *Critical*. By June 1756, only six months after the founding of the *Critical*, the *Monthly* endorses a kind of criticism it had repudiated just seven years earlier: "Criticism is the result of Judgment, and the perfection of Taste. It neither extenuates beauties, nor aggravates errors; but, placing both in a proper point of light, teaches when to applaud, and when to censure, with reason" (*Monthly* 14 [June 1756]: 528).

By 1773 the *Monthly* was routinely adopting military metaphors, a hallmark, as I will show next, of the *Critical*. A review of Hannah More's *The Search of Happiness*, for example, describes reviewers as "liege knights of the Muses" (*Monthly* 49 [September 1773]: 202). By this point in their history, both journals looked roughly the same: each issue of both the *Monthly* and the *Critical* opened with about ten long reviews (with extensive extracts) and concluded with a Monthly Catalogue of very brief reviews of less important publications, and each number of both cost a shilling. Though important ideological distinctions remained—the *Monthly*, as one can discern from its Monthly Catalogues, continued to express more liberal views on religion and especially politics—the two journals increasingly managed the difficult triangular relationship between themselves, authors, and readers in the same way.

As the *Monthly* and the *Critical* came to resemble each other as journals, their respective editors worked hard to differentiate them. Their attempts to do so take the form of a sophisticated professional discourse that quickly emerged in the pages of both the *Monthly* and the *Critical* during the late 1750s, and that took on a greater importance to both journals than their respective conceptions of reading. Professional language is a claim to power that derives from what Magali Larson describes as a "monopoly of competence"[33] and entails a commitment to neutrality. The *Monthly* and the *Critical*'s emergence at midcentury, roughly as the medical profession took form, makes them part of turbulent developments in the professionalization of English society during the early modern period. The Reviews' sustained regularity and rigorous specialization both define them as examples of institutional criticism and mask the struggle that helped create that institution. The formative years of the *Monthly* and the *Critical* markedly illustrate this process because these journals saw as their special service a particular way of reading and sought market control over the English reading public: their emergence signals a new phase in English letters, in which reading practices are conceived as distinct commodities, and readers as consumers with collective tastes.

The crude polemics that mark the early rivalry between the *Monthly* and the *Critical* have long been taken as evidence that mid-eighteenth-century reviewers were no more than latter-day Grub

Street hacks (that is, mercenaries without standards or principles). Ralph Griffiths, editor of the *Monthly*, and Tobias Smollett, editor of the *Critical*, did indeed try hard to discredit each other, and the first few years after the founding of the *Critical* in 1756 are replete with examples of their colorful, if ridiculous, rhetoric.

One exchange in particular has stood for at least 140 years as an emblem of their primitive conflicts. It was first cited in John Forster's *Life and Adventures of Oliver Goldsmith* in 1848, and then handed down through G. B. Hill's monumental edition of Boswell's *Life of Johnson*, to Derek Roper's *Reviewing Before the Edinburgh* (1978). All three use this exchange as proof that the early reviewers are hacks. Griffiths asserts:

The Monthly Review is not written by physicians without practice, authors without learning, men without decency, gentlemen without manners, and critics without judgment.

Smollett responds:

The Critical Review is not written by a parcel of obscure hirelings, under the restraint of a bookseller and his wife, who presumes to revise, alter, and amend the articles occasionally. The principal writers in the Critical Review are unconnected with booksellers, unawed by old women, and independent of each other. (*Critical* 7 [February 1759]: 141)[34]

Properly contextualized, though, this bombastic exchange provides a fascinating list of the essential criteria for professional standards as both editors understood them. The content of this attack and counterattack, considered apart from its inflated rhetoric, allows us to deduce a great deal of information about the emergent profession of reviewing.

The exchange between Griffiths and Smollett identifies either straightforwardly, or by negation, or by implication the characteristics that define their enterprise. Each editor begins by observing that the other is not a reviewer by profession, but has rather turned to reviewing after mismanaging his original line of work. Griffiths tells us that Smollett is, after all, a physician, who apparently edits the *Critical* because he is unable to maintain a medical practice. But if Smollett is an amateur reviewer, Griffiths is worse. Smollett identifies him as a bookseller, an accusation that carries two different negative associations. First, Smollett is implying that Griffiths runs the *Monthly* as though it were a shop: treating his writers not like gentlemen, but like tradesmen, and presuming to alter their work as he would alter the work of a printer. (Indeed, Smollett suggests, they may deserve nothing better, since they are in fact "hirelings.") Moreover, Griffiths runs a poor shop, one in which his wife is constantly allowed to interfere. Worse still, Griffiths's real profession as a bookseller will inevitably force him into conflicts of interest that ought to disqualify him as a literary arbiter. He cannot judge impartially books from which he hopes to profit.

The force of the emerging category of "professional" remains difficult to assess in this exchange. The term is never mentioned, even though the notion of being a reviewer by profession is precisely what is being debated, and the corollary debate about whether authorship counted as a profession was well underway during the 1750s.[35] In addition, the competitors draw a sharp division between professional and mercenary considerations: Smollett, in fact, makes that issue the centerpiece of his attack on Griffiths. The result is extremely complex: we find an exaggerated version of the professional rhetoric of our own day, one more zealous in severing connections between social function and material reward, more sanctimonious in mystifying both by means of an anachronistic, at times chivalric, vocabulary ("decency," "manners").[36] But this rhetoric is coupled with a basic uncertainty about the definition and social value of professionals.

As I will suggest in the next section, broader questions remain about the professional standards that the Reviews attempted to impart to their readers. In practice, the oppressive nostalgia of these categories threatened to suffocate the market that the editors of the *Monthly* and the *Critical* hoped to nurture. When Griffiths or Smollett addressed or spoke on behalf of the reader of candor and taste, they overlooked some potentially embarrassing questions: Are there enough readers of candor and taste in the English reading public to support a Review? Do such readers *need* a Review? The reviewers' enterprise, that of reforming and homogenizing the taste of the reading public, would, if it were successful, erode their own authority.

Hence their confused conceptions of and attitudes toward their more promising readers are understandable.

Moreover, the *Monthly* and the *Critical* were in all likelihood never in touch with the unambitious among their clientele. Large groups of readers (the consumers of popular novels, for example) showed no signs at all of responding to the Reviews' exhortations to reform, an illustration perhaps of Sartre's claim that, beginning in the eighteenth century, the needs of the masses are addressed ineffectually, in writing produced and read by the bourgeoisie.[37] The *Monthly* and *Critical* seemed, at some awkward moments, not only to have mismanaged their relationship with subscribers and other potential regular readers, but also to have badly misjudged the scope of their market as a whole.

One thing at least becomes clear if we look at this exchange and others like it during the years 1756–60: the foundation of the *Monthly* in 1749 did not in and of itself signal the beginning of professional popular criticism, for the *Monthly* first promised to "enter no farther into criticism just so far as may be indispensibly necessary to give some idea of such books as come under [their] consideration" (*Monthly* 2 [February 1750]: 260). Rather, the anxious rivalry between the two that began seven years later initiated a struggle that was conducted in a rhetoric of professionalism even as both parties sought to define the profession of reviewing. The rapid development of the Reviews to a position of prominence on the literary scene resulted chiefly from a dialectic made possible by the establishment of the *Critical Review* in 1756, after which the professional qualifications of popular critics became the subject of open debate. The contest between the two journals raised the issue of critical authority in an emerging professional context.

II

The word "critic" receives a significantly peculiar treatment in Samuel Johnson's *Dictionary* (1755). His primary definition of the word is "a man skilled in the art of judging of literature; a man able to distinguish the faults and beauties of writing," but his illustrations are the following three quotations:

This settles truer ideas in men's minds of several things, whereof we read the names in ancient authors, than all the large and laborious arguments of *criticks*. (Locke)

Criticks I saw, that other names deface,
And fix their own with labour in their place. (Pope)

Where an author has many beauties consistent with virtue, piety, and truth, let not little *criticks* exalt themselves, and shower down their ill-nature. (Watts)[38]

All three examples are pejorative in exactly the same way: they imply that the real definition of "critic" is "a man who *pretends* to be skilled in the art of judging of literature," and who does so in order to usurp a cultural authority that rightly belongs to authors. The discrepancy between Johnson's examples and the neutral definition to which they supposedly attest reveals a rupture, a locus of conflict in the field of mid-eighteenth-century literature. It posits a huge gap between the ideal and the actual and implies that no "true" critics exist in 1755, for the definition of the word remains in Johnson's mind fundamentally unresolved.

Another slightly earlier definition points to the same problem in a very different way. In the introductory chapter to Book 8 of *The History of Tom Jones* (1749), Henry Fielding defines the word "critic" as follows: "By this word here, and in most other parts of our work, we mean every reader in the world."[39] Fielding's definition is willfully idiosyncratic: by making "every reader in the world" a critic, Fielding radically democratizes the term, erasing the conventional discrimination between critic and common reader, denying the special skill and training by which his audience would recognize a critic as a privileged judge of letters. Like Johnson, Fielding wishes, without explicitly announcing his desire, to disempower those of his contemporaries who claim to possess special qualifications that define them as critics. Johnson implies that critics are charlatans; Fielding, that critics are no different from any other readers. Both authors are clearly concerned, though, that critics present a danger to literary culture because they threaten to encroach upon a conceptual space big enough for authors and readers alone.

The expressions of concern by authors in the 1740s and 1750s, such as Johnson and Fielding, that the office of critic was fraudulent were answered in a sense by the origin of institutionalized criticism marked by the founding of the *Monthly* and the *Critical*. One of the Reviews' key rhetorical strategies was to forge a formal separation between authors and readers, that is, to posit and side with the elite of the reading public, as though such readers existed as a discrete group. The critics, claiming to act on behalf of elite readers, in effect seized an exclusive forum in which to articulate their principles, justify their claims to expertise, and answer their detractors. Articles in the early issues of these journals are often particularly explicit about establishing a critical platform and staking a claim by the reviewers to the role of arbiter of literary taste.

Prefaces to two early volumes of the *Critical*, one which appeared in 1761 (vol. 11) after the journal had been in existence for five years, the other in 1765 (vol. 19), illustrate that journal's agenda quite clearly, and they reveal as well the kind of opposition and frustration that both Reviews experienced.[40] These prefaces, which function as manifestos of their early work, illustrate the *Critical*'s first attempts to construct its relationship with authors and with the English reading public. The reviewers had to identify that stratum of the reading public that they wished to address, then to decide how to address those readers. They had great difficulty determining the contours of literate England, and as these prefaces reveal, they were uncertain as well about whether to approach the public as their superior or their subordinate. Authors, on the other hand, were all too well known to the reviewers. Strenuously objecting to misrepresentations of their work, questioning the qualifications, abilities, and practices of their critics, authors as a class positioned themselves from the start against the major Reviews.[41] The early reviewers' struggle to ground this difficult triangular relationship is the subtext of many *Monthly* and *Critical* articles, but it is given a uniquely suggestive expression in the two prefaces from the *Critical* that I will discuss here.

The Reviews attempted to situate themselves in the increasingly commercialized literary culture of the mid-eighteenth century chiefly by treating authors and readers as mutually exclusive entities, as though readers could not also be authors, and vice versa. This represents a conceptual difference from reigning notions of the seventeenth century, when, as Sartre puts it, "the reader, if not strictly identical with the writer, was a potential writer."[42] The Reviews tend to speak of readers in vaguely condescending terms, but are in a sense compelled to specify either positive or negative opinions about authors.[43] Yet the prefaces I will examine suggest that the editors of the *Critical* are hostile toward both, that they are aware of the artificiality of separating authors from readers, and that they attack authors in part because they cannot safely attack the more serious source of their alarm, the emerging English reading public whose tastes they fear might prove to be both unsophisticated and uncontrollable. Thus, the militarism that often characterizes the reviewers' rhetorical stance is ambiguous: they conceive of themselves as involved in a battle, but the precise reasons for fighting and the identity of their enemies is never entirely clear.

The general ambiance of war is as central to mid-eighteenth-century literary culture as it was to the culture of Grub Street a generation earlier (a fact often obscured by traditional characterizations of midcentury, such as the Age of Sensibility). The idea, voiced by Sterne, that "the life of a writer, whatever he may fancy to the contrary, was not so much a state of *composition* as a state of *warfare*"[44] is echoed in the work of Tobias Smollett, Oliver Goldsmith, and Richard Sheridan, and it is epitomized in the figure of Johnson as Boswell presents him. These prefaces are thus typical of the age's perception of literary society, a perception in which "striving" against and "overcoming" some unspecified adversary are crucial aims for the man of letters. Competition and combativeness were just as essential to the literary world of midcentury as they had been to the world of Swift and Pope—only, by 1760, professional institutions, such as the Reviews, and the new possibility that readers or authors might function as collectives made such competition more complex.

In both prefaces, authors are first figured as the military enemies of the reviewers, and then, even more unsympathetically, as animals. In the 1761 preface, the editors describe the *Critical* as having "sustained all the complicated assaults of dulness, whose name is Legion," and pursue this metaphor by claiming that "dulness, tho formidable in her own strength, is not the only adversary that hath taken the field against the Critical Review," listing as well "the rage of jealousy, the fury of disappointment, the malevolence of envy, the heat of misapprehension, and the resentment of overweening merit." The second preface (1765) imagines an imperial struggle, with the editors of the *Critical* as governors of a "province" that is "perhaps the most ungrateful and difficult in the republic of letters," and hostile authors as a "formidable and busy band" of natives.

The image of authors as equal adversaries or hostile natives quickly degenerates in both prefaces into images of authors as pests. In the 1761 preface, authors are compared to "the insects of a summer's day" that "have buzzed, and stung, and stunk and expired." The 1765 preface unites the two metaphors—author as combatant and author as vermin—into a single grotesquely formulated vow: "Armed thus with integrity and independency, they [the editors of the *Critical*] are determined to proceed in the paths of candour and conscience; regardless of those porcupines who, irritated through disappointment, dart their fretful quills at the writings or persons of the Reviewers, who fear them no more than Pyrrhus did the weapon of Priam, which fell upon his buckler—*Imbelle sine ictu.*"[45]

The shift in characterization from author as soldier to author as pest is not mere rhetorical flourish, chiefly because it implies a change from deliberate opposition to unthinking havoc. By comparing authors to insects or porcupines, the editors of the Review wish to characterize them as mindlessly hostile, and implicitly to dismiss the more threatening notion that those authors might be organized and purposeful. That second possibility is more threatening, it seems to me, because it would confirm a legitimate pluralistic conception of taste. The *Critical* instead grounded its authority in the possibility of a catholic, monistic taste in reading and construed lack of unanimity in the public's opinions about books as a failure of education. Thus, contentious authors could be most safely dismissed as unlearned, irrational mavericks—or, in the extreme, as pests. Were it acknowledged, however, that those authors spoke from a specifiable position, that they had rational cultural dispositions of their own, the *Critical* would have had to concede that the first principle of its project of reform was open to debate.[46] The unfocused resentment that the Reviews imputed to bad authors was, they believed, ultimately manageable, but cogent opposition would not be.

Within these descriptions of authors we can identify a fissure, a point at which the Reviews struggle to find a way to legitimate their authority in literary culture. The prefaces patch together two very different rhetorics of authority, bringing each to bear upon their adversaries in the literary culture. The first is the anti–Grub Street invective employed by Pope and Swift during the 1720s and 1730s.[47] The personification of dullness, and dehumanizing metaphors for authors, had become clichés by 1760, but could still be used to invoke the authority wielded by the powerful writers of an earlier generation and to historicize the reviewer-author relationship by aligning it with Swift's and Pope's triumphs over their detractors. But the comparison with Swift and Pope is ironically self-reflexive, for Swift's and Pope's defenses of the integrity of authorship frequently involved attacks on critics of their own day. The *Critical's* attempt to occupy a Popean position in the literary society of midcentury is undercut by the lasting currency of the *Dunciad's* representation of the very office that the reviewers occupy.

The other, wholly positive rhetoric signals the emergence of a new, professional criticism. Through normative values such as "integrity and independency," "candour and conscience," the reviewers attempt to define a distinctly corporate kind of authority, different from the personal integrity championed by Swift and Pope, and calculated to be effective in the more expansive, thoroughly professionalized literary environment of the later eighteenth century. The awkward fusion of these two rhetorics suggests that neither was entirely adequate: the anti–Grub Street vocabulary was fast becoming merely conventional, while the newer professional rhetoric was not yet convincing enough to stand without bolstering.

The *Critical's* attitude toward authors suggests that there existed a power vacuum, one that the journal's editors were aggressively trying to fill. More significant, though, is that in 1765, after only nine years of operation, the *Critical's* editors appear exasperated by the failures of these strategies to overcome growing suspicions that they were relatively powerless over literary production. Their frustration is nowhere more evident than in the choice (in the 1765 preface) of the beleaguered colonial governor as a metaphor for their own situation. As Mary Douglas has argued, institutions are founded on analogies: "There needs to be an analogy by which the formal structure of a crucial set of social relations is found in the physical world, or in the supernatural world, or in eternity, anywhere, so long as it is not seen as a socially contrived arrangement."[48]

The Reviews predominantly use the analogy of the state to legitimate what they do. Almost as if they took the figure of the "Republic of Letters" literally, the Reviews present themselves as a police force or an army whose official capacity licenses them to regulate the behavior of authors and readers. As one would expect, the *Critical* makes use of this analogy first, as early as the 1765 preface, and continues to repeat it. For example, in 1767 the *Critical*'s editors say they have "declared war" on the "harvest of poor writers" (*Critical* 23 [January 1767]: "Preface"), and in 1772 they assure their readers that "our phalanx is not composed of mercenaries" (*Critical* 34 [December 1772]: "Preface"). The *Monthly* first uses less militaristic metaphors, describing their role in 1755 as "tasters to the public" (*Monthly* 13 [November 1755]: 399). But as I noted earlier, by 1773 they also refer to themselves as "liege knights of the Muses."

The analogy by which the editors of the *Critical* image themselves as the governor of an "ungrateful and difficult" province, plagued by a "formidable and busy band" of authors, alludes to the volatile state of affairs in the American colonies during the 1760s. The Treaty of Paris returned St. Pierre and Miquelon to France, and Cuba and the Philippines to Spain in exchange, respectively, for Canada and Florida, both undeveloped and potentially hostile tracts of land that many thought would prove far too difficult to colonize profitably. Moreover, the Great Indian Uprising during the same year, which threatened British outposts throughout the western frontier, immediately underscored the apparent dubiousness of the treaty's terms.

The resulting controversy over management of the colonies unleashed an enormous number of opposition pamphlets that pointed out the folly of the government's policy and set the stage for more extreme statements, such as the infamous issue number 45 of the *North Briton*, in which John Wilkes accused the Bute administration of treason. The swarm of charges that England had foolishly overextended itself makes the prominifisterial *Critical*'s identification with colonial governors deeply problematic, though in a curious way it is quite appropriate as well.[49] Laurence Henry Gipson in *The Triumphant Empire* describes the predicament of the typical governor in terms that would have been very familiar to the reviewers:

In reality, the power of a royal governor was not nearly so impressive as an enumeration of his powers would indicate. . . . If he were to maintain bearable relations with the inhabitants of the colony, he could not be forgetful of their interests, which might not be compatible with the free exercise of many of his powers. . . . At best his situation at all times was one of great delicacy in guarding, on the one hand, against a summary recall from his superiors at home for neglect of his office and, on the other, against the development of an opposition within his province that might leave him helpless to perform his duties.[50]

Like a governor in the colonies, the editors of the *Critical* felt themselves in 1765 to be caught in a thankless mediating position, between a clear (though self-appointed) set of duties and the incorrigible practices of authors. Like the anti–Grub Street rhetoric, this ambiguous metaphoric alignment with the colonial governor ultimately calls attention to the Review's own inadequacy, by asserting its authority only as an appeal for help.

Though most of the *Critical*'s efforts to anchor its authority in the field of literature were directed at authors, I contend that readers ultimately constituted a far more "formidable and busy" opposition to reviewers. Vocal and identifiable, authors presented a tangible threat that could be met head-on in the arena provided by the Review itself. Readers, however, were another matter—the ever-present material foundation of the Reviews' existence, they were nevertheless always silent. The editors of the *Critical* could speculate on the identity of these readers, but never engaged them in the medium of print.[51] Indeed, neither the *Critical* nor the *Monthly* followed the lead of the earlier *Gentleman's Magazine* (founded in 1731), which seemed to imagine a far more fluid relationship between itself and its readers. The *Gentleman's* gradually expanded from its omnibus format to characterize much of its feature articles as "original correspondence" (even if much of it was in fact written by the editors). Its radically

democratic motto, *E Pluribus Unum*, sharply differentiated its concerns from the Reviews' attempts to police the boundaries between
reviewer, author, and reader.

The absence of textual exchanges between readers and reviewers
in the *Critical* and the *Monthly* does not mean, however, that the
Reviews' readership was an enigma. On the contrary, readers were
capable of expressing their desires very powerfully *as consumers* of
literature. Thus, the reviewers could contain or rebut the articulated
opposition of authors, but the unwritten, material opposition of
readers filled them with a sense of frustration at their own power-
lessness—a frustration they could conveniently vent only at authors.

The *Critical*'s general recourse in the face of this resentment was
to incorporate its dissatisfaction with what it perceived as wayward
reading practices into a comprehensive social critique. The journal
resituated its exasperation with readers and the books that they purchased within a general campaign against luxury and the corruption
of taste. All the public's undisciplined or unprincipled desires in reading posed a threat, the *Critical* theorized, to the cultural and moral
stability of the nation. The terms of this position were in fact quite
powerful throughout the eighteenth century. John Sekora identifies
luxury as "the greatest single social issue and the greatest single commonplace" of the mid–eighteenth century and notes that the British
Museum and the London School of Economics possess more than
460 books and pamphlets on the subject from the years 1721–71,
most of them overwhelmingly against luxury.

As the object of attack, according to Sekora, the term "entered
two distinct levels of usage": on the one hand, luxury was "a nuclear
and organizing concept in an elaborate social and political system";
on the other hand, it was "a springboard for vulgar controversy . . .
inherently polemical and customarily vague, and, one could add,
applicable to any social or cultural evil, including bad literature."[52]
Luxury served as a bogeyman—it allowed the editors of the *Critical*
to justify their fear of failure by suggesting that everyone should be
afraid. Rather than castigating readers directly, they attacked bad
taste as a symptom of luxury, and constantly reasserted the principles
on which they believed writing should be predicated. As the 1765
preface reveals, however, such assertions were by no means guaran-

teed to succeed, and for all their attempts to neutralize popular opinion by embedding it in a rationalized and abstract critique, the un-
manageable tastes of the general public remained a constant source
of concern to the editors of the *Critical*.

Perhaps the best illustration of the acuteness of this fear is the
journal's treatment of the most famous attack on luxury written during midcentury, John Brown's *Estimate of the Manners and Principles of the Times*. The *Estimate* epitomized the ferment that I have
touched upon here: the first volume ran through seven authorized
and pirated editions in 1757 alone, and as Sekora points out, it is
immediately distinguishable from contemporary works on the subject by the "breadth and particularity of Brown's indictment."[53] One
might expect such a treatise to be right in line with the philosophy
that informs the *Critical*, but the journal instead said that the *Estimate* should be deplored and repudiated, not so much because of its
argument, but because of its appeal to anarchical, mass emotions.
This discrepancy, puzzling as it seems at first glance, goes to the heart
of the subtle but potentially volatile tensions that mark the relationship between reviewer and reader. The very popularity of the *Estimate* is enough to make it seem dangerous to the Review's editors,
and they take that popularity to be a more persuasive argument than
anything Brown has to say *against* anarchic public opinion. The *Critical*'s fear of the public is, in other words, more urgent than Brown's,
and the editors seem compelled by that fear to take an even more
radically reactionary stance than Brown himself took.

If we turn, however, from this general critique to the *Critical*'s
direct and specific characterizations of its readers, and of the
reviewer-reader relationship, the problems and the rhetoric become
far more nuanced. The difficulties arise chiefly out of a conflict inherent in the reviewers' project. In order to succeed in one sense, the
Monthly and *Critical* reviewers had to present their journals *as
books*, as salable commodities competing with the productions of
other writers for the patronage of a finite assortment of readers. Yet,
at the same time, the reviewers had to present themselves as *above*
the literary marketplace—offering a disinterested perspective on all
other kinds of published writing, in order to police the reading practices of the very audience they wished to attract. Thus, in 1761 the

editors of the *Critical* thank a neutral and undifferentiated "public," but express the hope that their work will be agreeable to the more particular "reader of ingenuity and candour." They acknowledge that they owe their success to the favor of that larger public, yet promise to "continue to exert their best endeavours for the regulation of taste," that is, paradoxically, to remake the audience that has so far supported them. The *Critical Review* hoped, in other words, to deny the possibility that the reading public on which they depended may have been unreformable—that the reader who buys the *Critical* may have had no wish to become a "candid and judicious" reader (*Critical* 34 [December 1772]: "Preface").

In addition to these prefaces, there are numerous instances in both Reviews of "interpellation" as Althusser has described it. That is, the Reviews hail, as he would put it, the "candid and judicious" reader, differentiating him (the Reviews' ideal reader is putatively male) from other imperfect readers, and thereby claiming him as their subject.[54] The imperfect readers are represented in stereotypes with which no one would want to identify. Novel readers are, for example, uniformly described in negative terms. They are "idle templars, raw prentices, and green girls, that support the circulating libraries of this learned metropolis" (*Critical* 2 [November 1756]: 379). The audience of *Tristram Shandy* comprises "novel-readers, from the stale maiden of quality to the snuff taking chambermaid" (*Critical* 11 [January 1761]: 36). Such readers (with the exception here of the "stale maiden of quality") chiefly include either young women and members of the lower classes, a profile meant to reinforce the Reviews' warning that the spread of reading, and the inclination of those new readers to choose harmful books, are actually a single, urgent problem.

In fact, though, the *Critical*'s greatest fears about the uncontrollability of the reading public were realized in the early 1760s, forcing the editors to acknowledge, in the preface of 1765, insoluble problems in the relationship between reviewer and reader. They note in that preface that, since George III's accession to the throne (1760), "political writings have engrossed the attention of the public of England more than they have done at any time since the Revolution," and that they, "the Critical Reviewers, according to the plan of their undertaking and their constant practice, could not help reviewing political as they did other works." But this practice laid them open to charges of partiality, and they thus found themselves accused of taking part on the government's side in the controversy. Their denial of this charge is a curious abdication of responsibility, a tacit, reluctant, deferral to the reading public:

It happens, however, as the most indifferent bystanders may observe, that the papers and pamphlets against any administration, are brought up with much greater avidity than those written in its defense; and consequently the opposition writers are, of late, more numerous than those for the government, as well as more indecent, more shallow, and more incorrect, because the bulk of them write only for the profit of their publications; and therefore the Reviewers have, perhaps, censured a greater number of antiministerial than of ministerial productions.

Having committed themselves to making a comprehensive account of contemporary writing, they now find themselves compelled by their own rules to review a barrage of pamphlets that they would almost certainly like to ignore. An occasional single work they could choose not to review, but not a flood of books written on the same subject or in the same style. A trend in literary production such as the glut of antiministerial pamphlets of the early 1760s demonstrated by its sheer volume the limitations of the Reviews' control over English readers. Nor are these pamphlets a unique case: the issue of what to review and what to ignore, and the uncertainty associated with these decisions, are revisited in the 1767 and 1772 prefaces.

The history of the *Critical*'s responses to novels, in particular, mirrors the progressive discouragement that led to the 1765 preface. Early articles present novels as "innocent amusement" and even apologize for reviewing them negatively.[55] But in later articles (from about 1760) reviewers seem exasperated by the productions of "the common herd of novelists,"[56] which they see as indistinguishable from one another. A review of *The History of Mr Byron and Miss Greville* archly summarizes the standard plot: "As usual, the hero and heroine are all perfection, in person, sentiment, morals, and conduct; and of course they are persecuted by their ill-fated stars, and the in-

flexibility of parental opposition. However, they at length come together, and are necessarily then at the very pinnacle of felicity" (*Critical* 16 [September 1763]: 217).

Reviewers also begin to move from attacks on the novels to
broader social critique, such as an article that speaks of the "youth
of the present age" as "corrupted by romances" (*Critical* 23 [March
1767]: 210). An article about yet another product of booksellers
John and Francis Noble's "novel *manufactory*" quickly becomes a
comprehensive indictment of a cycle of production and consumption
that the reviewer feels has spun out of control:

> The booksellers, those pimps of literature, take care every winter to procure
> a sufficient quantity of tales, memoirs, and romances for the entertainment
> of their customers, many of whom, not capable of distinguishing between
> good and bad, are mighty well satisfied with whatever is provided for them:
> as their female readers in particular have generally most voracious appetites,
> and are not overly delicate in their choice of food, every thing that is new
> will go down. The circulating librarians, therefore, whose very beings de-
> pend on amusements of this kind, set their authors to work regularly every
> season, and, without the least grain of compassion for us poor Reviewers,
> who are obliged to read their performances, pester the public with their pe-
> riodical nonsense. (*Critical* 16 [December 1763]: 449)

The tone of exasperation anticipates the preface of 1765. It registers the same complaint in a more elaborate way, describing a literary culture modeled on prostitution, with booksellers as pimps, authors as their prostitutes, and circulating libraries as a kind of brothel
that facilitates this disreputable kind of reading. The readers are described first as indiscriminate customers and unwitting victims.
Then, in an intriguing reversal of gender roles, they are figured in particular as women with voracious appetites. At the end of this chain
of commercial dependencies are "us poor Reviewers," critical policemen rendered helpless by a system in which producers and consumers alike are complicit.

It is significant that in both this particular review and in the preface of 1765, the editors of the *Critical* are careful to represent abuses
in the literary system in metaphors that mitigate the responsibility of
readers. The analogy between aesthetic taste and gustatory taste had
become standard by midcentury, after Addison introduced it to read-

ers of the *Spectator* (no. 412; June 19, 1712). Although Addison balanced the analogy with the argument that one acquired good taste chiefly by reading classical literature, the idea that taste is an individual, indisputable property threatens to open the door to a relativist aesthetics. As Colin Campbell observes, "The appetite analogy . . . is fraught with danger, raising as it does the possibility of *de gustibus non est disputandum* being applied to aesthetics."[57]

The *Critical* clearly stood against the idea that taste is relative. This particular review ingeniously skirts the uncomfortable analogy between gustatory and aesthetic taste by giving "appetite" a strongly sexual connotation, and making readers into the clientele of prostitutes, manipulated into bad choices by the criminal element in the book industry. These excuses for readers excuse the reviewers as well, since they qualify what would otherwise be indisputable evidence of their failure to influence the public's consumption of literature.

The treatment of novels in the *Monthly* has a slightly different career, since that journal (or more properly its editor, Ralph Griffiths) had from its beginnings held particular contempt for prose fiction.[58] After a couple of decades, however, that Review's tone also shifts to one of exasperation, as, for example, in this review of the sequel to a novel, *The Man of Honour; or the History of Harry Waters*, that the journal had earlier disparaged: "Vain were the hopes we expressed, on reading the first of these stupid volumes, that we should never be troubled with any more of them. The public, or the circulating libraries, have formed a different judgment of the merit of this work; and lo! the sequel is before us" (*Monthly* 48 [January 1773]: 71).

The notion that the "different judgment" about *Harry Waters* is formed by "the public, or the circulating libraries," bears a clear similarity to the *Critical*'s analogy of booksellers as pimps. The reviewer seems to shift, in midsentence, from blaming the public directly for the appearance of another bad novel, to blaming the institution of circulating libraries—as if circulating libraries could exist independently of consumer demand.

In *Women and Print Culture*, Kathryn Shevelow makes the important point that any periodical's representation of its audience is a "textual *projection*—sometimes idealized, frequently ideological—whose constitution and influence" are distinct from any empirical account of its actual readers.[59] This distinction entailed a special dilemma for the Reviews, whose aim was, in effect, to make their textual projection into reality, to turn all subscribers into versions of the ideal reader. The friction between the *Critical* and its readership that I have described arose from the journal's growing exasperation with thousands of particular readers who showed no signs of cooperating with the Review's program of reform. Both the *Critical* and the *Monthly* were able to articulate one version of the eighteenth century's ideal reading practices, but were unable to enforce them in a way that affected the publishing industry.

The discrepancy between ideal and actual readers engages the workings of taste itself, which is always uncomfortably self-reflexive: taste is an aesthetic judgment that is passed on one's ability to make aesthetic judgments. Claiming the right to prescribe or judge the judgments of others became more and more difficult to justify as the eighteenth century's debate about taste escalated. Though a great many philosophers (perhaps Kames and Gerard addressed the issues most directly) agreed that there were empirical standards of taste, no one could adequately articulate them, and the plurality of theories only served to undercut each other. The Reviews entered the scene at the peak of this philosophical dialogue, and they occupied a far more conservative position than any of their interlocutors. Rather than trying to demonstrate an empirical standard of taste in reading, the reviewers preferred to assume that self-evident standards were already in place, that these tendencies and norms in reading were shared by an elite subset of the bookbuying public, and that they could eventually be conveyed to everyone else. But they overestimated both the size of that subset and their own ability to reform the judgment of the rest of the public.

If the *Critical Review* so plainly failed in its attempts to police the reading habits of the English public, and if the idea of normalizing that public's tastes was so resolutely reactionary, then it seems that we need to reinvestigate the "function" of this very successful kind of popular criticism.[60] We need to account for the continued survival both of the *Critical* and the *Monthly*'s attempts to establish a universal standard of taste on the one hand, and to account on the other for the fashions that resulted in countless romances or antiministerial pamphlets. We need to ask, in other words, why the conservative rationale from which review criticism sprang was not dislodged by the nascent laissez-faire consumer culture with which it seems so much at odds.

In perhaps the most provocative discussion of what John Brewer, Neil McKendrick, and J. H. Plumb have identified as the "consumer revolution," Colin Campbell describes what he calls "modern autonomous imaginative hedonism" which instills an inexhaustible array of desires in the English public of the eighteenth century. He describes the "key to the understanding of modern consumerism" as the recognition of "longing as a permanent mode, with the concomitant sense of dissatisfaction with 'what is' and a yearning for 'something better.' "[61] I suggest that one central, though perhaps paradoxical, aspect of that longing was the desire for a means of assessing those very wants themselves. Perhaps nowhere was that need more acutely felt than in the field of literature. The period 1650 to 1750, as Plumb has described, saw books transformed from "semi-precious objects . . . carefully and beautifully bound," and read largely by the affluent, to plentiful, everyday objects within the purchasing reach of the bourgeoisie.[62] The Reviews answered a crucial need not merely by claiming to offer, hypothetically, an impartial and independent judgment about books, but by offering the consumers of those books an orderly and comprehensible way of participating in the literary culture of their day.

The success of the *Monthly* and the *Critical* is perhaps most dependent on the fact that in 1760 (as well as today), reading a Review and abiding by its recommendations were two very different and not necessarily related activities, even though the two usually go hand in hand. Indeed, it is no exaggeration to say that in the modern era the complexity of the act of reading has been severely underestimated. As books became more widely available and affordable, and as literacy became more widespread, reading became an activity at once more commonplace and more taken for granted. This development, a function of the new consumer society, unfolded at such a rapid pace that one could mistakenly come to assume that reading books was and is a cultural practice with a single meaning. It is easy to recognize that differences in social class, educational background, and gender would very likely make for different preferences in books (the cliché among reviewers that the typical reader of novels is female is but one example).

Once again, we are drawn back to questions attendant on the complexity of the act of reading. Too little attention has been paid to the corresponding differences in *how* the representatives of these social groups read what they read. The meaning of reading, so to speak, can be almost anything. It can be a coerced deference to dominant ideological interests, in which "I can read" means "I know how to behave."[63] But reading can also be what Michel deCerteau describes as a pervasive "poaching," an endless series of particular subversions of the official texts of the social elite. Reading, for deCerteau, is ideally "reading underneath scriptural imperialism."[64]

It is crucial to keep in mind, however, that the notion of the reading process as a symbol of one's place in the cultural spectrum is possible only in a society where reading itself has been commodified. The beginnings of book reviewing mark the advent of this development, for they indicate that not just books but the ways of reading them have become so numerous and so varied that someone (the reviewers) must regulate them. This is at once the urgent goal and the impossible hope of the early Reviews. They approach their goal only in that the act of regularly reading or subscribing to a Book Review indicates a sophisticated and comprehensive level of consumer awareness; it is an attempt at intellectual self-definition in relation to the ideal reader implied by the journal. But the act of reading one or more books at a reviewer's suggestion, and recognizing the correctness of his assessment, is at best merely a coincidental function of that larger ambition, if it is even that—and therein lies the certain failure of the *Monthly* and *Critical*'s ambition. The desire to peruse the whole range of printed matter available for purchase in a given month is nevertheless a vital step in the history of the consumption of culture. The determinants of that desire will always remain elusive, but their existence is confirmed dramatically by the very emergence of the *Monthly* and the *Critical*.

A final important context for understanding the relationship between review criticism and literary careers is provided by published attacks on the Reviews. Claude Jones lists more than a hundred attacks on the *Critical* alone, and Basker adds several more, so it is safe to assume that such attacks were a very common occurrence. Many of these publications are ephemeral, and few can bear much interpretive scrutiny. As for those that can, they help clarify the nature of reviewer-author relationships. If we ask to what extent authors accepted as true the notion that the Reviews represented England's elite readers, and thus anyone's most desirable reading audience, two contradictory answers present themselves: in theory (that is, in their writing about critics), authors reject the critics' claims and draw a sharp distinction between the opinion of reviewers and that of "the public in general."

In practice, however, there are cases, Laurence Sterne's perhaps the most dramatic among them, that suggest that some authors did indeed act on the assumption that the Reviews articulated the consensus of discerning readers. These conflicting reactions—the openly voiced inclination to resist the authority of the reviewer, and the always unstated suspicion that his authority may be legitimate—form the foundation of the volatile relationship between author and reviewer.

A great many of the attacks on the Reviews employ the same, predictable rhetorical strategy of challenging the analogy on which the Reviews found themselves. They tend to do this in one of two ways: either they directly dispute the Reviews' claim to a statelike official place in literary society, or they go behind the scenes to reveal the "real" character of the anonymous reviewers, and to demonstrate that the Reviews' claims to impartiality and professional competence are fraudulent. Of the direct attacks, the simplest are those that point out that no one designated the Reviews as critical authorities. The *Monthly* and the *Critical* are called by one detractor "a set of *self-erected* critics," and are described by another as having "*set themselves up* as the Judges of the Labours of the Learned, and Censors in the Republic of Letters."[65] They are described as tyrants or usurpers rather than legitimate authorities, or as "Goliahs," in an allusion that casts the imbalance of power between reviewers and authors in biblically heroic terms.[66]

Perhaps the most ambitious attack along these lines, Charles

Churchill's *The Apology Addressed to the Critical Reviewers*, is effective precisely because it inverts the *Critical*'s founding analogy,
stressing that the Review is a vehicle for crime, not official justice.
The chain of events consisting of the misinformed review of Churchill's *The Rosciad* (March 1761), which provoked Churchill to answer with the *Apology* in May of the same year, which in turn provoked a hostile notice in the *Critical* (May 1761), makes up the case
of a controversy between a man who would become a major midcentury literary figure and one of the two major Reviews. The debate
focuses on the Review's policy of anonymity and the way in which
that policy obscures both the degree and the sources of the *Critical*'s
power. Ironically, the episode began because the *Rosciad* was published anonymously (common practice for a young, as yet obscure
author such as Churchill), and the Review mistakenly suggested that
its author(s) were Robert Lloyd, George Colman, and Bonnell
Thornton. In the *Apology*, which calls this mistake to the *Critical*'s
attention, Churchill comprehensively attacks the standard reviewing
practices of the day, comparing reviewers first to papists and then to
highwaymen. The first analogy appears in a description of the reviewer's place in literary society:

> Who shall dispute what the Reviewers say?
> Their word's sufficient; and to ask a reason,
> In such a state as theirs, is downright treason.
> True judgment, now, with Them alone can dwell;
> Like church of Rome they're grown infallible.
> Dull superstitious readers they deceive,
> Who pin their easy faith on critic's sleeve,
> And, knowing nothing, ev'ry thing believe![67]

Churchill's is a pessimistic account of the English reading public.
For him, there is no possibility that the public might act as a higher
tribunal, by which an author's work might be judged: the public's
behavior is dictated by a uniform doctrine of reading to which they
assent without examining. Readers are presented as numerous but
powerless, subject to the tyranny of the Reviews. Their passivity
makes possible the Reviews' influence over authors.[68]

Churchill supplements this anti-Jacobite nightmare vision with a
historical thesis about the decline of Criticism:

> A Critic was of old a glorious name,
> Whose sanction handed merit up to fame:
> His Judgment great, and great his Candour too.
> No servile rules drew sickly taste aside;
> Secure he walk'd, for Nature was his guide.
>
> (48–54)

His description of a literary state of nature is a nostalgic fantasy that preempts all the pressures that a market economy brings to bear on authors and critics alike. It is a strict meritocracy, one in which self-evident, "natural" judgment makes "servile rules" unnecessary. In midcentury London, however:

> our Critics bawl
> In praise of Candour with a Heart of Gall.
> Conscious of Guilt, and fearful of the light,
> They lurk enshrouded in the veil of night:
> Safe from detraction, seize the unwary prey,
> And stab, like bravoes, all who come thy way.
>
> (55–60)

A sharp dissociation exists between the reviewers' cant and their true sympathies. Their guilt over this hypocrisy deprives them of the security felt by critics of old, and forces them to become secretive criminals.

Churchill is at a loss to explain this radical change, just as he is unable to answer the question, "How could these self-elected monarchs raise / So large an empire on so small a base?" (84–85). He goes on to wonder, more specifically, how the *Critical* can "rule in Letters and preside in Taste," when

> The TOWN's decisions they no more admit,
> Themselves alone the ARBITERS of WIT;
> And scorn the jurisdiction of that COURT
> To which they owe their being and support.[69]
>
> (259–63)

Churchill's cynical perplexity, expressed over a variety of issues in the *Apology*, is ultimately the poem's organizing rhetorical scheme. How the Review's hypocrisy could survive undetected, how the *Critical* could keep its readers in tow, and most of all, how the journal could nonchalantly misattribute Churchill's own *Rosciad*—none of these questions are answered, and Churchill's inability to obtain the answers remains the focus of the poem.

The *Critical's* review of the *Apology* sardonically underscores the unequal relationship between the journal and the authors it considered. After observing that Churchill has become an annoying "gadfly," the reviewer addresses the journal's policy of anonymous articles in a way that all but taunts the poet:

The reviewers pass no censure but in the face of day; censures, which if they are unjust, may be openly and fairly refuted by reason and argument, without any scurrility or recrimination. Common sense might have told him that no man, supposing himself qualified for the office of reviewer, would chuse to lay himself personally open to the illiberal revenge of every vulgar dunce, or low bred railer, who must naturally be supposed to smart from the critic's correction. (*Critical* 11 [May 1761]: 410)

In order to reclaim the *Rosciad* as his own, Churchill would have to identify himself and refute the *Critical's* attribution of the poem to Colman, Lloyd, and Thornton. The *Critical*, by contrast, could flaunt the empowerment that comes with anonymity, framing the practice of anonymous reviews in its typically professional vocabulary. Its censures, though "public," remain impersonal, institutional. Churchill can only rail against the unfairness of the *Critical's* self-presentation, but even by 1761, just five years after the journal's inception, he is powerless to overcome it.

While Churchill raged against the *Critical's* institutional facade, T. Underwood refused to grant the journal institutional status at all. In *A Word to the Wise* (1770), he pretends to depict a typical meeting of the *Critical's* editorial staff, which is represented as the military hierarchy of a Scottish clan: Archibald Hamilton, general; William Guthrie, captain; William Robertson, lieutenant; and Edward Thompson, ensign. Underwood's premise ingeniously demystifies these figures, revealing them to be not a powerful, impartial agency operating solely out of refined, gentlemanly taste, but rather an assortment of egotistic Scottish critics, quarreling among themselves, and terrified that they might not really possess the power that they claim to.

Hamilton calls the meeting, sending his servant, Mungo, to summon the "Caledonian Band."[70] They begin to arrive, first Guth-

rie: "Not Age alone—by Learning most,/ He's render'd—sapless,
as a Post" (6), then Robertson, who "greets, *sincerely* greets,
his Brother—/ But Harpies prey on one another" (8), and finally
Thompson. After waiting in order to build his confederates' antici-
pation, Hamilton makes his ridiculously grandiose appearance:

> Ye pitying Gods!—Spare your surprise,
> Observe—nay look with steady Eyes,
> A pigmy Mouse—no more—no more
> *Pomposo* Hamilton's at Door.
>
> (12–13)

The urgent issue that has led to this convocation is Hamilton's
concern that the Review's power is quickly eroding. He explains the
problem at length:

> How must it then distract my Soul,
> To think—to feel—our vast Controul,
> Our Pow'r, so absolute of late,
> Despotic—in the *lettr'd State*,
> How must it grieve—afflict—dismay,
> To see our Kingdom pass—away,
> Its Influence fade, from Day to Day—
>
> . . .
>
> For know, my *Caledonian* Band,
> Our Dissolution's near at hand;
> A Spirit, obstinate in Ill
> Which dares oppose your—utmost Skill,
> Has spread Contagion far and wide—
> Nor will it suffer, to preside,
> Your *polish'd* Labours—or admit
> Yourselves—sole arbiters of Wit—
> The Public—or a factious Crew,
> Who late implicit bow'd to You,
> Confess'd no Judgment of their own,
> But all Submission to your Crown,
> Now, (by that Demon, *Common Sense*,
> To which they madly feign Pretence)
> Declare—resolve—by Reason's Aid,
> They'll quite extirpate this sweet Trade;
> Judge for 'emselves—no longer wear
> Those Chains—which Nature cannot bear—
>
> (17–18)

Underwood, in "Hamilton's" voice, describes a scenario that Churchill, writing only nine years earlier, could not have thought possible. The Review's power deteriorates under pressure from an increasingly sophisticated reading public that more and more employs common sense and reason to cultivate tastes in reading that are independent of the Review's judgments. Hence Hamilton fears that the *Critical's* "dissolution's near at hand."

The aged Guthrie, second in command, is asked to speak first, and he proposes that the *Critical* issue an edict against booksellers, accusing them of "Treason—'gainst their letter'd State" (25). But Guthrie adds that this aggressive attempt to reclaim the Review's lost power must be accompanied by a pay raise of ninepence a day to the editorial staff. This last request infuriates Hamilton, but, fortunately for him, Guthrie no sooner finishes his speech than he dies (28–29). In a shortsighted return to business as usual, Hamilton claims that he will veto both the edict and the pay increase, and begins to speculate on the best procedure for replacing Guthrie. Only Thompson's threat of resignation brings Hamilton back to his senses, reminding him that the present emergency is more important than the mechanisms by which the Review's internal hierarchy will be preserved. Hamilton then agrees to the raise and sends his editors out to put together the next issue of the Review.

Underwood subtly represents the reviewers as growing out of touch with a changing reading public, and becoming preoccupied with the internal affairs of their journal. Their stagnant military organization is part of a futile attempt to rule consumers of literature by force. Guthrie's death occurs ironically at the conclusion of his recommendation about preserving the *Critical's* power. This central incident, together with frequent analogies between the editors and a highland clan, underscores the impression that the Review's mission has become antiquated. Underwood's attack is, moreover, all the more effective because it accurately reflects the anxieties that the editors of the *Critical* admitted to having.

The *Monthly* is the object of an attack in Samuel Foote's *The Lyar* (1761) that is similar to Underwood's in its pretense to inside information. Papillion, the mentor to the play's hero, Young Wilding, relates the details of his first employment in London, working for the *Monthly*. He presents the process of reviewing as ridiculously formulaic:

> Our method was very concise: We copy the title-page of a new book; we never go any farther: if we are order'd to praise it, we have at hand about ten words, which scattered through as many periods, effectually does the business, as, "laudable design, happy arrangement, spirited language, nervous sentiment, elevation of thought, conclusive argument;" if we are to decry, then we have, "unconnected, flat, false, illiberal stricture, reprehensible, unnatural:" . . . These are the arms with which we engage authors of every kind. To us all subjects are equal; plays or sermons, poetry or politics, music or midwifery, it is the same thing.[71]

What is perhaps most astounding about the phenomenon of pamphlet attacks on the *Monthly* and the *Critical* is that the Reviews took them so seriously, responding to brief, hastily written publications with what now seems an unwarranted zeal. The ensuing chapters will serve, I hope, to put these local skirmishes in a clearer perspective. Except for Churchill, the writers of pamphlet attacks either did not aspire to, or failed to attain, significant status as professional authors. The more substantial antagonism between the Reviews and major writers offers a more valuable means of delineating the relative power of each. The case studies that follow illustrate possible resolutions to the relation between author and critic, as well as possible ways for an author to enact a career. As these examples make clear, not only is the model for authorship at midcentury unstable, but the relations between authors and the critics who in effect predict their careers are highly volatile.

"I wrote not to be fed but to be famous"

Laurence Sterne

Laurence Sterne offers perhaps the most valuable case study of a mid-eighteenth-century literary career. His decision at age 45 to "turn author" is uniquely premeditated, yet his uncertainty about the conditions of authorship in the literary world he so assertively entered is equally remarkable. Both his self-consciousness and his confusion can be traced with considerable accuracy in letters, *Tristram Shandy*, and *A Sentimental Journey*. They make up the history of his struggle to discover what it meant to be an author in his time. We can mark each stage of his unsteady progress toward attaining celebrity and understanding the nature of his own fame. We can also observe, in the rise and decline of the *Tristram Shandy* fashion in the early 1760s and the subsequent success of *A Sentimental Journey* in the late 1760s, how one author responded to gaining, then losing, then regaining the adulation of the various publics that defined him as a cultural figure.

Sterne's case is an especially illustrative one for this study because he reenacts the transition from patrons and a coterie audience to booksellers and a consuming public that had transformed authorship as a whole during the late seventeenth and early eighteenth centuries. Though that transformation took place over a period of more than a century, Sterne, I will argue, experienced it all during his brief career as a writer. In a way that is matched perhaps only by Samuel Johnson's indignant rejection of Lord Chesterfield's patronage in 1755, the story of Sterne's career is emblematic of the most basic changes in cultural production that took place during the eighteenth century, and through him we can assess with some precision what authors lost and what they gained as the conditions of literary production were realigned.

Though the influences on Sterne's behavior throughout his seven years as a celebrated author are numerous, I would like to isolate four stages in his professional life as the focus of my inquiries in this chapter. At first, Sterne relied on the Church of England, the central organizing feature of which was a system of individual patronage, for his understanding of professional advancement and success. His initial beliefs about patronage as a universal means of public validation made his transition from clergyman to author almost seamless. The second stage is characterized by Sterne's reimagining the function of patron, and by his earliest awareness of a mass audience. I argue that by soliciting David Garrick's aid in the promotion of *Tristram Shandy*, Sterne sought to combine a patronage that consisted exclusively of publicity with a uniquely theatrical appeal to potential readers. He behaved as though Garrick were his aristocratic patron (though he received no money from him), and with Garrick's help he courted a broad readership by means analogous to those that the actor had perfected. The third stage is marked by Sterne's uncertain reaction to the flood of public attention that followed the publication of the first two volumes of *Tristram Shandy*. Sterne first saw the pamphlet attacks and imitations as flattering, but quickly grew disillusioned with them. Throughout this period, which spanned from May 1760 to the publication of volumes three and four in January 1761, Sterne struggled to regain authorial control over the book and characters that he had released to the English reading public in the previous year. Finally, Sterne's complex relationship with the *Monthly* and the *Critical* is the focus of the final stage of his career and culminates an intensive process of professionalization. Though nothing about the reception of *Tristram Shandy* could be called ordinary, this last set of influences encompasses Sterne's normal interaction with the newer, institutional forces that were so prominent in the literary culture of his day.

My aims are broadly biographical: I wish to chart the path by which Sterne came to redefine his job as an author. How, in other words, did he go from seeking the personal validation that only an important patron could offer, to thoroughly commodifying himself, "both inside and out," in order to embrace the anonymous validation of the largest possible audience?[1] At the same time as I tell the story of Sterne's professional life, I make the broader argument that biographies are invented, not disclosed. By exploring the powerful forces that prompted detour after detour in Sterne's crusade for fame, I hope to show how his career is an amalgam of his own ambitions and various expressions of consumer demand, the most significant of which proved, ultimately, to be the Reviews. In virtually every case, Sterne had limited latitude in his attempts to come to terms with this demand. Thus, the narrative of his career is not entirely his own; ultimately it belongs more properly to his reviewers.

The topics that I address in this chapter bear only a tangential relationship to the conventional concerns of Sterne criticism.[2] From the following pages, one might deduce my opinions about whether Sterne is in control of his narratives or whether he is inseparable as a presence in the novels from Tristram or Yorick, or whether we should hold Sterne's work by the comic or sentimental "handle."[3] I hope that the questions that I ask here encompass these thematic problems and allow them to be reframed in light of the more significant issue of how Sterne's career was made.

The most fascinating moment in all of Sterne's correspondence occurs in a letter to Eliza Draper, written in 1767, in which he recollects his first meeting with the great Lord Bathurst in 1760, shortly after the first two volumes of *Tristram Shandy* appeared in print:

He came up to me, one day, as I was at the Princess of Wales' court. "I want to know you, Mr. Sterne; but it is fit you should know, also, who it is that wishes this pleasure. You have heard," continued he, "of an old Lord Bathurst, of whom your Popes, and Swifts have sung and spoken so much: I have lived my life with geniuses of that cast; but have survived them; and, despairing ever to find their equals, it is some years since I have closed my accounts, and shut up my books, with thoughts of never opening them again: but you have kindled a desire in me of opening them once more before I die; which I now do; so go home and dine with me." (*Letters*, 305)

Established by 1767 as an immensely popular author, Sterne expresses a wish to cement his position in the literary tradition of his century. Bathurst, the patron of Swift and Pope, and 76 years old at the time, is the superannuated symbol of the continuity between Sterne and the giants of the previous age, and Sterne ventriloquizes that connection explicitly through Bathurst. He presents this meeting, with all the affective force of the best episodes of *A Sentimental Journey*, as one of the most important events of his life.

The real relationship between Sterne and Bathurst, however, bears only slight resemblance to the kind of bond we might expect to follow from Sterne's highly stylized account of its beginnings. Bathurst did subscribe to the first two volumes of *The Sermons of Mr. Yorick* in 1761, and he occasionally entertained the author as a dinner guest. But his financial support thereafter was nominal, and he did not, as Sterne implies, unreservedly invite the author into his private life and social circle. Indeed, the dialogue that Sterne ascribes to Bathurst in the letter is curiously inappropriate as well: in Sterne's fantasy, the noble patron is rendered into a shrewd businessman. Bathurst closes his accounts and shuts up his books when he fails to see a promising investment, behavior fitting for a member of the merchant class, but grossly out of place for a nobleman. Having never witnessed firsthand the relationship between an aristocratic patron and an author (unaware perhaps of how unlikely was the image of Lord Bathurst as corporate accountant), Sterne fills in the blanks as best he can.

The letter raises, if obliquely, a host of questions that this section will attempt to answer, questions about the status of noble patronage in the eighteenth century, and also about the sources and nature of the fame authors attain in an environment no longer dominated by patronage. How, for example, do we reconcile Sterne's sense of the significance of meeting Bathurst with the token financial support that he actually received from the lord? Since Sterne clearly did not benefit in a practical way from Bathurst, what need did meeting Bathurst satisfy? And how do we weigh the endorsement of the most selective of noble patrons against other, more immediate indexes of Sterne's success as an author?

Sterne's personal transition from a fantasy of individual patronage to the realities of the open market was significantly incomplete: he never fully relinquished the belief that being an author entailed a special affinity with the aristocracy. Yet, astonishingly, he seemed to realize without prompting that he would have to present both his writing and himself as commodities in order to succeed. His reluctance to let go of the old conception of patronage, even as he embraced the new, is a compelling testimony to the confusion caused by the changing conditions of literary production during the middle decades of the century.

In order to make sense of Sterne's attachment to the idea of noble patronage, we need first to recognize the importance of his first career as a clergyman and to explore how his decision to write *Tristram Shandy* emerged.[4] Sterne's strategies for advancement in the field of literature are, I suggest, adapted from traditional means of advancement in the Church of England: he reasonably assumed that his new career, like his old one, would be enabled by a patron. Even a much more detailed account of the clerical profession than this chapter allows would not easily clarify the significance of Sterne's accomplishments during his 22 years in the full-time service of the Anglican Church. Geoffrey Holmes accurately characterizes the Church as the "most haphazard of professions" during the eighteenth century.[5] The chief flaws in its career structure were, as he observes, the "insecurity of tenure" that resulted from intense overcrowding and a byzantine system of patronage that did not reward merit with any consistency. Although it is impossible to assess Sterne's clerical career until 1759 as typical or atypical, we can identify, in his letters especially, frustrations and disappointments that were common for those in situations like his. What is extraordinary about Sterne's case, of course, is that he ultimately exorcised his frustrations by writing *Tristram Shandy*.

It is worth pausing, however, to consider the nature of those frustrations. Joseph Addison joked in the *Spectator* (no. 21; March 24, 1711) that the clergy in England "are not to be numbered," and that should they "enter into the corrupt Practice of the Laity, by the splitting of their Freeholds, they would be able to carry most of the Elections in *England*."[6] The claim was perhaps less hyperbolic in 1740, when Sterne was ordained, than when Addison wrote. Those without "the advantages of birth and influence" were, as Norman Sykes describes, involved in "a lottery in which the number of blanks was alarmingly high, and the proportion of small prizes still higher."[7]

Compounding the problem of simple overcrowding was the arbitrary nature of the sponsorship of would-be clerics. Throughout the first half of the century, the upper clergy remained a "closed shop for the well-connected."[8] As for the rest, a bewildering but inefficient array of sources of patronage existed. At the beginning of the century, there were more than 1,000 livings in the Lord Chancellor's gift. The Church of England's hierarchy itself determined about one-quarter of all pastoral appointments. In the first three decades of the century, Oxford and Cambridge colleges "embarked on a systematic spending spree, picking up patronage of livings where and when they could in order to be able to place their Fellows advantageously."[9] But an inordinate number of these positions went to relatives of those who assigned them. Moreover, Holmes estimates that "perhaps two-thirds" of the Anglican clergy numbered among "the shabbily genteel, the straitened, the depressed and the submerged."[10] Many of these depended on subscriptions for their subsistence, and could effectually be starved out if the subscribers refused to honor their pledges.

Sterne's own career includes many of the successes and disappointments of a typical clerical life. His progress was promising at first: aided by his uncle Jaques Sterne, he acquired a living at Sutton-on-the-Forest in 1738, and a second, at Stillington, in 1744.[11] By 1756 he had good prospects for a third living, and, as Arthur Cash speculates, "had he waited patiently, he might have ended his life as a prosperous Yorkshire clergyman."[12] But he could not contain his ambition. After this promising uphill climb, his hopes received an irrevocable setback when he sided with John Fountayne (the Dean of York, with whose help Sterne hoped to gain his third living) in a controversy with Dr. Francis Topham. Sterne led the pamphlet attack on Topham, who had schemed to reserve an important clerical position for his son (then only seven years old). He culminated his efforts with *A Political Romance* (1759), but on the eve of its publication, John Gilbert, Bishop of York, summoned Fountayne, Topham, and Sterne to London and—by means that remain a mystery—settled the quarrel. The publication of *A Political Romance* was summarily canceled, and Sterne blamed his wasted efforts on Fountayne, who, he felt, did not reciprocate his loyalty.[13] Beginning *Tristram Shandy* in 1759 was the first step in a career change he initiated because he ceased to see hope for further advancement in his original field.

His letters during this transition period reveal the remarkable extent to which he saw the two careers (authorship and the clergy) as interchangeable, both possible means to a level of professional or social fulfillment that he wanted to reach. He confesses that his motivations for "turning author" are first despair over the slow pace of his professional advancement in the clergy—"Ought I know I may not be preferr'd till the Resurrection of the Just" (*Letters*, 76)—and then resentment of the toil for his superiors that would earn such advancement. The letters bear no evidence that Sterne saw his decision to turn to writing as a radical redirection of his life. They suggest both how narrow and how uniform his conception of professional life is. The advancement he hopes for is an unspecified kind of prestige as a public figure, one that could be won just as easily by an author as by a prebendary.

In the same letter, written in November 1759, Sterne admits, in a particularly cryptic apology, his most secret hopes for what a literary career will do for him. Discussing *Tristram Shandy*, he draws the analogy between the clerical and writing professions even more tightly: "I deny I have gone as far as Swift—He keeps a due distance from Rabelais—& I keep a due distance from him—Swift has said a hundred things I durst not Say—Unless I was Dean of St. Patrick's" (*Letters*, 76). The significance of the condition "Unless I was Dean of St. Patrick's" can only be appreciated fully in light of the relationship Sterne himself draws between his frustration in the Church and his decision to embark on a writing career. In fact, only a few months later, once *Tristram Shandy* had been published and its author made instantly famous, Sterne deliberately aligned himself with Swift. Writing to Richard Berenger on March 8, 1760, about the possibility that Hogarth might sketch the frontispiece to the second edition of *Tristram Shandy*, volumes one and two, Sterne recalled, "Oft did Swift sigh to Pope in these words—*Orna me*" (*Letters*, 99).

In short, Sterne felt that *Tristram Shandy* would guarantee him a literary preferment. It would not make him Dean of St. Patrick's, but it would make him independent of the Dean of York. That step, he hoped, would end his professional stagnation and make it possible for him someday to advance to a position of power sufficient for him to get away with saying things as outrageous as Swift had. As for the problem of how he would go about acquiring this literary preferment, Sterne claimed to know only enough in the summer and fall of 1759 to say, "I depend much upon the candour of the publick" (*Letters*, 84).

In fact he knew much more, specifically, that there was no unmediated path to the "candour of the publick." He realized that he would require assistance to succeed as an author just as he needed (and did not get) it to succeed in the Church. All of Sterne's assumptions about professional advancement came from his experience with the Church of England's intricate and nepotistic patronage system, its practices and customs firmly entrenched since Walpole's rise to power nearly a generation before Sterne was ordained. Thus, Sterne's initial methods, as well as his aim, were no different than those of a prebendary politicking for ecclesiastical preferment. He assumed, first, that there was an equivalent literary hierarchy and, second, that it operated in a similar way, but this vision, complete with potential patrons at every level, was no longer accurate by 1760.

Sterne's choice of a benefactor, David Garrick, reveals both his shrewdness and the limits of his ability to assess the literary culture of his day. Sterne correctly realized the value of Garrick's favorable opinion. Garrick was, by his thirteenth year as Drury Lane's manager and part owner, a patron of great stature, a man who could not supply an author with money, but who had complete control over the production of plays at his theater. The recipients of Garrick's patronage, though, formed a fairly small, closed circle; indeed, some of them enlisted titled friends to intercede with the manager on their behalf. Moreover, Garrick was in a position to offer tangible help only to playwrights. He was extremely well connected, and Sterne benefited from his circle of acquaintances, but he could not serve as the traditional patron Sterne probably envisioned he would be.[14]

Nevertheless, Sterne began his efforts to ensure the favorable reception of *Tristram Shandy* with a baldly strategic address to Garrick. His only means of access to Garrick was the actress and singer Catherine Fourmantel, with whom Sterne was at the time carrying on a flirtation. Sterne took advantage of her slight acquaintance with

Garrick by sending her a letter, "with intention that she recopy it and send it as from herself" to Garrick. The letter served to identify Sterne, and to recommend his book:

There are two Volumes just published here which have made a great noise, & have had a prodigious Run; for in 2 Days after they came out, the Bookseller sold two hundred—& continues selling them very fast. It is, The Life & Opinions of Tristram Shandy, which the Author told me last night at our Concert, he had sent up to London, so perhaps you have seen it; If you have not seen it, pray get it & read it, because it has a great Character as a witty smart Book, and if You think it is so, your good word in Town will do the Author; I am sure great Service; You must understand, He is a kind & generous friend of mine. . . . His name is Sterne, a gentleman of great Preferment & a Prebendary of the Church of York, & has a great Character in these Parts as a man of Learning & wit. (*Letters*, 85–86, January 1, 1760)

Amazingly, the letter accomplished everything that Sterne could have hoped. Garrick wrote to Sterne asking for a copy and was favorably impressed (as he had been set up to be).

On January 27, 1760, Sterne himself wrote to Garrick and mentioned that he had heard that the actor "had actually spoke well of my Book" (*Letters*, 86). That first letter is a further attempt to secure Garrick's approbation and is as carefully calculated as the Fourmantel letter. Sterne thanks Garrick for his good opinion, and half apologizes for not having sent him the two volumes before publication. He even hints coyly at his motives for seeking out Garrick: "I know not what it was (tho 'I lye abominably,' because I know very well) which inclined me more to wish for your Approbation, than any Others" (*Letters*, 86).

Significantly, this and subsequent letters to Garrick are written in a prose style no different from that of *Tristram Shandy* itself. He begins the first letter, for example, by recording in Shandean fashion his recent worries about writing to such a famous man:

I had a strong Propensity when I did myself the pleasure of sending You the two vols to have accompanied them with a Letter to You:—I took up my Pen twice—hang it!—I shall write a vile insinuating Letter, the english of which will be,—to beg Mr. Garrick's good word for my Book, whether the Book deserves it or no—I will not, the Book shall go to the Devil first. (*Letters*, 86)

He then reiterates that the book "has therefore gone forth into the world, hot as it came from my Brain, without one Correction:—'tis however a picture of myself, & so far may bid the fairer for being an Original." In fact, Sterne had revised *Tristram Shandy* extensively after Robert Dodsley initially showed no interest in it, but he was anxious to convey the impression that everything he wrote—from *Tristram Shandy* to everyday correspondence—was spontaneous and "Original."[15]

His second letter is written even more eccentrically, more in the style of the novel. Alluding to the rumor about the powerful Bishop of Gloucester, William Warburton, appearing as Tristram's tutor in future volumes, Sterne writes: "Twas for all the world like a cut across my finger with a sharp penknife.—I saw the blood—gave it a suck—wrapt it up—and thought no more about it" (*Letters*, 92).

During the first few months after the publication of *Tristram Shandy*, Sterne relied on the Shandy style whenever he sought an important ornament for his growing reputation: specifically Garrick's friendship, Warburton's goodwill, and a Hogarth frontispiece for the second edition, volumes one and two. For this last favor, Sterne/Shandy wrote to Richard Berenger, whom he had met through Garrick: "Prithee sally out to Leicester fields, and when you have knocked at the door (for you must knock) and got in—begin thus 'Mr. Hogarth, I have been with my friend Shandy this morning'— but go on yr own way—as I shall do mine. . . . Yrs most Shandaically L Sterne."[16]

Sterne's estimation and exploitation of Garrick's position of influence in fashionable London society says a great deal about how he conceived of his literary practice at this early stage. Certainly one can infer that he perceived fashionable London as indisputably the most desirable readership. But a more important conclusion is to be drawn from the nature of the fame Sterne sought and the methods by which he sought it. He struggled to reconcile his complete willingness to commodify himself with the fantasy that his best readers, at least, could still stand as discrete individuals—a personal network in which he hoped to enlist with the help of its leader, whom Sterne presumed to be Garrick. Even as he deliberately set about to capture the attention of a mass audience, Sterne measured his fame in purely

personal terms: celebrated acquaintances, a heavy slate of dinner en-
gagements, occasional gifts from the nobility, and meeting the prince.
Boswell describes him:

> By Fashion's hands completely drest
> He's everywhere a welcome Guest;
> He runs about from place to place,
> Now with my Lord, then with his Grace,
> And mixing with the brilliant throng,
> He straight commences Beau Garcon.
> (*Letters*, 106)

Boswell caricatures the defining features of Sterne's ambitions to
upward mobility, fixing, like Sterne himself, on all the details that
suggest he is now welcome in (perhaps part of) the aristocratic social
circles to which *Tristram Shandy* has given him access. Far more
clearly than Sterne, however, Boswell sees the absurdity of the rural
parson's "mixing with the brilliant throng." As the recollection about
Bathurst suggests, Sterne clung to the fantasy of the rewards of personal patronage—an affiliation with the nobility and social elite—
throughout his life as a writer, but his unfounded faith that one advances in literature as one does in the Church of England is never so
apparent than in these first few months of the Shandy vogue.

That particular misjudgment, however, did not blur the uncanny
self-consciousness with which Sterne marketed himself during this
period. His correspondence with Catherine Fourmantel (an insider
from the start) is particularly revealing in its differences from the letters designed to further his popularity. He does not adopt the Shandy
style. He seems genuinely astounded by his sudden popularity and
openly eager to help it along. He boasts to her in March 1760 about
receiving a stipend of £160 per year from Lord Fauconberg, and
again in April that "there is a fine print going to be done of me" (the
first one by Reynolds) (*Letters*, 101–2). In his most straightforward
and astonishing admission of his surrender to a consumer public, he
writes to her, "I shall make the most of myself & sell both inside and
out" (*Letters*, 105).

For the most valuable insight into this confusing juxtaposition of
attitudes we must look to Sterne's relationship with Garrick. Sterne's

solicitation of Garrick and the means by which he secured him as a benefactor are usually attributed to the aspiring author's entrepreneurial skill aided by the coincidence of Fourmantel's acquaintance. But these general speculations leave key questions unanswered: where did Sterne acquire his entrepreneurial skill, and why did the tactics he chose work so well on Garrick? I contend that courting the attention of Garrick was Sterne's first attempt to define himself professionally after abandoning hope of advancement in the Church. In the absence of a conventional career pattern or public image for writers of fiction, Sterne looked to the theater as the best available model for capturing the attention of a mass audience.

Garrick epitomized the London theater in 1760. He had not yet reached Olympian heights as a cultural figure—he was not elected to Johnson's Club until 1767. Although his power as manager of one of the two patented theaters was considerable, he still existed in the public imagination foremost as an actor. But Garrick's complete identification with acting is also precisely what made him controversial, the subject of critiques of fame by Johnson, Goldsmith, and, most acerbically, Joshua Reynolds.

Reynolds echoes the complaint of his contemporaries that "great as Garrick was on the stage, he was at least equal if not still superior at the table, and here he had too much the same habit of preparing himself, as if he was to act a principle part."[17] Garrick seems, in Reynolds's description, a "slave to his reputation," driven by his desire for fame to extend the premeditated behavior of the stage into every aspect of his public life. The practice jeopardized the possibility of his relating to individuals rather than large groups: Johnson described him as having "friends but no friend."[18] Reynolds offers an even subtler theory of the incompatibility of fame and intimacy: "An inordinate desire after fame produces an entire neglect of their old friends. . . . Their whole desire and ambition is centered in extending their reputation by showing their tricks before fresh new men. That moment you begin to congratulate yourself on your new acquaintances, your intimacy ceases."[19] Ultimately, he concludes, people who, like Garrick, are motivated by "greediness [for] . . . immediate gratification" forfeit any sense of themselves as consistent subjects:

"From having no great general principle they live in perpetual anxiety what conduct to take on every occasion to insure this petty praise."[20]

The characteristics of Garrick's path from slavery to his reputation to an unprincipled thirst for praise from any audience are replicated in the early stages of Sterne's career. They are the inevitable features of any author's relationship with a consumer public. That public can only apprehend the author as a commodity akin to an actor on stage, and only within the confines of this framework can the ready audience be construed as the author's "friends." (Johnson, had he lived later, would perhaps have said that Garrick had fans but no friends.) Sterne and Garrick's affinity for one another—Cash describes them as "fascinated with each other"[21]—can be traced in part to the virtuosity they shared in commodifying themselves for the emergent mass audiences, and to the restlessness that seemed to compel both of them always to show "their tricks before fresh new men." Similarities in their visions of the ideal relationship with an audience reach as far back as Sterne's sermons, which were occasionally prefaced with a list of "dramatis personae," and were originally to be published under the title, *The Dramatic Sermons of Mr. Yorick*.[22]

What makes Sterne's intuitions about presenting himself strategically as Tristram significant is that he extended practices that have their origins in the theater not merely to "the table," as Garrick had, but to the printed page. He was Tristram or Yorick to a reading public consisting of thousands who had never even seen him, a point that Boswell makes concisely in the conclusion of the epigram cited above:

> A buzzing whisper flys about;
> Wher'er he comes they point him out;
> Each waiter with an eager eye
> Observes him as he passes by;
> "That there he is do, Thomas! look,
> Who's wrote such a damn'd clever book."
>
> (*Letters*, 106)

Indeed, the first two volumes of *Tristram Shandy* precipitated a kind of cult surrounding the author. Dr. John Hill observed in May 1760:

"The discourse, where I was, turned not upon the book, but upon the man. . . . We long to know something of the man, whose exploits astonish us, or whose wit has charmed us."[23]

Sterne as an author, though, as his correspondence with Garrick suggests, is so adeptly grafted to his characters that the distinction between the book and the man quickly became impossible to draw. The identification of author and character in Sterne's life and work suggests the presence of a remarkable (and distinctly modern) alertness to the nature of consumer demand in the field of literature. In the past, literary works had not determined the public image of their authors. Though Pope and Swift, for example, both made use of elaborate personae, no one conceived of Pope and Martinus Scriblerus as a single identity, and the character of Isaac Bickerstaff, when it was appropriated by Addison and Steele, did not remain fused with Swift.

Over the course of the next few decades one can observe, however, several other examples in which "the book" and "the man" are conflated. The public identities of both M. G. "Monk" Lewis and William Beckford, the "Caliph of Fonthill," were intimately bound up with the fictional works that had first brought them notoriety. The development culminates in the early nineteenth century with the Byronic hero—a creation whose defining feature is the capacity for being identified with Byron himself, and for behaving in a way that one can recognize from Byron's personal life. But the centrality of character, of "personality" per se in *Tristram Shandy* is unprecedented. What is perhaps most remarkable is that Sterne began this professional lifetime of passing before his public undifferentiated from the characters of his book by addressing the most accomplished of role-players, Garrick.

More needs to be said, however, about why Sterne and Garrick were able to captivate their respective publics as they did. What accounts for the attractiveness of the public images that these two men were so skillful at manipulating? For an answer we need to look to the growing appeal during the middle of the eighteenth century of "natural" acting on stage and its literary equivalent, "sensibility." In different settings, Sterne and Garrick were perceived by consumer publics as breaking new ground: they both appeared, in a richly detailed way, to be recovering authentic emotions either on stage or in the pages of *Tristram Shandy*.

Garrick and Charles Macklin were the central figures in what has come to be known as the Acting Revolution, a transformation in acting style so radical that it dominated discussions of theater during the middle decades of the century, and prompted a widespread interest in the theory of acting.[24] By all contemporary accounts, Garrick's charisma on the stage derived from his ability to represent characters and emotions in a way that audiences perceived as lifelike. Virtually all of his peers appeared, by contrast, to be declaiming. Persuasive acting during this revolutionary period, in other words, came to depend on the interdependency between real emotions and those portrayed on stage, a relationship that worked to minimize obvious artifice. The association informs the oratorical revival as well—Thomas Sheridan, in *Lectures on Elocution*, concludes a chapter on delivery by asserting: "The chief aim of all public speakers is to persuade, and in order to persuade, it is above all things necessary that the speaker should at least appear himself to believe what he utters, but this can never be the case where there are any evident marks of affectation, or art."[25]

Manuals on acting urged students to investigate the range of emotions as they had experienced them, and to draw from that archive when performing on stage. The emphasis, to be sure, was on simulating rather than reliving emotional responses—extensive practice before mirrors was highly recommended. Johnson and others regularly observed that while Garrick represented rage, sorrow, and so on, convincingly, he felt nothing himself while doing so. But the very need to make such an observation suggests that, by midcentury, acting and feeling stood in closer proximity than they had in previous generations on the London stage. Indeed, the possibility that Thomas Betterton or Elizabeth Barry might have been feeling what they represented would not have been conceivable to a Restoration audience—the emotional distance between the actor and the performance seemed, to those audiences, to be greater.

The analogue to the Acting Revolution in letters is the rise of fictional narratives such as *Tristram Shandy*. Sterne, like Garrick, captured his audiences by appearing to tap his own real emotions, and he aroused their suspicions, as well, that no emotions so extensively chronicled and so widely published could possibly be heartfelt. *Tristram Shandy* crosses the boundary between "natural character" and "personality" that Richard Sennett uses to distinguish eighteenth-century psychology from that of the nineteenth century. Natural character presumes that the range of human emotions is universal and unchanging, that it can be encompassed through "variations in rage, compassion, or trust." Personality, by contrast, is self-conscious and individual, and requires chiefly "the capacity to 'recover' one's emotions."[26] A work such as *Tristram Shandy* invites a universal reaction, particularly to its sentimental episodes; a person's readiness to shed a tear at the appropriate moments is evidence of that person's sensibility and defines him or her as an ideal reader.

Yet *Tristram Shandy* was unprecedented and unsurpassed in its recovery of one person's emotions. Beginning as it does with Tristram's conception, the book describes an inner life in a way that is radically different than the myriad of novels bearing the title "The History of . . ." And in a way very different from *Pamela* or *Clarissa*, private correspondences deemed instructive by their "editor," *Tristram Shandy* promotes its hero's inner life shamelessly.

Sterne and Garrick, then, bear similarities that are crucial to the developments that I wish to illustrate. Both revolutionized the artist's relationship with an emergent mass audience. At a time when the affective power of theater seemed in danger of eroding, Garrick re-energized it by psychologizing the function of the actor, by redirecting the audience's focus to the vibrant and emotionally integrated individual before them. A generation later, Sterne redirected the thriving cultural practice of fiction writing in precisely the same way, by intertwining his own identity with that of his characters and presenting the undifferentiated amalgam to the public. Thus Sterne's initial dreams of a career in literature boosted by a patron were thereby transformed and modernized.

Sterne's public and thoroughgoing identification with his characters predictably played itself out in the reception of the first two volumes of *Tristram Shandy*. Both the disparity and the similarity of the responses are neatly captured in the following two excerpts. In a letter from an unidentified correspondent to the *Grand Magazine*, entitled "Animadversions on *Tristram Shandy*," the writer lingers on "Tristy's" physical appearance:

I have the pleasure to acquaint you that I am one of the jolly sons of Comus, and that we are all in raptures with his facetious disciple, that paragon of mirth and humour, *Tristram Shandy*. We are firmly persuaded, with friend *Tristy*, that every time a man smiles, but more so when he laughs, it adds something to this fragment of life. This being the case, we pronounce *Tristy* the best physician [in] the world, for there is no reading him without laughing; nay the very sight of him is reviving—for his long sharp nose, and his droll look altogether, affect our risible faculties so strongly, that there is no looking at him without laughing.[27]

In a slightly different context, the *Monthly Review*'s article on Sterne's *The Sermons of Mr. Yorick*, published in May 1760, called the ploy of placing Yorick's name on the title page of a collection of sermons actually preached in church "the greatest outrage against sense and decency that has been offered since the first establishment of Christianity": "Must obscenity then be the handmaid to Religion—and must the exordium to a sermon, be a smutty tale? Tillotson, Clarke, and Foster found other means of raising attention to divine truths; and their names will be respected, when those of YORICK and TRISTRAM SHANDY will be forgotten or despised" (*Monthly* 22 [May 1760]: 42).

The two passages express sharply opposed opinions about the same set of relations that make up Sterne as a public figure. The letter makes no distinction between Sterne and Shandy, and celebrates "Tristy's" mere presence as an inducement to laughter. The writer does not present Sterne as an author but as an image, not as a wit but as the physiognomic epitome of wit. He speaks of Sterne, in other words, more as a character than an author. And yet the thrust of the sketch is to present Shandy/Sterne as the letter writer's kindred spirit. The reviewer for the *Monthly* is also drawn to the ways in which Sterne is united with his characters, specifically to the use of Yorick's name on the title page of Sterne's sermons. But the reviewer describes this strategy for enhancing the public profile of the *Sermons* as a case of obscenity being rendered "the handmaid of Religion." He is outraged by Sterne's decision to place marketability above all else, including traditional standards of decency, when he chose the title of his sermons, and he resents as well that Sterne accomplishes that end by conflating his own public identity with that of his fictional parson.

Contrasting assessments, such as these, of the packaging of Laurence Sterne soon raised urgent complications for the author. Imitations, pamphlets, spin-offs, and fan letters in magazines, taken as a whole, constituted one chief legible source of the reception of *Tristram Shandy*, and the Reviews constituted the other. Sterne's initial hopes that Garrick would circulate *Tristram Shandy* among an elite clique of London readers, who would stand as the book's ideal audience, were quickly exploded by the enormity of the Shandy fashion. His immediate, overwhelming popularity made it impossible, at this stage, for him to gauge the predilections of his audience or audiences.

In the months that followed the initial printing of *Tristram Shandy*, volumes one and two, and the social connections made possible by Garrick, I contend that Sterne was forced to revise, sometimes enthusiastically, sometimes grudgingly, his idealistic notion that the relationship between author and reader could be a one-to-one correspondence between equals, or a show of public deference to a noble patron. As he sought new means of identifying, in order to appeal to, the desires of his new larger audience, the discourses that most readily presented themselves as indexes of that public's taste were the Reviews and "Sterneiana." The former purported to reflect the judgments of erudite and discerning readers, and the latter—the productions of imitators, parodists, and other pamphleteers—could be counted on to reproduce what they considered to be the most salable aspects of *Tristram Shandy*.

Sterne was, in effect, confronted with a choice between two barometers—reviews and Sterneiana—of a range of public tastes that increasingly defied comprehensive representation. Moreover, as the passages with which I began this section suggest, the reviewers and the pamphleteers approached the moral possibilities of the book from opposite directions. Plainly, the pamphleteers aimed to sensationalize the "hints and whiskers" of obscenity that the reviewers, as literary policemen, wished to suppress. More substantively, the pamphleteers and the reviewers entertained radically different opinions of the Sterne/Shandy or Sterne/Yorick amalgams that drew their attention. The second installment of *Tristram Shandy* (volumes three and four, which Sterne composed from June through November 1760), then, entailed a momentous choice about the relative desirability of two very different audiences. As I will argue, Sterne chose in that second installment to disparage the reviewers and write in the vein of the pamphleteers.

The scope and popularity of the Sterneiana that appeared in 1760 alone was astonishing. Pamphlet attacks and imitations began to appear and came to Sterne's attention in the spring of 1760. At first he welcomed them all, eager for publicity but misjudging the distinctions among the kinds of people who read *Tristram Shandy*. He remarked in a letter to Stephen Croft on May 1, 1760: "There is a shilling pamphlet wrote against Tristram—I wish they would write a hundred such" (*Letters*, 107).

Sterne got his wish. *Two Lyric Epistles*, by the author's friend John Hall-Stevenson (published April 17, 1760), was the first of a flood of publications praising, defending, attacking, or imitating *Shandy*. Twenty such pieces appeared by January 1761; they became more elaborate as well, growing from shilling pamphlets to small books that sold for three shillings sixpence. Perhaps the most popular, *The Clockmaker's Outcry Against the Author of the Life and Opinions of Tristram Shandy* (a complaint against the sexualizing of clocks brought about by Walter Shandy's domestic habits) was originally published on May 9, 1760, and had already reached a fourth edition by June 20.[28] Jeremiah Kunastrokius's *Explanatory Remarks on the Life and Opinions of Tristram Shandy* was so popular that the author felt sufficiently encouraged to satisfy the reading public's curiosity about his own life in *The Life and Opinions of Jeremiah Kunastrokius*.

Despite the astounding scurrility of many of these pamphlets, critics occasionally suggested that Sterne himself had written them. The *Critical*'s reviewer of *Explanatory Remarks* wrote, "We harbour some suspicions that the author himself is here giving breath to the trumpet of fame" (*Critical* 9 [April 1760]: 319). Even those who could tell the difference between Sterne and his imitators blamed him for setting a bad example, such as the writer for the *London Magazine* who claimed in June 1760: "If *Tristram Shandy* had done any mischief, 'tis in raising such a swarm of filthy pamphleteers, to din the ears and poison the eyes of the public."[29]

Sterne was just as quickly disillusioned by the great success of the *Tristram Shandy* pamphlet industry as he had been delighted by its beginnings. Less than a month after welcoming the publication of such pamphlets as *The Clockmaker's Outcry*, he complains, "The scribblers use me ill" (*Letters*, 112) and later implores, "God forgive me for the Volumes of Ribaldry I've been the cause of" (*Letters*, 118). Sterne's quick reversal of opinion about this popular body of writing stems from his as yet incomplete sense of the complex sources of his own fame. The pamphlets contributed greatly to the cult of *Tristram Shandy* and thereby helped popularize Sterne himself, since as a public figure he made himself virtually indistinguishable from Shandy.

At the same time they further undermined his initial understanding of the author-reader relationship as a bond modeled upon personal patronage. The pamphlets made it clear that "Laurence Sterne" had been turned into an institution. Each time a pamphleteer capitalized on the suggestion of bawdiness in *Tristram Shandy*, or brought forth some fictional anecdote about the "real" Sterne, or simply attacked him for immorality, Sterne's control over his own fictions of authorship, specifically the character of Tristram, and over his own wishes about how his book should be read, were diminished. Sterne was powerless to halt these developments—he was, as I will suggest, soon co-opted by them and became, in effect, one of his own imitators. As of the summer of 1760, however, he was simply chagrined that *Tristram Shandy* had outgrown the regulated setting into which he had introduced it and had, along with the image of its author, escaped his control.

Sterne returned to Yorkshire in June 1760, at the peak of this conflicted reception, to resume writing his book. Pamphlets of all kinds boosted *Tristram Shandy*'s popularity but appropriated Sterne's public identity in ways he did not always approve. The *Monthly* and the *Critical*, though they were favorably impressed by volumes one and two (*Critical* 9 [January 1760]: 73–4; *Monthly* appendix to July–December 1759: 561–71), partially blamed Sterne for the abundance of scurrilous pamphlets. The *Monthly*'s review of the *Sermons*, the most negative response to the new author's debut, tacitly condemned

Sterne's whole enterprise of conflating his own identity with his fiction. Finally, and predictably, the appearance of a spurious continuation of *Tristram Shandy* late in the summer of 1760 that was accepted as genuine by "a good many people"[30] demonstrated the urgent need for Sterne to produce volumes three and four. It also underscored the importance of the choices that lay before him about who his desired audience was and how to sustain their interest.

Sterne expressed his decision straightforwardly in volumes three and four by attacking the *Monthly* directly and by implicitly aligning himself with his imitators. Near the beginning of volume three, he responds with an elaborate metaphor to the *Monthly*'s excoriation of his *Sermons*:

A Man's body and his mind, with the utmost reverence to both I speak it, are exactly like a jerkin, and a jerkin's lining;—rumple the one—you rumple the other. There is one certain exception however in this case, and that is, when you are so fortunate a fellow, as to have had your jerkin made of gumtaffeta, and the body lining to it, of a sarcenet or thing persian. . . .

I believe in my conscience that mine is made up somewhat after this sort:—for never poor jerkin has been tickled off, at such a rate as it has been these last nine months together,—and yet I declare the lining to it,—as far as I am a judge of the matter, it is not a three-penny piece the worse. . . .

You Messrs. the Monthly Reviewers!—how could you cut and slash my jerkin as you did?—how did you know, but you would cut my lining too. (190–91)

He vows in addition to remain indifferent to any future assaults by reviewers, "being determined as long as I live or write (which in my case means the same thing) never to give the honest gentlemen a worse word or a worse wish, than my uncle Toby gave the fly which buzz'd about his nose all *dinner time*,—'Go,—go poor devil,' quoth he, 'get thee gone,—why should I hurt thee? This world is surely wide enough to hold both thee and me'" (191). Sterne's is an ingenious version of the standard midcentury claim by authors that reviewers have no real power. He reminds the reviewers that he remains an enigma to them—his jerkin is impenetrable and its lining exotic ("a sarcenet or thing persian")—and that this guarantees that they can inflict only the most superficial wounds on him. And he transforms them into flies in a hyperbolic demonstration of his own magnanimity.

Less direct but more insistent evidence of Sterne's decision is the almost relentless use of double entendre and innuendo to be found in volumes three and four. These choices constitute a measure of respect for the many imitators who used the Shandean style as a vehicle for the crudest ribaldry. But they are also Sterne's attempt to reclaim *Tristram Shandy* for himself: at times he seems to be trying to outdo the pamphleteers at their ("his") own kind of writing, a sort of mimicry to the second power. Indeed, Sterne's sense that he was competing with his imitators for the right to speak authoritatively in Tristram's voice may have been the dominant reason for his dismissal of the Reviews. The reviewers spoke a language drawn primarily from moral philosophy, in which Sterne, the author, at this point, had no interest. Nor does he in the passage from volume three seem to conceive of the reviewers as commanding any substantial audience— they are merely critics speaking their own minds. Sterne saw the pamphleteers, by contrast, as rivals vying for the attention of the *same* audience that he wished to continue entertaining. In fact, when he came to compose volumes three and four, Sterne seems to have not yet fully realized that the "general public" was far from homogenous, but instead seems to have mistaken part of it for the whole.

In the wake of *Tristram Shandy*'s initial success, Sterne looked to a larger audience for valorization, to move beyond Garrick's circle and "show his tricks before new men." The two distinct readerships that presented themselves to him, the readers of the Reviews and the readers of pamphlets and imitations, represented separate, opposing constituencies that might legitimate him as a public figure. In volumes three and four, Sterne underestimated the Reviews and overestimated the pamphleteers. By the spring of 1761, the production of Sterneiana had dwindled sharply, and the Reviews became the putative spokesmen for Sterne's increasingly impatient and dissatisfied readers. The *Monthly*, in its review of volumes three and four of *Tristram Shandy*, which were published in January 1761, made it clear that the novelty of the book had completely worn off: "Dull, *very dull*. . . . We are sick of your uncle Toby's wound in his groin" (*Monthly* 24 [February 1761]: 103). Both the *Monthly* and the *Critical* castigated Sterne for being grossly indiscreet, and the *Monthly* responded specifically to the jerkin-lining metaphor: "We wish . . .

that we could rumple the *lining of his jerkin*, as it is the best expedient we know of, to make the owner ashamed of exposing it, for though he assures us, that it is not yet frayed, yet all the world may see that it is in a filthy pickle. Our former animadversions of the Reverend Yorick were intended as a warning to Mr. Shandy to hide his dirty lining" (*Monthly* 24 [February 1761]: 105).

The *Monthly*'s "warning" foreshadows a confrontation that would result in Sterne's redirection of his work toward yet another audience: the readers whom the Reviews claimed to represent. This final orientation is most revealing because Sterne so strongly resisted it. Unlike his courtship of Garrick, or of the mass audience indicated by the Sterneiana of the early 1760s, Sterne's acknowledgment of the Reviews was both reluctant and unarticulated. Indeed, he never retreated from the claim he made upon beginning volume five of *Tristram Shandy* in June 1761: "I care not a curse for the critics" (*Letters*, 140).

In fact, crucial forces coalesced to prompt Sterne to care a great deal. With the publication of volumes five and six in December 1761, the Shandy fashion began to show signs of having crested. Not only had the production of pamphlets subsided, but in the spring of 1763, Sterne was shocked to learn from his bookseller, Thomas Becket, that a quarter of the sets of volumes five and six (printed in an edition of 4,000) remained unsold, an unprecedented bad performance. He wrote to Becket four times during the year, expressing hope that sales had improved, or asking outright, "Have you sold any Shandys? . . . How many? (*Letters*, 199, 203–4, 211). Sterne's anxieties about the continued marketability of *Tristram Shandy* were accompanied by increasing critical confidence among the reviewers, who, having grown accustomed to Sterne's tendencies through the first four volumes, began to reach a remarkably clear consensus in their assessments of volumes five and six.

The uniformity of the critical reception of these volumes was in part elicited by Sterne's alertness to objections raised by the *Monthly* and the *Critical*'s reviews of volumes three and four. He directly, though sardonically, defends the structure of these volumes by presenting a series of graphs at the end of volume six to prove that he has curbed his tendency to digress, a habit for which he was faulted in nearly every previous review. Sterne made more substantive changes as well. Although Tristram's injury from a falling window sash (which like everything else in the Shandy family is not well hung) is an incident typical of the first four volumes, it is surrounded by other episodes in volumes five and six that suggest a significant move away from subjects that might be judged obscene. Sterne carefully details the effect on various members of the Shandy household of the news of Bobby's death, and volume six includes the story of Le Fever, the first pathetic tale of any length that Sterne introduced into his fiction.

Those last few affecting episodes were very favorably received. The writer for the *Critical* concludes his review by suggesting that "if our author has sometimes lost sight of Rabelais, he has directed his eye to a still greater original, even nature herself." He then quotes from the "beautifully pathetic" Le Fever episode, which he claims must appeal "to every reader of sensibility." He refers to the passage as "glowing with the warmth of a heart truly sentimental" (*Critical* 13 [January 1762]: 68–69). The *Monthly* reviewer invokes the moral obligations of his office to justify the Review's rough treatment of volumes three and four: Sterne's obscenity, particularly in those volumes, had according to this reviewer all but forced the *Monthly* to censure him. Though "they are not without their stars and dashes, their hints and whiskers," volumes five and six, the reviewer notes, seem to portend a change (*Monthly* 26 [January 1762]: 33). The reviewer quotes the Le Fever episode in its entirety, and claims that it "does greater honour to the abilities and disposition of the Author, than any other part of his work" (*Monthly* 26 [January 1762]: 40). He concludes with an appeal to the *Monthly*'s readers, asking them to declare their preference: "Since Mr. Sterne published his Sermons, we have been of the opinion that his excellence lay not so much in the humourous as in the pathetic; and in this opinion we have been confirmed by the above story of Le Fever. We appeal to the Heart of every reader whether our judgment is not right?" (*Monthly* 26 [January 1762]: 41).

The reception of volumes seven and eight, published in January 1765, follows an almost identical pattern, isolating for praise Toby's courtship of Mrs. Wadman, and offering it as proof that Sterne's real talents lay in representing pathetic scenes. Ralph Griffiths pays Sterne the highest compliment by comparing him favorably to Richardson: "Richardson—the delicate, the circumstantial Richardson himself, never produced a thing equal to the amours of Uncle Toby and the Widow Wadman" (*Monthly* 32 [February 1765]: 136). He then concludes his review with an eloquent plea that repeats the *Monthly*'s assessment of volumes five and six:

One of our gentlemen remarked *in print* Mr. Shandy—that he thought your excellence lay in the PATHETIC. I think so too. In my opinion, the little story of LE FEVRE has done you more honour than every thing else you have wrote, except your Sermons. Suppose you were to strike out a new plan? Give us none but amiable or worthy, or exemplary characters; or, if you will, to enliven the drama, throw in the innocently humourous. . . . Paint nature in her loveliest dress—her native simplicity. Draw natural scenes and interesting situations—awake our hearts—arouze, transport, refine, improve us. Let morality, let the cultivation of virtue be your aim—let wit, humour, elegance and pathos be the means. (*Monthly* 32 [February 1765]: 138–39)

This time, however, both Reviews add to their exhortation that Sterne cultivate his best talents the proviso that he do so in a new book. The *Critical* reviewer laments that *Tristram Shandy* has become like Uncle Toby's red breeches, which "were worn so long that they became thin, threadbare, and rotten" (*Critical* 19 [January 1765]: 66). Griffiths also expresses consternation at the thought that *Tristram Shandy* would go on for yet another two volumes: "Ah, Mr. Shandy, your *ninth* and *tenth*!—that's talking of things at a great distance. Better take a friend's advice. Stop where you are. The Public, if I guess right, will have *had enough* by the time they get to the end of your eighth volume" (*Monthly* 32 [February 1765]: 138).

Taken in the aggregate, the reviews of volumes five through eight display in a strikingly consistent way the whole range of their rhetoric of judgment. Sterne's place as an established writer in 1765 enables the reviewers to consider his entire oeuvre and to measure out praise or criticism by comparing the current installments of *Tristram Shandy* with earlier ones or even with the *Sermons*. They were also able to situate him in a broad pantheon of writers, both continental (Sterne turning away from Rabelais) and English (Sterne improving upon Richardson). More powerful than these practices, which by the mid-1760s had become conventional in reviews, is the emphasis in both the *Monthly* and the *Critical* on the interdependency among nature, morality, and the pathetic, an armature pieced together specifically for Sterne's edification. Reviewers for both journals define the pathetic episodes, primarily Le Fever's death and later Toby's courtship of Mrs. Wadman, as true to nature. Griffiths appeals to Sterne's "honour" and sense of morality in urging him to "let the cultivation of virtue be your aim." The *Monthly*, in particular, characterizes the kind of readers who will be most receptive to these adjustments, should Sterne choose to make them, as people who consult their hearts rather than their minds, and who desire a book that will "arouze, transport, refine, improve" them.

The Reviews implicitly but programmatically oppose all the prominent features of volumes one through four of *Tristram Shandy*: obscenity, exaggerated wit, complexity. They exhort Sterne indirectly to abandon the genre of the learned satire and write a different kind of fiction. That new kind of fiction, derived principally from an interpretation of Richardson that privileges affect, is to follow the guidelines prescribed by Griffiths's review of volumes seven and eight.[31] The directions are so precise, I would argue, and the philosophy underlying them so coherent, that we need to give some credit to the Reviews for inventing (or at least preinventing) the English sentimental novel, the genre of which *A Sentimental Journey* is the first widely successful example.

Sterne continued, for a short time, to try to "care not a curse for the critics," but he found it increasingly difficult to write as if these latest reviews had made no impression on him. He published only one more installment of *Tristram Shandy*, in January 1767, and it was indifferently reviewed. Even as he composed volume nine in the summer of 1766, he had already begun to work out plans for *A Sentimental Journey*. He writes to Edward Stanley on June 23, 1766: "At present I am in my peaceful retreat, writing the ninth volume of Tristram—I shall publish but one this year, and the next I shall begin a new work of four volumes, which when finished, I shall continue Tristram in a fresh spirit" (*Letters*, 284). In a classic 1940 article, Rufus Putney argued that Griffiths's plea persuaded Sterne to make this decision, but I contend, in light of the presentation I have made here, that one cannot point to a single review as the occasion of his "conversion."[32] Instead we must look to the discourse of reviewing as a whole, and to its prestige at this time as perhaps the most important agency of evaluation in the literary culture.

Although he effectually complied with his critics by composing *A Sentimental Journey*, Sterne never acknowledged that the Reviews had altered the direction of his writing. In two particularly fascinating letters he carefully claims the new emphases as solely his own. He writes in November 1767 that *A Sentimental Journey* "suits the frame of mind I have been in for some time past": "I told you my design in it was to teach us to love this world and our fellow creatures better than we do—so it runs most upon these gentler passions and affections, which aid so much to it" (*Letters*, 400–401 [November 1767]). He goes even further in a letter written slightly later, this time denying that he had changed at all and instead revising the history of his whole career in a way that depicts him as a congenital sentimentalist: "In fact I have long been a sentimental being—whatever your Lordship may think to the contrary.—The world has imagined, because I wrote *Tristram Shandy*, that I was myself more Shandean than I really ever was—'tis a good-natured world we live in, and we are often painted in divers colours according to the ideas one frames in his head" (*Letters*, 189 [November 9, 1767]).

The subtexts of both letters are assertions about the origin of *A Sentimental Journey*, and Sterne shrewdly sketches chronologies in which his decision to write the book predates the reviews of volumes seven and eight of *Tristram Shandy*. In the first version, the new book is the fruit of Sterne's long-standing emotional state, and in the second it provides a corrective to misinterpretations of Sterne prompted by *Tristram Shandy*.

Perhaps the most noteworthy aspect of this redefinition of the trajectory of his career is that Sterne originally fused himself with Tristram and encouraged everyone to identify him with his book, but now he does the opposite—distancing himself from *Tristram Shandy* and hinting at the dangers of making precisely this kind of identification. The ease with which Sterne abandons what had ostensibly been the first principle of his writing since he began *Tristram Shandy* suggests that his most urgent concerns at this stage lay elsewhere.

Indeed, his correspondence, as in the case of this last letter, presents his relationship with his writing as a strategy to be employed in winning over audiences that he felt he had alienated. Sterne's letters as he readied *A Sentimental Journey* for publication show how prominent were his anxieties about who might read it and how they might react. He guesses that the new book will be "likely to take in all kinds of Readers" (*Letters*, 393 [September 3, 1767]). He expects that *A Sentimental Journey* will finally placate those who have always charged him with indecency: "If it is not thought a chaste book, mercy on them that read it, for they must have warm imaginations indeed" (*Letters*, 402–3). In the following passage, he combines these two intentions in his most entrepreneurial speculation about *A Sentimental Journey*'s potential: "I will send you a set of my books— they will take with the generality; the women will read this book in the parlour, and *Tristram Shandy* in the bed-chamber" (*Letters*, 412 [February 1767]).

This intriguing glimpse into the decorum of reading says a great deal about how Sterne had come to interpret his audiences in light of his acquaintance with the Reviews. He implies that even his most reputation-conscious readers—women of a social rank sufficiently high to enable them to live in houses with both parlors and bed-chambers—are not fastidious. They continue to read *Tristram Shandy*, but the book's improprieties (or the reviewers' strictures) have forced them to do so in secrecy, in the most private spaces in their houses. He wishes not to replace *Tristram Shandy*, but to supplement it with a book that can be displayed and read aloud without fear of scandal, in the most public room, where company congregates.

The new book was indeed received better than any of Sterne's work for several years. Griffiths exulted in the thought that Sterne had taken his advice, describing *A Sentimental Journey* as Sterne's "best production" (*Monthly* 38 [April 1768]: 310). Another long-time detractor, Horace Walpole, called the book "extremely good-natured" (*Letters*, 418, n. 2). But Sterne's careful description of how and where he hoped *A Sentimental Journey* would be read goes to the core of his new conception of his readership, particularly his relationship with the Reviews. As the parlor/bedroom analogy makes clear, two very different conceptions of Sterne's audience remained in play. Sterne never admitted that the audience of *Tristram Shandy* had diminished—rather, he implied that it merely read his work in private. The Reviews, on the other hand, had repeatedly claimed that readers were tired of *Tristram Shandy*. The difference of opinion was unresolvable because there was, of course, no means of demonstrating the desires or the practices of the reading public. Book sales alone were not conclusive, nor were posthumous comments about *A Sentimental Journey* particularly reliable. (Indeed, Sterne's death on March 18, 1768, just three weeks after the book was published, may have contributed most heavily to its popularity, a possibility that Yorick would have appreciated.)

Yet the contest between Sterne and the Reviews hinged on convictions and assumptions about these very matters, and what they did or did not impel him to do. Sterne wished to present the decision to write *A Sentimental Journey* as a free choice reflecting only his own state of mind, and his letter supports his presentation with a theory that the audience for *Tristram Shandy* was not shrinking. That is, if people are willing to continue reading further installments of *Tristram Shandy*, though only in their bedchambers, then he is under no pressure to write *A Sentimental Journey*, but simply wishes to do so. The Reviews, however, particularly the *Monthly*, hoped to take considerable credit for rehabilitating Sterne as an author by advising him about the strengths and weaknesses of his writing, and all but instructing him to write a new book along the lines of *A Sentimental Journey*. In their account of Sterne's decision, then, the erosion of an audience for *Tristram Shandy* is crucial. It confirms the reviewers' claims that they alone possess an accurate sense of the public's reading tastes, and *Tristram Shandy*'s waning popularity inevitably led Sterne to turn to them for direction.

If there is no material resolution to these competing accounts of the tastes of the English reading public, there may at least be some clues in the book that Sterne produced. The sincerity of Sterne's claim to have written a "chaste book" has been perhaps the focus of the critical debate about *A Sentimental Journey* at least since Ernest Dilworth's *The Unsentimental Journey of Laurence Sterne* was published in 1948. The opposing poles in this debate, which still informs Sterne criticism today, are by now so familiar that they need not be rehearsed in depth: Gardner Stout's introduction to his edition of *A Sentimental Journey* remains the cornerstone of defenses of the book's earnestness, while John Stedmond and Melvyn New have argued that the book's sentimentality is consistently subverted or satirized.[33] My examination of the institutional forces that contributed to Sterne's identity as an author allows us to cast this debate in a materialist light. It could be that Sterne's aim, in compliance with the Reviews, was to write a book that would be *both* presentable in the parlor and titillating in the bedchamber. It is possible, in other words, that he carried out the reviewers' prescription, but all the while continued to address the audience of *Tristram Shandy* (which he believed lived on) in ways that they would appreciate.

I want to restate my hope, however, that the approach I have pursued encompasses and moves beyond these narrower thematic concerns. Sterne's career, as he improvised it in order to appeal to Garrick, imitators and pamphleteers, and the Reviews, is most importantly a study in alienated labor. Because he entered the literary culture so naively, yet at a period when that culture was rapidly becoming more complex, Sterne was especially sensitive to the nature and strength of the forces that alienated him as an author. Although at times he realized, intuitively it would seem, that the institutions of author, reader, book, and bookseller were not at all discrete and independent, he also seemed to be stunned whenever he was confronted with these interdependencies and their possible consequences for him. He proceeded accordingly, throughout his career, as if recovering from one trauma after another. When he claimed in 1760, "I wrote not to be fed but to be famous," he did so in ignorance of the nature of fame at midcentury. In particular, he was unaware that the famous author now bore no resemblance to his heroic classical or even Renaissance predecessors, but was rather the site of an assortment of institutional forces that combined to legitimate him.

Amid this relatively new and astonishingly confusing set of relations, only the Reviews claimed to have the power to tell the official story of the working writer's professional self. Their decisive role in the representation of Laurence Sterne is powerful evidence that literary fame in the later eighteenth century could best be conveyed in the narratives that the Reviews alone could construct.

"He never gives us nothing that's *low*"
Oliver Goldsmith

Sterne's literary career reflects a naïveté about the writing profession that he eventually grudgingly admitted and overcame only through a long process of trial and error. Goldsmith's, by contrast, epitomizes even at its earliest stages an insightful pragmatism that is driven by a sophisticated understanding of the literary culture of his day. From his very first book-length production, *An Enquiry into the Present State of Polite Learning in Europe* (1759), it is evident that he conceives of literature in ways very similar to the editors of the *Monthly* and the *Critical*, and that he sees his work as occupying the same discursive space as popular criticism. Drawing perhaps from his first literary employment, writing reviews for these journals in the late 1750s, Goldsmith, like the editors he worked for, conceived of literature as the site of a struggle between critics and authors for the legitimating attention of English readers.[1]

On the surface, Goldsmith saw critics as pedantic levelers of all cultural accomplishment, and he represented them as such in the *Enquiry*. But that same treatise, while offering a ruthless critique of popular criticism, nevertheless accords critics a considerable amount of institutional power over what is written and read. At no point does he abandon this carefully balanced perspective, in which the Reviews' misguided and illegitimate judgments are weighed against their real power in literary culture. Unlike Sterne, Goldsmith became too shrewd too early in his professional life to dismiss outright the opinions of reviewers, and his opinion of their claims to cultural authority is, in a sense, never finally resolved.

Goldsmith gravitated toward genres that afforded him a comprehensive perspective on culture roughly analogous to that to which the Reviews aspired. Indeed, as an author he enjoyed a degree of freedom that was unavailable to reviewers, who could, after all, only assess culture through discrete commentaries on other people's published writing. He could pretend to occupy the fictional vantage points of a gentleman writer, a Chinese visitor to London, a rural parson, or a world traveler, not to mention the more conventional roles of historian, biographer, and essayist. But he consistently and more or less explicitly redirected the kinds of writing that he selected toward the larger aim of a general critique of culture, the basic terms of which, as stated earlier, he shared uneasily with the *Monthly* and the *Critical*.

After exploring the principles of this critique in various works from the first decade of Goldsmith's fifteen years as a writer, I would like to advance the more speculative claim that he turned his familiarity with the particular discursive mode of popular criticism to practical use in his last years. Specifically, I will argue, he strategically promoted his plays, *The Good Natur'd Man* and *She Stoops to Conquer*, in effect by dictating to critics the proper cultural contexts in which to assess his own work. His skill in outmaneuvering his reviewers in their own rhetoric, I will argue, included inventing the so-called laughing-sentimental debate on the English stage. That debate, I conclude, was waged not in drama itself but in popular criticism, and Goldsmith's victory in it engineered the success of *She Stoops to Conquer*. Goldsmith's protracted negotiation with the reviewers of his plays typifies his mastery of the dynamics of literary production and reception. His recognition of both the power and the vulnerabilities of the institution that would legitimate him as an author is unparalleled. Several years before Frances Burney's politic dedication of *Evelina* to the "Authors of the *Monthly* and *Critical Review*," Goldsmith demonstrated a sophisticated awareness of the means by which the Reviews packaged literature for consumption, an understanding that while critics were crucially influential guides to public taste, they were necessarily also responsive to it.

This chapter is organized around Goldsmith's various definitions of and prescriptions for literary culture. He consistently wrote with a self-consciousness about the predicament of the professional author that is missing from the writings of Smollett and Sterne. I pursue the development of that self-consciousness largely along chronological lines, taking the *Enquiry*, pertinent letters of Lien Chi Altangi in *The Citizen of the World*, *The Vicar of Wakefield*, and the plays as my central texts. But since Goldsmith wrote so much else, and since one cannot mark definite stages in his career as one can with Sterne and Smollett, the result is an analysis that is more episodic than linear, more thematic than biographical.

It is ironic that the eighteenth-century author who perhaps best understood the relationships that lead to the formation of a literary career never really had one himself, in the sense that the disparate nature of his publications makes it impossible to analyze the trajectory of his writing in the same way I do Sterne's and Smollett's. It is unfortunate as well that the lack of a "plot" to his professional biography is compounded by his image among his contemporaries as the "inspired idiot" of Johnson's circle.[2] Though my primary aim is not to rehabilitate Goldsmith, it is nevertheless true that he must be accorded more credibility than he currently has if my claims about the value of his cultural critique are to carry any weight.

The *Enquiry into the Present State of Polite Learning in Europe* is a uniquely theoretical overview of cultural production in the mid–eighteenth century. It appeared in two substantively different editions, the first published in 1759 and the second revised by the author late in life and published posthumously in 1774. In its first manifestation, this monograph of 200 pages served two purposes for its author: it contributed to an active debate taking place during the 1750s about the state of culture in England; second, it functioned as Goldsmith's critique of his own working conditions as a writer during that period. The most popular tract about the decline of culture, John Brown's *Estimate of the Manners and Principles of the Times* (1757), went through five editions in its first year. Other books on related issues, such as John Gilbert Cooper's *Letters Concerning Taste* (1754), John Campbell's anonymously published *The Present State of Europe*, which reached a fifth edition in 1756, and James Ralph's *The Case of Authors by Profession or Trade* (1758), also sold extremely well, encouraging Robert Dodsley to publish the *Enquiry* and leading Goldsmith to apologize in its first chapter for adding to the glut of writing about the decline of literature.[3]

In contrast to the nervous and insistent alarmism of Brown's *Estimate*, the chief book against which it is situated, Goldsmith's treatise is, as Robert Hopkins has described, a dispassionate diagnosis of the pathology of European culture.[4] Goldsmith describes most complaints about the "degeneracy in literature" as "enforced . . . with the ardor of devious declamation," whereas his own will be marked, he promises, by the "calmness of deliberate enquiry" (1: 258). But Goldsmith's *Enquiry* not only differs from Brown's *Estimate* in tone but perhaps more importantly in organization. The *Estimate* obsessively focuses on concerns that Brown presents as specific to England. Brown, who would defend the *Estimate* in a pamphlet written the following year, places the blame for the decline of culture in England on luxury and effeminacy of manners. Both his argument and his urgency can be attributed in part, at least, to immediate national concerns. England had entered, in effect, a world war in 1757 (later to be known as the Seven Years War) and had lost two crucial early battles. One of them, at Minorca, was clouded by allegations of cowardice that ultimately resulted in the trial and execution of Admiral Byng for abandoning British troops.[5] Brown's argument was shaped by these events in that he worried only about England, and he derived his critique from very pressing doubts about the country's political and moral failures.

Goldsmith, by contrast, writing two years later, as the tide of the war had begun to turn in England's favor, draws a more tenuous, less insistent connection between moral and political stability and that of culture. He also arrives at conclusions about literature in England chiefly by means of a survey of the standing and history of literature throughout Europe. But Goldsmith's is a pseudocosmopolitanism, one that he continued to practice in the forum of the polite essay (in *Citizen of the World* and in his poem *The Traveller*). His audience is explicitly English, and his assumptions are largely chauvinistic. The brevity and lack of seriousness that characterize his descriptions of polite learning in most of Europe foreground the fundamental virtues of English culture and present France as England's only competitor in that field as it was in the world's political scene.

The *Enquiry*'s lack of urgency has also been ascribed, correctly I think, to its function as Goldsmith's farewell to the very scene that it describes.⁶ Goldsmith composed it during the period 1757–59, during which his publications consisted of a miscellaneous assortment of reviews for both the *Monthly* and the *Critical*. After he had left both journals, he wrote the *Enquiry* as an abstract summation of his unpleasant experience. It appeared in print just as Goldsmith was hoping to leave writing as a profession altogether and pursue a medical career abroad. But his hopes were not fulfilled, and he returned to the life of writing from which he had so recently and carefully articulated his departure.

Goldsmith's success as a writer of an assortment of genres (none so theoretical, though, as the *Enquiry*) led him to take a very different perspective on the complexities of literary society in 1774, near the end of his life, than he had fifteen years earlier. The differences between the first edition of the *Enquiry* and the second are crucial for what they reveal about the dialectic that produces the man of letters in the later eighteenth century. At the center of the first edition is a prescribed course of action for aspiring authors and an outline of a philosophy of taste. It is hardly surprising that Goldsmith, immersed for the first time in the everyday concerns of the "writing trade," would wish to define directly the ideals of authorship and the habits of reading that ultimately generated the demands placed upon him as a hired writer.

What is remarkable, however, is that all of the passages dealing explicitly with the proper conduct of authors and readers (including an entire chapter on taste) were deleted from the second (1774) posthumous edition. So drastic and numerous were Goldsmith's professional compromises as an author, and so changeable were his convictions about the nature of taste among consumers of literature, that he retracted virtually every general conclusion he had drawn about these subjects less than fifteen years earlier.

In the first edition, Goldsmith amplifies the general plight of hired writers, describing them in terms reminiscent of Pope as "living among vermin" (*Enquiry*, 1: 314) and dying "among the dregs of mankind" (1: 316), two phrases that he removed from the 1774 edition. But he also posits a class of "gentlemen writers" whose wealth makes them independent of the literary market (and even misleadingly implies that he is a member). It is they, described as "having the leisure to polish what they write, and the liberty to choose their own subjects," whom Goldsmith exhorts, "*Write what you think, regardless of the critics,*" adding that "to persuade to this was the chief design of this essay" (1: 317). At a later point, he ascribes to these writers significant power to establish the best writing style: "As our gentlemen writers have it . . . so much in their power to lead the taste of the times, they may now part with the inflated stile" (1: 322).

This characterization of the worst and best conditions for writing is at once too pessimistic and too optimistic, and it is likely that Goldsmith deleted all of these passages once he realized that such extremes were not representative of the existing writing trade. As he continued, during the next decade, to generate income from his own publications, he came to see that the typical hired writer was exploited but not destitute. More significantly, he came to abandon the notion that the gentlemen writers were numerous enough to constitute a class, or that they would be inclined to act in unison.

The gentlemen writers hypothetically occupied a position exempt from the demands of the market, but they could nevertheless influence professional writers by their example. Abandoning the idea that they existed in numbers great enough to effect changes in writing, Goldsmith was forced to compromise his fantasy of reforming the literary market. In the first edition, he expressed the hope of "rescuing genius from the shackles of pedantry and criticism" (1: 258). But that rescue was to be abetted by the gentlemen writers. Their absence from the picture that Goldsmith paints in the 1774 edition greatly diminishes the persuasive force of his argument. Indeed, the gentlemen writers are ostensibly the audience of that first edition, and the lack of a particular addressee in the second renders the rhetorical purpose of the *Enquiry* ambiguous.

Even more alarming contradictions arise from conclusions that Goldsmith found himself drawing in his chapter on taste, the centerpiece of the 1759 edition, which is omitted entirely in the revised version of the *Enquiry*. He outlines gradations of taste that depend on the experience and expertise of the perceiver of objects both natural and cultural, using a guinea as his prime example:

Thus the Barbarian finds some small pleasure in the contemplation of a guinea; the enlightened European, who is acquainted with its uses, still more than him; the chymist, who, besides this, knows the peculiar fixedness and malleability of the metal, most of all. This capacity of receiving pleasure may be called Taste in the objects of nature. The polite arts in all their variety are only imitations of nature. (1: 296)

In the face of the inference that in the world of literature the critic is the equivalent of the chemist, Goldsmith abruptly reframes taste as an aspect of the *production* rather than the reception of writing. He emphasizes the axiom "Taste in writing is the exhibition of the greatest quantity of beauty and of use that may be admitted into any description without counteracting each other" (1: 296). "Exhibition" has an ambiguous standing, though it seems easier in this formulation for a writer to exhibit taste than for a reader to do so. In his concluding paragraphs, however, he finds himself completing the analogy that he had earlier aborted, asserting that "critics should, therefore, imitate physicians" and even suggesting that "every country should have a national system of criticism" (1: 296).

Far from accomplishing his original intent—"I have assumed the critic only to dissuade from criticism" (1: 317)—the chapter on taste only serves to strengthen the position of criticism. By arguing that the capacity to judge derives from experience and careful, systematic training, Goldsmith oddly seems almost to ratify the institution of criticism that he had set out to discredit, and in so doing he secures the place of critics as the logical authorities over literary production. The metaphor is thus ultimately quite confused and is all the more intriguing because it represents Goldsmith's first position on popular criticism. He revised that position, as I will show, at several crucial junctures, then returned to this same text, the *Enquiry*, and omitted it altogether.

The deletion of the chapter on taste from the 1774 edition leaves the "man of taste" as the most influential agent in the effort to stop the decline of literature:

The man of taste, however, stands neuter in this controversy, he seems placed in a middle station, between the world and the cell, between learning and common sense. He teaches the vulgar on what part of a character to lay the emphasis of praise, and the scholar where to point his application so as to deserve it. . . . By means of polite learning alone, the patriot and the hero, the man who praiseth virtue, and he who practises it, who fights successfully for his country, or dies in its defense, becomes immortal. (1: 306)

The *Enquiry* suggests then, that between 1759 and his death in 1773, Goldsmith relinquished the hope that a national system of criticism would crystallize or that a cadre of gentlemen writers would show the way to a reform of writing. His loss of faith in these institutional solutions to the decline of literature leaves him with only the heroic man of taste, who figures so greatly in both editions. Moreover, the hero of Goldsmith's narrative is not the author (who, unless he is independently wealthy, is victimized by the book trade and the institution of criticism) but the "man of taste," who is described in terms no different from the "reader of candour and taste" to whom the Reviews address themselves and who is typified by the Review editors themselves.

The question that the *Enquiry* poses, quite boldly for its time, is whether taste and the assumptions on which the reviewers predicate their judgments are the same. Goldsmith concludes that they are not: critics, he argues, enforce a rigid, exclusively rational set of rules on the literature that they read. Goldsmith, instead, following Hume as one of "those who found morality on sentiment, more than on reason," locates taste as an aspect of feeling rather than intellect.[7]

The 1774 version of the *Enquiry* is a text eviscerated by Goldsmith's many subsequent reconsiderations of the literary market in which he worked. The 1759 edition represents his first primitive attempts to work out the proper relations between author, critic, and reading public. Of all Goldsmith's works, the *Enquiry* is the one most transparently indebted to the Reviews for both its terminology and its overarching vision of the cultural world. The *Enquiry* shares with the Reviews a general sense of dissatisfaction over interrelated crises in politics, morality, and culture. Both the *Enquiry* and the Reviews advocate interventions in the cultural field that would reestablish standards of taste that would in turn direct writers and readers, and help literature to right itself. Goldsmith, as a reviewer turned author, predictably argues that critics have no authority to make these important determinations: he confers that authority in the 1759 edition on the gentlemen writers, and in the 1774 edition on the man of taste. But though Goldsmith rejects the Reviews' conclusions about literary culture (chiefly their claim to being its highest tribunal), he cannot escape the assumptions and perceptions from which those conclusions are drawn.

Shortly after publishing the *Enquiry*, Goldsmith contracted with John Newbery to compose two letters a week for the *Public Ledger*, the first of which appeared on January 24, 1760. The letters, written in the much imitated genre of Montesquieu's *Lettres persanes* (1721) and published in May 1762 as *The Citizen of the World*, form the correspondence of Lien Chi Altangi, a Chinese merchant temporarily residing in London. The fictional device of the Chinese letters infinitely extended the boundaries of Goldsmith's satire by permitting him to place a naive observer and informant in the midst of an assortment of situations that typify corruption in English society. Like Goldsmith's own dispassionate authorial voice in the *Enquiry*, Lien Chi's tone is restrained throughout. Indeed, he is a parody of the ascetic Oriental: described by Goldsmith in a preface as possessing learning and gravity "within one degree of absolute frigidity," he stoically quotes Confucius upon hearing that his family has been seized by the Chinese government (*Citizen of the World*, 2: 39). But Lien Chi's comical matter-of-fact delivery is the ideal medium for Goldsmith's most acerbic critique of culture. Nearly a quarter of the 119 letters touch directly on some aspect of the English cultural scene: most notably Lien Chi reports on his visit to a play, and to a club of authors, and is himself visited by a bookseller. The fiction of a man witnessing the everyday business of culture for the first time, and describing it often as a foreign convolution of Chinese cultural customs, allows Goldsmith to pose, in a plausible way, basic questions about the production and consumption of literature.

As in the *Enquiry*, the focus of Goldsmith's attention is the relationship of author, reader, and critic in what Lien Chi, scoffing at the myth of a republic of letters, calls the "anarchy of literature" (2: 85). Lien Chi marvels at the daunting logistics of book production in England, reckoning that a publication rate of 23 books a day, or 8,395 a year, must leave the learned of England with an impossible responsibility should they wish to remain current: even a scholar reading a thousand books a year will cover "but an eighth part of the works which daily come from the press" (2: 124).

This apparent glut of publications leads him to wonder who is writing and reading them. Until he is corrected by his friend, the Man in Black, Lien Chi imagines that only "learned seminaries" could produce writers "in sufficient number to throw off the books I daily saw crowding from the press" (2: 124). But the Man in Black disabuses him only by synecdoche, as it were, by introducing him to a club of authors. The club consists of an assortment of literary types: a metaphysician, a lawyer, and two hack writers, all of them devoted to prolificacy for its own sake, while at the same time so satiated by the surfeit of writing they have helped to produce that they do not allow a member to read from his own work until he first pays an initial fee of sixpence and a shilling per hour thereafter.

But the merciless satire on the club of authors does not explain the patterns of production about which Lien Chi inquired. Rather, it shows him only a few compulsively productive professional writers, and leaves the authors of the rest of the 23 books per day, and more importantly the constant demand for all those books, a mystery. In a much later letter, however, Lien Chi advances the following, powerfully original theory:

In proportion as society refines, new books must ever become more necessary. . . . In a polite age, almost every person becomes a reader, and receives more instruction from the press than the pulpit. The preaching Bonse may instruct the illiterate peasant; but nothing less than the insinuating address of a fine writer can win its way to an heart already relaxed in all the effeminacy of refinement. Books are necessary to correct the vices of the polite, but those vices are ever changing, and the antidote should be changed accordingly; should still be. (2: 212)

Though this hypothesis accounts for the proliferation of books, and the demand for them, it does so in a way that compromises authors and readers alike. That the "fine writer" must craft an "insinuating address" if he is to reach the reader "relaxed in all the effeminacy of refinement" indicts both as conspirators responsible for the continued deterioration of culture. This unappealing prospect, in which refinement equals effeminacy, is rendered even more disturb-

ing by the presence of only one alternative model of cultural trans-
mission, that of the preaching Bonse who instructs the illiterate peasant. The account is thus deeply conflicted: no one would aspire to be
either the Bonse or the peasant, yet we are pushed toward the simplicity and unaffected nature of their communication in the face of
Goldsmith's construction of the fine writer and the effeminate reader.

The relationship anticipates both the attacks on refinement in
The Vicar of Wakefield and the opposition between Marlow and
Tony Lumpkin in *She Stoops to Conquer*. In all three texts, Goldsmith makes the necessity of choosing between these cultural alternatives all the more significant by placing the moral condition of England at stake, but his position in *The Citizen of the World* is ultimately unresolved. He promotes a progressive justification of the
expanding book trade by arguing that a changing society of readers
requires a constant supply of new books. But he delivers this message
in terms reminiscent of Brown's *Estimate*.

Perhaps more significant than Lien Chi's observations about the
excess of printed works in England is that he begs the question of
demand. In the letter totaling the 8,395 books published per year, we
are left to wonder how Lien Chi's typical hyperactive scholar goes
about choosing the fraction of those books that he actually reads.
The scene in the club of authors, far from illuminating the problem
of demand, satirically inverts the relationship between producer and
consumer by making the author, not the reader, pay the cost of
publication.

Lien Chi assigns booksellers a purely passive role in this process,
presenting them as slavishly responsive to a reading public that they
see as driven by vanity. Any time a book sells successfully, Lien Chi
observes, the instinctive reaction of every bookseller is "to bring out
several more upon the same plan, which are sure to have purchasers
and readers." The production of sequels on the popular subject continues until "the sated reader turns from it with a kind of literary nau-
sea" (2: 387). In another letter, a bookseller describes for Lien Chi
his marketing policy: "Others may pretend to direct the vulgar; but
that is not my way; I always let the vulgar direct me; wherever popular clamour arises, I always eccho the million. For instance, should
the people in general say that such a man is a rogue, I instantly give
orders to set him down in print a villain; thus every man buys the

book, not to learn new sentiments, but to have the pleasure of seeing his own reflected" (2: 214).

Although the "anarchy of literature" that Lien Chi describes seems to cry out for some rational mediating agency that would recommend some books and steer readers away from others, Goldsmith consistently denies the reviewers, whom Lien Chi compares to wolves—they attack each other when their preferred prey, authors, are in short supply (2: 86)—any legitimate claim to that role. He calls attention to the pretensions rather than the qualifications of critics as judges both in the literary and theatrical worlds. Lien Chi remarks that the critics in the pit of a theater where he has gone to observe a play "seemed to consider themselves as judges. . . . They assumed the right of being censors because there was none to contradict their pretensions. . . . Every man who now called himself a connoisseur, became such to all intents and purposes" (2: 89).

The critic of literature, by the same token, treats his readers with an unwarranted condescension. He "pretends to take our feelings under his care, teaches where to condemn, where to lay the emphasis of praise, and may, with as much justice, be called a man of taste, as the Chinese who measures his wisdom by the length of his nails" (2: 88). In a much later letter, Lien Chi attributes the critical quackery that he sees plaguing English letters to the absence of an official tribunal that, in "China," guarantees its own impartiality by judging publications submitted under a policy of blind submission. He asserts that in England, "If any chuse to be critics, it is but saying they are critics; and from that time forward they become invested with full power and authority over every caitiff who aims at their instruction or entertainment" (2: 236).

Through Lien Chi, Goldsmith drives home the point that any claim to critical authority is baseless. In every case, the critic in question has had no formal training and possesses no formal qualifications to superior taste. By making these discriminations, Goldsmith implicitly discredits the shows of institutional authority, of which the *Monthly* and the *Critical* were so fond, by measuring them against the traditional professional standards that might certify a doctor or a clergyman.

But, as in the case of the *Enquiry*, Goldsmith's formative experiences as both a writer of reviews and a firsthand witness of the am-

bitions and procedures of both the *Monthly* and the *Critical* leave
him far too well informed to dismiss reviewers entirely. In an astonishing rhetorical tour de force, he anticipates and lists the most likely
critical responses to *The Citizen of the World* in a single letter. Em-
ploying a tactic that he would resort to on a grander scale to direct
the reception of his plays, Goldsmith defuses the opinions of the major Reviews by making them appear utterly predictable, and by de-
picting the reviewers who would write them as acting by rote. The
bookseller who relates the story praises the talents of his employee,
the reviewer—"There is no work whatsoever but he can criticise"—
and then, addressing Lien Chi, proceeds to make the following archly
prescient speculation: "Suppose you should take it into your head to
publish a book, let it be a volume of Chinese letters for instance;
write how you will, he shall shew you the world you could have written better" (2: 216).

This prediction, which appeared on June 23, 1760, is in a sense
a pointed advertisement for *The Citizen of the World*, which did not
appear until May 1762. But Goldsmith seems here already to have
imagined several specific possibilities for its reception. The bookseller rehearses, in a dialogue with Lien Chi, the repertoire of auto-
matic responses that his natural critic will deliver:

Should you, with the most local exactness, stick to the manners and customs
of the country from whence you come; should you confine yourself to the
narrow limits of eastern knowledge, and be perfectly simple, and perfectly
natural, he has then the strongest reason to exclaim. He may with a sneer
send you back to China for readers. He may observe, that after the first
or second letter the iteration of the same simplicity is insupportably te-
dious. . . .

   Yes, cried I, *but in order to avoid his indignation, and what I should fear
more, that of the public, I would in such a case write with all the knowledge
I was master of. As I am not possessed of much learning, at least I would
not suppress what little I had, nor would I appear more stupid than nature
made me.* Here then, cried the bookseller, we should have you entirely in our
power, unnatural, uneastern, quite out of character; erroneously sensible
would be the whole cry; Sir, we should hunt you down like a rat. *Head of
my father!* said I, *sure there are but the two ways; the door must either be
shut, or it must be open. I must either be natural or be unnatural.* Be what
you will, we shall criticise you, returned the bookseller, and prove you a
dunce in spite of your teeth. (2: 216–17)

This exchange is one of the few instances in which Lien Chi loses the composed tone that characterizes all of his letters. Faced with this disturbing hypothesis about the inevitable disparagement of his future work as an author, he abandons his normal pose—almost that of an early ethnographer—and defends the book that he has yet to write.

The source of his exasperation is that his book is not to be judged at all, but rather condemned programmatically. If the author disappears as a central figure in literary culture from the second edition of the *Enquiry*, the critic is finally absent from *Citizen of the World*. Lien Chi presents a literary society filled with poseurs masquerading as critics; in this final case, he shows us a critic by profession who does not really assess the book that he reviews. Indeed, the reviewer is presented as simply another facet of the publishing industry. He is recruited by a bookseller (an obvious reference to Ralph Griffiths's dual capacity as bookseller and editor of the *Monthly*) who recognizes his special talent for a particular kind of writing. That genre, the review, is different from but in no way superior to any other popular literary form. Moreover, the bookseller markets the skills of his reviewer just as he does those of the other writers in his employ. Collapsing criticism into generic professional writing devalues the opinions of reviewers perhaps more effectively than Lien Chi's simple assertions that critics have no authority. Goldsmith uses this episode to demonstrate that professional reviewers cannot be disinterested.

The Citizen of the World is Goldsmith's most cynical assault on the institutional influences on the production and consumption of literature. Not long after its publication (in book form) he began to take a more analytical and a more pragmatic approach to the concept of taste. Here, though, he subjects criticism and pretensions to cultural expertise to the same invective that he had in the *Enquiry*, but without offering the saving hope of the man of taste.

The crucial issues in cultural production and consumption are not central to *The Vicar of Wakefield*, composed during the early 1760s and published in 1766, as they had been to Goldsmith's earlier two works. But the luxury of a sustained prose fiction narrative allows him to address some key topics in the production and consumption of culture in a way that reveals his deepening awareness of the ideological assumptions that underpin them. Indeed, Goldsmith is able to construct vignettes that represent phenomena as diverse and intricate as the practices of hired writers and the power of the magazine industry to construct the social identities of its readers. His treatment of the field of culture in *The Vicar* continues to move away from the nostalgia for a simpler time that the *Enquiry* evokes, and gives up as well the utopian "Chinese" alternatives that were available to Lien Chi in his critique of current English conditions. In particular, Goldsmith scrutinizes far more carefully than he had before the relationship between class and culture, the delineation of which would become central to his plays.

The critical history of *The Vicar of Wakefield* correctly characterizes the novel as diffuse; there is no conclusive proof that it was even finished when Samuel Johnson submitted it for publication on Goldsmith's behalf.[8] Rather than treat the book as a structured whole, then, I will restrict myself to four episodes, two concerning authorship and two concerning taste, that seem especially significant.

Shortly after beginning his long sojourn to London, the consequence of the Primrose family's financial catastrophe, the vicar's eldest son, George, tries to become a writer. In only a brief span of time he attempts, unsuccessfully, to occupy three distinct positions on the spectrum of authorship as the mid–eighteenth century defined it. George's disappointments allow Goldsmith to anatomize and critique the writing trade far more specifically than he had in his earlier writing, where the hired writer was represented as more or less an undifferentiated class. These episodes begin when George's cousin, himself a writer and the young man's initial contact in London, first suggests that George, "a lad of spirit and some learning," might be suited for the profession. George's cousin makes this proposal in strongly antiromantic terms: "You have read in books, no doubt, of men of genius starving at the trade: At present, I'll shew you forty very dull fellows about town that live by it in opulence. All honest jogg trot men, who go on smoothly and dully, and write history and politics, and are praised" (*Vicar*, 4: 108).

But George, clinging to outmoded idealisms and determined to "pursue a track which Dryden and Otway trod" before him, ambitiously resolves to "write a book that should be wholly new." He envisions an overwhelming and controversial reception for the collection of paradoxes that will make up his book: "The whole learned world, I made no doubt, would rise to oppose my systems; but then I was prepared to oppose the whole learned world" (4: 109). To his astonishment though, the whole learned world ignores his book, sentencing him to "the cruellest mortification, neglect" (4: 110).

As he meditates on this failure to gain an audience, George is approached by another kind of writer, a scholar who begs him to subscribe to a new edition of Propertius. When the scholar discovers the extent of George's poverty, he shares with him his secret of living entirely upon income generated by proposals for books which he never actually writes:

The moment a nobleman returns from his travels, a Creolian arrives from Jamaica, or a dowager from her country seat, I strike for a subscription. I first besiege their hearts with flattery, and then pour in my proposals at the breach. If they subscribe readily the first time, I renew my request to beg a dedication fee. If they let me have that, I smite them once more for engraving their coat of arms at the top. Thus, continued he, I live by vanity, and laugh at it. (4: 110)

His proposition is not that George become a writer of any kind, but rather that he masquerade as one in order to deceive a nobleman whose porter already recognizes the scholar. George refuses, as he later explains to his father: "A true poet can never be so base; for wherever there is genius there is pride. The creatures I now describe are only beggars in rhyme" (4: 110). Unwilling to "stoop to such indignities" as impersonating an author, and too poor to finance his own publication in a second attempt to become famous, George finds himself "obliged to take the middle course, and write for bread" (4: 111). But he discovers that he is "unqualified for a profession where mere industry alone was to insure success." His inability to give up the hope of being famous causes him to take excessive care in his writing, and ultimately to struggle financially compared to others who "all wrote better, because they wrote faster" (4: 111).

George leaves the writing trade shortly after making these discoveries, but his short-lived attempts to find a place of some kind in literary society are instructive. The idea, espoused by Goldsmith in the first edition of the *Enquiry*, that England's gentlemen writers should write what they want, "regardless of the critics," is repudiated by the silence that greets George's first book. He had mistakenly believed that the sheer originality of his paradoxes would guarantee interest among the public. He made no attempt to determine or whet the tastes of his would-be consumers, "the whole learned world," and seemed as well to have ignored the implications of his cousin's characterization of the 40 writers who live in opulence by industry alone.

At the other extreme is the scholar who lives by generating consumer interest and nothing more. He arrests the ordinary cycle of production and consumption at the patronage stage, cashing in on the desire of the wealthy to be perceived as patrons, not necessarily readers, of literature. Indeed, his practice creates a perverse literary system in which there are neither authors (in the sense of people who actually write books) nor readers, but only patrons whose vanity keeps the scholar's assortment of proposals in constant circulation. They care not about books, but only that the subscription list and dedication page reflect their own magnificence. The scheme continues to succeed, moreover, only if the sham author *evades* rather than gains recognition by his sponsors. This latter prospect horrifies George, who had, after all, anticipated that a writing career centers on the spirited exchange between author and reader. He turns finally to hack writing, where, paradoxically, his intelligence and desire for a lasting fame hinder his success rather than aid it.

Irrational as the world of the hireling writer is, however, Goldsmith by this point in his own career offers no alternative to it. Another episode concerning authorship in *The Vicar* is a subtly historicized sketch of a coterie of poets. Goldsmith's vicar records a conversation between Lady Blarney and Miss Carolina Wilhelmina Amelia Skeggs, the two prostitutes who pass themselves off as aristocratic ladies, about the private circulation of manuscripts as an alternative to publication through print. They discuss a recent trivial scandal among the peerage, and wonder why the incident has not made its way into the coterie verse that circulates among them. Each of their comments in this exchange is punctuated by Burchell's puzzling, disgusted cry of "Fudge!" Burchell, who will later reveal him-

self as the benevolent Squire Thornhill, knows the two women to be
frauds, but casts suspicion by his interjections on the whole practice
of privately circulated writing as well:

"Besides, my dear Skeggs," continued our Peeress, "there is nothing of
this in the copy of verses that Dr. Burdock made upon the occasion." *Fudge!*
"I am surprised at that," cried Miss Skeggs; "for he seldom leaves any
thing out, as he writes only for his own amusement. But can your Ladyship
favour me with a sight of them?" *Fudge!*
"My dear creature," replied our Peeress, "do you think I carry such things
about me? Though they are very fine to be sure, and I think myself something
of a judge; at least I know what pleases myself. Indeed I was ever an admirer
of all Doctor Burdock's little pieces; for except what he does, and our dear
Countess at Hanover-Square, there's nothing comes out but the most lowest
stuff in nature; not a bit of high life among them." *Fudge!* (4: 62)

This rich piece of satire offers additional evidence that suggests
that Goldsmith further qualified his understanding of the privileged
status that he had earlier accorded to gentlemen writers. The coterie
is absurdly self-reflexive, shut off, as Lady Blarney's assessment of the
state of writing in her day suggests, from the literary mainstream.
With no reason to worry about consumer demand or critical censure,
Dr. Burdock writes without discrimination, descending to so extreme a level of triviality that the ladies are surprised when he leaves
anything out of his verses. If the world of the hired writer corrupts
or undermines the integrity and sincere message of aspiring authors
such as George, the coterie, as Goldsmith presents it, is worse because it is a world in which authors have nothing to say anyway.

The issue of critical judgment is likewise more fundamentally
confused in the coterie than in commercial literary society. When she
rules on Dr. Burdock's poems, "They are very fine to be sure, and I
think myself something of a judge; at least I know what pleases myself," Lady Blarney makes her own taste the indisputable standard,
the very same unfounded claim that Goldsmith accuses the reviewers
of making. In the coterie there can be no alternative to idiosyncratic
but definitive judgments like those of Lady Blarney: there is no reading public, per se, but only a series of isolated individuals among
whom the poems are circulated. The protocols of that circulation,
moreover, ensure so strict a degree of privacy that the two women

cannot read Dr. Burdock's poems at the same time even though they want to—Lady Blarney's excessive refinement forbids her from carrying them about with her. By presenting at a much later point the travails of a lowly professional writer as the sympathetic George Primrose has experienced them, Goldsmith implies that the present state of writing, while it allows for the possibility of fraud, is at least not predicated upon it.

The Vicar delineates extremes in the consumption as well as the production of literature, and brilliantly explores taste as a volatile component of class instability. In a chapter archly entitled "The family use art, which is opposed with still greater," the vicar describes a long-standing "sort of rivalry in point of taste" between his own family and their neighbors, the Flamboroughs. The rivalry leads the Primroses to commission an itinerant limner to paint a family portrait that will outdo the Flamboroughs' seven individual portraits, done by the same painter, in which each member of the family is pictured with an orange.

The Primroses arrive at the choice of a "large historical family piece," on the mixed grounds that "this would be cheaper, since one frame would serve for all, and it would be infinitely more genteel; for all families of any taste were now drawn in the same manner" (4: 82). Each member of the family chooses to be drawn as an independent "historical" (that is, mythological) figure, a plan that results in a montage that iconically undermines everything that the vicar stands for. Prudence is abandoned, since the members of his family are painted as richly dressed and decorated in jewelry. More ridiculous still is the image of the vicar, holding his books on the Whistonian controversy (in which he adopts a strict monogamist stance), surrounded by four emblems of enthusiastic promiscuity: his wife (who is drawn as Venus), his two youngest sons (Cupids), and his elder daughter Olivia (an Amazon). The portrait is finally completed on literally too grand a scale: "It was so very large that we had no place in the house to fix it. . . . The picture, therefore, instead of gratifying our vanity, as we hoped, leaned, in a most mortifying manner, against the kitchen wall . . . much too large to be got through any of the doors, and the jest of all our neighbors" (4: 83).

The problems with the Primrose family portrait can be traced to their desire to combine frugality with gentility, for it is that unlikely mixture that leads to the confused and useless finished product. The Primroses seem on some level to recognize that, on the eighteenth century's register, historical paintings were considered more prestigious than portraits. But their conflicting impulses make it impossible for them to give up the idea of portraits altogether. The result is a grotesque that satisfies neither impulse. That is, the vicar is unsure whether saving money or appearing genteel is the higher priority, mentioning both in the same breath, even though the two motives are incompatible. The size of the portrait presupposes that its owners also own a house large enough and genteel enough to display it, whereas frugality, a cornerstone virtue of the middle class, would most likely dictate that no portrait at all be commissioned. The Primroses wish to enter the scene of cultural consumption in grand style, but they do so without relinquishing the provincial modesty that normally informs their spending habits. Perhaps more importantly, they fail to foresee the consequences of their aspirations to upward cultural mobility.

The lesson to be learned from this fiasco is, as the vicar points out, that "rivalry in point of taste" always has an embarrassing material result. He generalizes about his family's repeated attempts to overstep the bounds of culture that are also the bounds of class: "Our family had now made several attempts to be fine; but some unforeseen disaster demolished each as soon as projected. I endeavoured to take the advantage of every disappointment, to improve their good sense in proportion as they were frustrated in ambition" (4: 68).

The implied conclusion of the portrait episode is that taste, like water, always finds its own level, and that affecting taste above one's economic class is a foolish ambition that cannot be attained. But this conclusion is complicated later in the novel by an episode that presents a butler who, by assiduously completing the reading list of periodicals that would be required of a country squire, turns himself into a perfect replica of a man from a higher social station. When the vicar arrives at "one of the most magnificent mansions" that he encounters during his stint on the road, he is greeted by a man who presents himself as the owner. The man wishes chiefly to discuss national politics and lists an assortment of periodicals as his means of

staying abreast of current events: "I read all the politics that come
out. The Daily, the Public, the Ledger, the Chronicle, the London Evening, the Whitehall Evening, the seventeen magazines, and the two
reviews; and though they hate each other, I love them all" (4: 98). He
engages the vicar in an animated debate about the proper extent of
sovereignty, predictably adopting the standard argument used by
country Tories during the period (that the property rights of the
landed gentry must be upheld against encroachments by the mon-
archy).⁹ The conversation is aborted when the real owner of the estate
returns unexpectedly. The vicar is amused by the butler's attempt "to
cut a figure," and by his skill at impersonation: "to say the truth, he
talked politics as well as most country gentlemen do" (4: 103). He is,
in other words, not outraged by the butler's audacity and even in-
tercedes with the master of the house to prevent the man's dismissal.

Taken together, these last two ingeniously nuanced episodes have
such neatly opposed ramifications that they render Goldsmith's position on the relationship between culture and social class indecipherable. Contemporary sociologists and cultural anthropologists,
in particular Pierre Bourdieu and Bryan Turner, have made the case
that culture helps ensure social closure. A whole array of factors—
economic, educational, political, gender-based (what Bourdieu calls
the *habitus*)—combine to determine, or at least to predict, cultural
dispositions. In turn, those instinctive habits in the consumption
of culture help stratify society, offering a kind of lexicon in which
a person's (or class's) tastes invariably give away his or her economic status, education, or politics. Culture thus plays a central role
in clarifying social distinction and holding the social hierarchy in
place. Bourdieu argues that "it is an immediate adherence . . . to the
tastes and distastes, sympathies and aversions, fantasies and phobias
which, more than declared opinions, forge the unconscious unity of
class."¹⁰

Taste generates the heuristics by which we consume the artifacts
of culture and allot our leisure time. It has obvious ties to economic
standing: money makes leisure time possible in the first place, and it
also fixes the limits of formal education. But taste, because it is in-
tangible and extends across so broad a range of social practice, can

also be quite slow to respond to simple economic mobility. Beginning in the eighteenth century, taste becomes a kind of cultural capital, which during an era of intense industrialization and economic upheaval keeps money from being the sole indicator of social rank. As Colin Campbell observes, the idea of taste in this period draws on "the classical ideal in which intimate association with noble birth inevitably leads to the exclusion of all inferior classes from the possibility of aesthetic privilege."[11]

All of these features of the relationship between cultural consumption and social class are played out in the family portrait episode. Though they strain to accumulate money, the Primroses do have enough to commission the painting. But their incomplete understanding of this new kind of consumption ultimately defeats them. Driven by a desire to gain an edge in refinement on their neighbors, the Flamboroughs, the Primroses step up to a level of cultural practice for which their unrefined tastes leave them inadequately prepared. They become confused about whether they want a history painting or a portrait; they forget their real characters when faced with unfamiliar decisions about how they would like to be represented on canvas; they ask the limner, almost certainly a portraitist, to attempt a more ambitious kind of painting; and, most embarrassingly, they lose sight of the painting's ultimate function as part of their house's interior decoration. Their failure reinforces the lesson that it is futile to try to exceed one's social standing. Cultural dispositions ultimately override money and doom such moves to failure.

The other episode, however, in which the butler impersonates his master, carries very different, radical implications. The butler's reading habits erase all appearances of the differences in social standing between himself and the landlord of the estate, and in so doing, they jeopardize the stability of the social order. The scene construes a certain kind of taste (reading periodicals) as a practice that, in some situations, can threaten to level class distinctions rather than uphold them. The point that Goldsmith seems to be making is that the commercialization of literary culture allows a whole range of sociopolitical and economic perspectives to be encapsulated in the pages of magazines and newspapers, mass produced at affordable prices, and made available to anyone who can read. This suggests that social class itself has become a commodity, something that can be bought and sold in the literary marketplace. Goldsmith's other writings during this period, particularly *The Traveller* (1764), make it clear that he would not have endorsed such a transformation. But the butler episode does, nevertheless, entertain the possibility of a bourgeois public sphere, such as Jürgen Habermas has described, a cultural space created through the butler's individual participation in the magazine culture of his day.[12]

Goldsmith leaves the episode tantalizingly open-ended. While the Primroses' motives in the painting episode are explicit, we never find out what drives the butler. We are left to wonder perhaps if his voracious reading in politics somehow motivated him to impersonate his master—as the only way he could show off his knowledge to an informed audience. It may be the case, in other words, that the butler's relatively lofty ambitions as a reader, like the Primroses' desire for a family portrait, inevitably drove him to transgress class boundaries in other, more radically material ways. Or perhaps the opposite is true: a fantasy of upward mobility motivated him to read broadly and carefully in order somehow to make his dream come true. We are also left to wonder what will become of him. He emerges from this violation of social codes unscathed. He is not punished by his master, and moreover, his aggressive contentiousness in conversation with the vicar is presented as unpleasant but not villainous, as were the disguises of Jenkinson, who defrauds both the vicar and his son Moses. More significantly, nothing is done to ensure that he will stop reading, or stop trying to use what he has read toward some other subversive end. The episode is thus unresolved and suggests that the social order can indeed be disrupted by certain patterns of consumption in the field of culture.

The issues that are the focus of these four episodes, particularly the last two, engaged Goldsmith throughout his writing life. He began as a reviewer for the *Monthly* and the *Critical*, the institutions most invested in prescribing and policing the practices of the English reading public. He went from there to pretend to occupy positions outside the cultural market altogether, writing as a gentleman author in the *Enquiry*, and as a Chinese observer in *The Citizen of the World*. But *The Vicar of Wakefield* marks the first time that he explored the complexities of the relationship between culture and social standing. He would go on to make this subject the center of his inquiry in his plays.

The culminating works of Goldsmith's life as a professional writer are his two plays, *The Good-Natur'd Man* (1768) and *She Stoops to Conquer* (1773), which mark his election into the highest London literary circles. The plays, along with *The Traveller* and *The Deserted Village*, ensured Goldsmith's lasting prestige among his contemporaries. They also concretely measure the distance he had come since his first literary project, a tragedy composed in the mid-1750s that he could not persuade anyone to produce.[13] Aside from assuring his steadily improving reputation, however, Goldsmith's ventures as a playwright put to the test his evolving theories about the cultural field in which he, his fellow writers, critics, and the consuming public operated. In *The Good-Natur'd Man* and *She Stoops to Conquer* Goldsmith not only continued to examine thematically the material conditions and consequences of taste, but he was also obliged to defend his conclusions and the plays that expressed them.

The Good Natur'd Man presents another in a series of explorations by Goldsmith of the relationship between cultural disposition and social class. But, as I will describe, critical dissatisfaction with the play (as "low") provoked Goldsmith's ingenious apology for his stance in the preface to the published version of the play. That preface looks forward to the more famous essay "A Comparison Between Laughing and Sentimental Comedy," published in *Westminster Magazine* on January 1, 1773, and *She Stoops to Conquer*, which was produced at Covent Garden just three months later. Taken as an aggregate, these texts make up a sustained engagement with his reviewers, a series of polemics designed to persuade them to adopt terms of Goldsmith's own choosing in their assessments of contemporary comedy, especially his own. Not only did he ultimately meet with astounding success, as the reception of *She Stoops to Conquer* attests, but his influence extended beyond his own work. So powerful were the sympathies evoked by the laughing-sentimental debate that popular criticism of comedy throughout the 1770s never found alternatives to these categories, which Goldsmith had suggested.

The "supposed" revolt of laughing against sentimental comedy was long ago championed by Arthur Sherbo and discredited by Robert Hume, and though the opposition of these tendencies is still a hobbyhorse of Goldsmith studies, it is of little relevance to the questions I ask here.[14] I do wish to stress, though, as a premise of my argument, that there was indeed a prevailing sentimental mode in comedy, not in the plays themselves but in popular criticism. Goldsmith initiated and established the key terms of a laughing revolt, one designed to counter critics rather than other playwrights. He was, as his earlier writing suggests, aware that the tastes and influence of reviewers was distinct from the desires of an amorphous playgoing or reading public. His efforts to win the support of important theater critics are entirely self-conscious and rhetorically adept, and they draw heavily on his decade of experience in literary culture that preceded his writing of *The Good-Natur'd Man*.[15]

Although Goldsmith did to a large extent determine the Reviews' response to his last two major works, he also depended on those journals. Were it not for the Reviews' capacity to present both of his plays as a single corpus, as part of a career, the effect of Goldsmith's campaign for a laughing revolt would have been greatly diminished. Only because the Reviews presented his plays as having a unified purpose did he stand as the leader of a theatrical revolution. The case of Goldsmith's plays persuasively bears witness to the inauguration at midcentury of a time when the functions performed by authors and critics were fast becoming interdependent, as they are today. His playwriting career was chiefly formed through that particular dialectic, the workings of which I will explore here.

The seemingly incontrovertible premise that an author's play would succeed if it satisfied the expectations of its audience was suddenly complicated by the emergence of a more powerful form of popular criticism, led by the *Monthly* and the *Critical*, that cast the identity of that audience in doubt. The *Monthly*'s editors' cryptic claim, for example, that to influence the reception of a play they must sometimes "appeal from the people to themselves" suggests that the play-going or reading public did not know its own tastes.[16] By claiming for themselves the task of articulating public taste, the Reviews threatened to render indeterminate even so simple a response as applause or hissing.

The predicament of the playwright attempting to please a variety of audiences whose tastes often conflict is reproduced in *The Good-Natur'd Man* itself, in which the benevolist Honeywood feels compelled to be "every man's man" (*Good-Natur'd Man*, 5: 19). Although he describes himself as motivated by selflessness and reserve, he is in fact driven by fear of situations in which he might be unable to accommodate conflicting tastes: precisely the playwright's dilemma as Goldsmith saw it. In the climactic scenes of the play, to choose the most striking illustrations, virtually all of the conflicting dispositions that Honeywood has been attempting to please are voiced on stage at the same time. This crisis begins at the end of act 4, when Honeywood is called in to resolve a dispute between Mr. and Mrs. Croaker over the best way to react to what the old man believes is an extortion attempt. Of course, Honeywood is unable to side with either party (Mr. Croaker believes he should fight back against the incendiaries; Mrs. Croaker believes he should ignore the threats), but can only agree first with the husband, then with the wife, with no hope of resolution.

In act 5 Honeywood, trying to help Croaker catch the incendiary, unwittingly leads the old man to Leontine (his son) and Olivia, whom Honeywood has tried to help elope against Croaker's wishes. In the midst of great confusion and general animosity, the good-natured man can only try in vain to explain the tangled story of his attempts to help everyone, even when his aid involves the most extreme conflicts of interest. The scene represents not only a universal benevolist's downfall, but the author's worst nightmare as well, caused as Honeywood's uncle, Sir William, observes by "errors of a mind that sought only applause from others" (5: 80). By the play's end, Honeywood himself is finally able to see "how I have overtaxed my abilities, lest the approbation of a single fool should escape me!" (5: 75). The benevolist/author analogy in *The Good-Natur'd Man* demonstrates that Goldsmith was already aware in 1768 of the dilemmas about audiences that would confront him, especially in his new venture as a playwright.

But if Goldsmith presents Honeywood's situation as untenable, he also displaces some of the responsibility for his hero's plight onto those characters whose tastes he hopes to accommodate. The positions held by Mr. and Mrs. Croaker in their argument, for example, are ridiculously exaggerated. One could plausibly claim that *they* place Honeywood in an impossible position. One scene in particular goes even farther, addressing the problems of the indeterminacy of taste itself. This scene, in which Honeywood must pass off two debt collectors as polite guests, provoked a great deal of critical debate and, I believe, triggered Goldsmith's campaign against popular dramatic critics.

By involving a bailiff and his follower in a debate about taste, specifically the advantages and disadvantages of cultural importation from France, Goldsmith makes the butt of his satire not the apparently vulgar characters, but the pretension to refined taste itself. Any critic who sets himself up as a man of taste and rebukes Goldsmith for lowness automatically incriminates himself, because he is doing precisely what the bailiff and his follower try to do. In an acute way then, the scene anticipates the very kinds of problems it would cause for critics. The satire on taste begins when Miss Richland responds to Honeywood's embarrassed attempt to pass the debt collectors off as officers in the navy:

Miss Richland. It has often surprised me that, while we have had so many instances of bravery there [in the navy], we have had so few of wit at home to praise it. . . . I'm quite displeased when I see a fine subject spoiled by a dull writer.
Honeywood. We should not be so severe against dull writers, madam. It is ten to one, but the dullest writer exceeds the most rigid French critic who presumes to despise him.
Follower. Damn the French, the parle-vous, and all that belongs to them.
Miss Richland. Sir!
Honeywood. Ha, ha, ha, honest Mr. Flanigan! A true English

officer, madam; he's not contented with beating the French, but he will scold them too.

Miss Richland.   Yet, Mr. Honeywood, this does not convince me that the severity in criticism is necessary. It was our first adopting the severity of French taste that has brought them in turn to taste us.

Bailiff.   Taste us! By the Lord, madam, they devour us. Give Monseers but a taste, and I'll be damned, but they come in for a bellyful!

Miss Richland.   Very extraordinary this!

. . .

Honeywood.   Ah! The vulgar rogues, all will be out! Right gentlemen, very right, upon my word, and quite to the purpose. They draw a parallel madam, between the mental taste, and that of our senses. We are injured as much by French severity in the one, as by French rapacity in the other. That is their meaning.

(5:48–49)

The bailiff and his follower, instructed beforehand merely to be silent, are eager to help Honeywood make his point. They side with him against the French, vehemently trying to convince Miss Richland that corrupted taste is of foreign origin. Much of the humor in the scene arises from Honeywood's ingenious though understandably strained attempts to translate their vulgar Francophobia into a cultured Francophobia, one that would be appropriate for his conversation with Miss Richland about writing. Thus the scene raises in two different ways the unsettling possibility that "high" and "low" might not be fundamentally different at all. Not only do the vulgar and the cultured attacks on the French become one through Honeywood's mediation, but in addition the bailiff and his follower are firmly persuaded (as any reviewer would be) that they know what taste is and how it is corrupted.

Unfortunately, the bailiff scene's inescapable logic was lost on the opening night audience and the critics. The scene was hissed in its first performance: "The people in the pit shouted that the language was low," and when the follower cried, "That's all my eye!" it was reported that "there were hisses from the gallery."[17] Reviews of the play provided a more specific, articulate response. One day later, on January 30, the *London Chronicle* advised, "The whole scene in which those fellows perpetually joined conversation, in language uncommonly low, gave some offence, and it is hoped that the author will for the future wholly omit it."[18] Goldsmith did omit the scene from the remaining shows to ensure a successful run, but he included it—along with a defense—for the printed version of the play, which appeared on February 5, 1768, midway through its run on the stage, and thus continued the controversy in the monthly periodicals.

The *Monthly*, which liked *The Good-Natur'd Man*, claimed that "the bailiff and his blackguard followers appeared intolerable on the stage, yet we are not disgusted with them in the perusal" of the text (note that the reviewer mistakenly exaggerates the problem, giving the bailiff more than one follower). The *Critical* concludes a largely unfavorable review by cautioning that "coarse characters should be touched by a delicate pencil. . . . Forcible situations should rather be softened than aggravated," and Goldsmith, in pursuing humor "into the recesses of the mean . . . should not wholly abandon the dignity of his own character." In what appears to be a review of the performance, the *London Magazine* echoes the complaint that "abilities so extensive as Dr. Goldsmith's are but meanly employed" in the play.

Not all of the notices were unfavorable—both the *St. James Chronicle* and the *Gentleman's Magazine* offered generous praise of Goldsmith and thoughtful comparisons between *The Good-Natur'd Man* and its rival at Drury Lane, Hugh Kelly's *False Delicacy*.[19] But so many of the reviews had singled out the bailiff scene for negative criticism that Goldsmith focused his future efforts on the rehabilitation of that scene's message.

Though it is impossible to know exactly why Goldsmith chose to include the bailiff scene in the published version of *The Good-Natur'd Man*, it is important to consider how he describes that choice and what sort of rhetoric he uses to defend it. Significantly, he presents both the moves first to delete the scene from the production and then to include it in print as concessions rather than independent decisions. Moreover, his description of the whole episode recalls his representations of Honeywood's dilemmas. The striking congruity between play and preface, character and author, suggests how deeply *The Good-Natur'd Man* is informed by Goldsmith's concern with his image before the public. He relates that he has made concessions: "In deference to the public taste, grown of late perhaps too delicate, the scene of the bailiffs was retrenched in the representation. In deference also to the judgment of a few friends, who think in a particular way, the scene is here restored" (5: 14). Of course, the "particular way" in which Goldsmith's friends (Johnson chief among them) think is no different from his own notions about the scene, and his phrasing may be mere convention. But he nevertheless presents the printed version of the play as the product of his friends' opinions rather than his own intentions.

Goldsmith's dissatisfied characterization of "public taste" is equally revealing. After having stated that public taste forced him to remove the bailiff scene, Goldsmith speculates on the potential effects of such pressure on the English stage. He "hopes that too much refinement will not banish humour and character from ours, as it has already done from the French theatre. Indeed the French comedy is now become so very elevated and sentimental, that is has not only banished Molière from the stage, but it has banished all spectators too" (5: 14). In other words, an author must not only worry about whether the scenes in his play are too "low," but he must also be careful not to err in the other direction—driving away audiences by filling his play with too many refined and sentimental episodes.

I will consider Goldsmith's more forceful adoption of this nationalistic stance in "A Comparison Between Laughing and Sentimental Comedy" shortly. First, however, I would like to consider *She Stoops to Conquer* (1773), which moves far beyond *The Good-Natur'd Man*'s strategy of making ostensibly vulgar characters discuss refined topics. In essence, Goldsmith's second play examines the laughing-sentimental debate by way of the class and cultural dispositions that underwrite it. It places the "high"-"low" opposition, which had been the focus of the critical debate over *The Good-Natur'd Man*, alongside similar familiar oppositions: country-city, "modest"-"impudent." By dramatizing the possibilities for confusion over these seemingly stable antinomies, Goldsmith undermines the critical position that he opposes. If refined characters can so easily be mistaken for vulgar, modest characters for impudent, etc., how can there exist a universal rationale that would make distinctions between these social poles possible?

The answer, Goldsmith persuasively argues, is that no essentialist standard is available: critics must always stumble trying to dismiss Tony Lumpkin's friend's glowing compliment, "I loves to hear him sing, bekeays he never gives us nothing that's *low*" (*She Stoops to Conquer*, 5: 117). But Goldsmith does not use the "mistakes of a night" to tear down the boundaries between modesty and impudence, or even those between high and low. Rather, he calls attention to the arbitrary nature of the conventions that characterize those boundaries, and to the vagaries of judgment by which they are identified. He wishes, in other words, to destabilize the very categories and capacities in which his critics place their confidence.

The play sustains, at least in some sense, a genuine social and cultural stratification. Though he claims to "love everything that's old" (5: 107) and complains about his wife's affected attempts to be fashionable, the country squire Hardcastle nevertheless drills his farmhands in a pathetic attempt to make them into the servants one might expect to find at a more luxurious country estate than his own (5: 125–27). Moreover, while he tolerates an endless stream of insolent remarks from his titled friend's son, Marlow, he is infuriated by an insult from the young man's servant and nearly throws Marlow out of his house as a result (5: 181). Mrs. Hardcastle, lecturing her son Tony Lumpkin about his ingratitude, reminds him, "Did I not work that waistcoat to make you look genteel?" (5: 153). The remark reveals both her awareness of high fashion, and her distance from it: unable to locate (possibly unable to afford) a London tailor, she cares enough to expend her own labor in an attempt to make Tony look fashionable. She is also a diligent student of London gossip, which she gleans from the *Scandalous Magazine*, and she dresses her own hair by copying styles from prints in the *Ladies' Memorandum-book* (5: 150).

Marlow, too, is constrained by his awareness of differences of class and learning. He confesses to his companion Hastings, "I don't know that I was ever familiarly acquainted with a single modest woman—except my mother," and in the company of such women he is "an ideot . . . a trembler" (5: 129). He can only assert himself in the presence of lower-class women, whom he seems to consider little more than commodities. He says of Hardcastle's daughter, Kate (during the period in which he believes she is a barmaid), "Take my word for it; there's nothing in this house I shan't honestly pay for" (5: 178). Both Marlow and Hastings consider Tony unworthy of their company because of his age (he has not come into his estate) and because he is illiterate (5: 192).

But the social and cultural dispositions of Marlow, Hastings, and Mr. and Mrs. Hardcastle are quickly shaken by Tony Lumpkin and Kate Hardcastle, each of whom demonstrates how easily manipulated distinctions such as "high" and "low" actually are. Tony's inspired plan of revenge against his stepfather displays considerable acumen about class differences, particularly an understanding of how much those differences rest on custom and manners. He misleads Marlow and Hastings into thinking that Hardcastle's estate is an inn, and that the innkeeper (Hardcastle), having grown rich, is about to retire and live as though he were a country squire: "So he wants to be thought a Gentleman, saving your presence, he, he, he. He'll be for giving you his company, and ecod, if you mind him, he'll persuade you that his mother was an alderman and his aunt a justice of the peace" (5: 124).

Everything said here about Hardcastle's character is true, but by slyly altering his situation from a country squire anxious to be a good host to an innkeeper who is paid for any services he renders to his guests, Tony ensures that Marlow and Hastings will treat the old man in precisely the way that will insult him most. Tony understands equally well how to embarrass Marlow and Hastings by taking advantage of their cultured fastidiousness. The two arrive at the Three Pigeons Alehouse in a post chaise looking "woundily like Frenchmen" (5: 119) and express great reluctance about taking any but the most luxurious accommodations. Tony plays on their fears, suggesting with mock seriousness that they sleep at the alehouse on "three chairs and a bolster." As a result, he is able to offer them, as a godsend, the prospect of spending the night at Hardcastle's "inn" instead (5: 123).

The immediate purpose of Tony's machinations is clear enough:

Hardcastle constantly disparages him, and the arrival of Marlow and Hastings presents an excellent opportunity for revenge. But his particular plan, a diabolical manipulation of class and cultural differences, hints at a more deeply rooted set of motives. That Tony has some independent ideas about how people ought to behave becomes apparent in act 5. Hastings treats Tony with near contempt throughout his stay at Hardcastle's estate, but when he realizes how much Tony has done to help him and Miss Neville elope, he tries to thank the boy. Tony responds indignantly: "Ay, now it's dear friend, noble 'squire. Just now it was all ideot, cub, and run me through the guts. Damn *your* way of fighting, I say. After we take a knock in this part of the country, we kiss and be friends. But if you had run me through the guts, then I should be dead and you might go kiss the hangman" (5: 203–4).

Tony's remarks address another opposition fundamental to the play: between urban and rustic mentalities, or more to the point, between affected and natural behavior. For Tony, Hastings's urban affectations erect barriers between people, making life-threatening confrontations out of what should be inconsequential incidents. By contrast, Tony's ideal vision, in which people "take a knock" and then "kiss and be friends," is a burlesque, in which no one is inhibited by social conventions from either spontaneously fighting or just as easily making up.[20] Goldsmith's management of this particular opposition, and the improvement of Tony's stock over the course of the play, are crucial elements in the playwright's debate with his critics. He wishes to alter our perception of the "high"-"low" opposition by replacing the notion of lowness with one of naturalness. Tony's perception of conflict between people and of class, as well as our increasingly favorable impression of him, all contribute to a rehabilitation of the "low"-"natural" position in the critical debate.

Repressive affectation and a naturalizing antidote for it also constitute the critical issue in the relationship between Kate and Marlow. Marlow's "reserve," which Hardcastle lists as an important "noble virtue" (5: 113), virtually prevents him from conversing with Kate when she is introduced to him as a refined woman. But when she wears "the dress . . . that every lady wears in the country but when she visits, or receives company," Marlow mistakes her class and pursues her (5: 168). His artificially modest manner makes his talk with Kate a "sober, sentimental interview" and buries the sexual attraction that emerges as soon as their class relationship appears to change and modesty is no longer the appropriate demeanor. The demands of his social rank make Marlow alternately a mouse and a rake. Kate "conquers" him by confusing him into dropping both facades. What is left, Goldsmith implies, are the natural virtues that are opposed to sentimentalism.

Virtually every example I have used to illustrate the means by which Goldsmith argued with his reviewers about the aims of comedy involves an opposition between France and England, and the strategy of campaigning for (and writing) a distinctly English kind of comedy produced remarkable results. Goldsmith's politics and his dramaturgy proved to be mutually empowering. The nationalistic rhetoric that he first applied to theater in the preface to *The Good-Natur'd Man*, and later in the "Comparison Between Laughing and Sentimental Comedy," as well as in the texts of both plays, was ultimately taken up by reviewers of *She Stoops to Conquer*. Thus the language of these reviews, both favorable and unfavorable, constitutes a kind of victory for Goldsmith. The widespread adoption of his terminology made it easier for supporters to praise *She Stoops to Conquer* and put his hostile critics on the defensive.

Why was nationalism so powerful a weapon for Goldsmith in his struggle with the reviewers? To answer this question we must turn to the preface of *The Good-Natur'd Man*, where Goldsmith first aligns himself with a native tradition of comic playwriting and opposes that tradition to a vitiated contemporary French theater. I have already quoted his description of how the French have banished humor, character, Molière, and finally all spectators from the stage; his characterization of his own undertaking as a playwright is equally crucial: "When I undertook to write a comedy, I confess that I was strongly prepossessed in favour of the poets of the last age, and strove to imitate them. The term, genteel comedy, was then unknown amongst us, and little more was desired by an audience, than nature and humour. . . . The author of the following scenes never imagined that more would be expected of him" (5: 13).

In 1768, a reviewer or reader well versed in popular criticism would have taken this as a revolutionary statement. The earlier comic dramatists whom Goldsmith, with seeming naïveté, claims as ancestors and models were scorned by popular critics throughout the 1760s. The prevailing view, as stated by the *Theatrical Review* in 1763, was that "indecency no longer usurps the place of wit, nor does any elevation of language gild over, in these days, an illiberal morality of sentiment," which meant that no author could be "confident enough to expect the approbation of the public at the expense of decency and virtue."[21]

Such attitudes were reflected in practice by favorable reviews of often heavily didactic, sentimental, or "genteel" comedies. Indeed, the *Critical Review*, which became more and more favorably disposed toward sentimental comedy as the decade progressed, condemned one play in 1770 solely because it lacked "a sentimental stroke."[22] The *London Magazine*, in its review of *The Good-Natur'd Man*, is extremely concrete in its didactic approach, going so far as to denounce the very poets whom Goldsmith implied were his models: "Dryden's comedies, Wycherly, Vanbrugh, and Congreve, are almost banished, indeed banished very justly from the theatre. . . . Thank God in these times we have too much understanding . . . to be charmed by obscenity because it may be brilliantly expressed."[23]

Phrases such as "in these days" and "in these times" incorporate this theory of comedy into a larger progressive philosophy of English society, which allows the critics to delineate the history of both British theater and British manners as a gradual, hard-earned victory over vulgarity. Thus one can see that Goldsmith was pitting himself against an extremely powerful, almost monolithic set of ideas. In order to make the reviewers regard him as something more than a peculiar heretic, his own aesthetic had to draw upon an ideology that would potentially be just as expansive and appealing as the progressive one from which he dissented. Nationalism proved to be the perfect alternative.[24] By claiming to fall naturally into a tradition of English comedy (in fact replacing "low" with "natural" as the opposite of "refined"), Goldsmith invokes a kind of nostalgic patriotism and implicitly pleads for sympathizers. He lends a sense of urgency to this plea by alluding to a degenerate contemporary French stage, and more to the point, warning of the great danger threatening the English if they continue to copy French taste.

Goldsmith returns to this same theme four years later, in the "Comparison Between Laughing and Sentimental Comedy," an essay that is ideologically more straightforward than the preface to *The Good-Natur'd Man*. Goldsmith begins the "Comparison" by directly challenging the progressive philosophy that underlies sentimental comedy: "The Theatre, like all other amusements, has its Fashions and its Prejudices; and when satiated with its excellence, Mankind begins to mistake Change for Improvement" ("Comparison," 3: 209). He concludes with an apocalyptic repetition of the warning he had first issued in the preface:

Humour at present seems to be departing from the Stage, and it will soon happen that our Comic Players will have nothing left but a fine Coat and a Song. It depends upon the Audience whether they will actually drive poor Merry Creatures from the Stage or sit at a Play as gloomy as at the Tabernacle. It is not easy to recover an art when once lost, and it would be a just punishment that when, by our being too fastidious, we have banished Humour from the Stage, we should ourselves be deprived of the art of Laughing. (3: 213)

The "Comparison" is a much more confident document than Goldsmith's earlier rehearsal of the same position. As the progressive reviewers had done before him, Goldsmith incorporates his theory of comedy into a broader philosophy of manners, only his of course is opposed to theirs. Even more powerful is his astonishment that comedy is virtually doomed on the English stage; it contrasts starkly with the humorously anxious suggestions about the fate of humor in the preface to *The Good-Natur'd Man*. The disappearance of comedy is now imminent, and the English people about to be deprived forever of laughter.

Despite the differences between the preface of 1768 and the essay of 1773, one can clearly recognize them as part of a single sustained campaign. The reception of *She Stoops to Conquer* reveals just how successful that campaign was. The most sophisticated reactions to Goldsmith's strategy came, predictably, from the *Monthly* and the *Critical*. The two journals take opposing positions, but both address the theme of French-English rivalry that he had introduced. In addition, both greatly elaborate the histories of comedy, laughing and sentimental, to which Goldsmith had alluded.

The writer for the *Critical*, who commends *She Stoops to Conquer*, seems to have borrowed heavily from the "Comparison." The French, he admits, have done well in eking out a place for comedy between tragedy on the one hand and farce on the other. The English, however, "have excelled other nations in the strength of their characters, the warmth and bustle of their plots and the variety of their incidents." The reviewer lists among the best comic playwrights Vanbrugh and Farquhar, both very recently considered unfashionable. Having stated his preference for the "old comedy," he then turns to the threat posed by the French influence on the English stage: "Comedy both in France and England has been seen to languish in recent years. . . . The *Comedie Larmoyant*, or Tradesman's Tragedy, has prevailed in France to the utter extinction of all other comic representation. As we often imitate not only the dress of that people, but also their manner of thinking, we have followed them in their domestic declensions; and it was supposed, by the lovers of the old comedy, that she was extinct among us" (*Critical* 35 [March 1773]: 229–30).

The whole review, particularly this last point, is far more effective because it is written about rather than by Goldsmith. The reviewer, who has license to take Goldsmith's hints to their didactic extreme, bullies his readers into supporting the play by implicitly (but hardly subtly) branding anyone who does not cheer Goldsmith's attempt to revive the old comedy a mindless Francophile.

The *Monthly*'s review is even more interesting because, though the reviewer dislikes the play, he has been defanged by the force of Goldsmith's nationalistic rhetoric. He cannot attack the fundamental aim of *She Stoops to Conquer* (to revive the old comedy) because Goldsmith has so cleverly associated it with patriotism; as a result, the objections he does raise seem almost trivial. For example, he feels obliged to praise the "poets of the last age," Vanbrugh, Congreve, Farquhar, Cibber, and Steele, and must strain to make the point that their merit lay in their ability to "represent the manners of the time."[25]

From this beginning, he proceeds to a standard version of the progressive theory of comedy:

Our customs and manners have undergone a gradual alteration. A general correspondence arising from trade, and the progress of the arts, has brought the nation . . . together, and worn off those prepossessions and habits which made every community with its peculiar character. The business of comedy is therefore changed. . . . Some of our late writers have therefore very judiciously had recourse to what is called *Sentimental Comedy*, as better suited to the principles and manners of the age. A general politeness has given a sameness to our external appearances; and great degrees of knowledge are everywhere diffused. An author, therefore, has not the variety of character, and that simplicity and ignorance to describe, which were the capital ingredients of the old Comedy.

But this theory, the trump card of drama criticism during the 1760s, must now be accompanied by an apology: "Modern writers may indeed have carried the matter too far, and perhaps kept their eyes too much on French models. They may have neglected some remains of English oddities which are still left, and would have very much enlivened their writings. They have erred only in the execution: they are right in their general principle" (*Monthly* 48 [March 1773]: 309–10).

The notice differs significantly from the negative criticism of *The Good-Natur'd Man*. The reviewer is keenly anxious to avoid appearing unpatriotic, and to defend his position as carefully as possible. His justification of sentimental comedy is circuitously conducted, so much so that a reader must work hard to draw the inference that he is criticizing Goldsmith for immorality. One is left with a sense that, though he wishes to attack the play comprehensively, the obstacles presented by Goldsmith's promotional rhetoric prevent him from delivering anything more than a mild reproof.

Though it may appear that Goldsmith used a convenient set of political assumptions to further his own strictly literary ambitions, the relationship between his politics and his dramatic production is in fact much more complex than that. He seems to have conceived of politics chiefly in literary terms, hence he never strays far from a specifically literary kind of nationalism in the preface, the "Comparison," and the plays, as he had, particularly, in the *Enquiry*. Thus, by virtue of being a literary issue, the laughing-sentimental debate is for Goldsmith of serious political import.

Goldsmith typifies an age in which new kinds of extraliterary

skills—those of the professional writer—came to figure very importantly in literary production. He was a master of those skills: his critical and strategic tour de force in reviving the old comedy soon extended beyond his own work and came to stand as a sign of his
achievement. In 1780 George Colman (who had only seven years earlier balked at the idea of producing *She Stoops to Conquer*) could
sum up Goldsmith's influence on the past generation of playwrights
in the following lines:

> When Fielding, Humour's fav'rite child, appear'd,
> *Low* was the word—a word each author fear'd;
> 'Till chac'd at length, by pleasantry's bright ray
> Nature and mirth resum'd their legal sway;
> And Goldsmith's genius bask'd in open day.[26]

But if the reviewers took their cue for treating *She Stoops to Conquer* from Goldsmith, they also provided the institutional arena in
which he won his victory. Just 24 years after the founding of the
Monthly, and seventeen years after the founding of the *Critical*, the
practice of reviewing had already become an essential element in the
reception of any literary publication. Goldsmith's is the most extraordinary instance of an author all but compelling change in the rhetoric
and critical intent of his reviewers. In order to challenge the Reviews'
endorsement of sentimental comedy, however, he had first to grant
their position some measure of legitimacy. That acknowledgment
fundamentally differentiates Goldsmith's literary practice from that
of Sterne, who, as we saw, denied the significance of his reviewers,
even as they prompted him to alter the course of his writing.

"It is better to be envied than despised"

Tobias Smollett

Perhaps because Tobias Smollett is now studied almost exclusively as a writer of fiction, his importance as editor of the *Critical Review* is generally underestimated.[1] In his own time this was not the case. His reputation as a novelist rested chiefly on the popularity of one book, *Roderick Random*, published in 1748.[2] Of the three novels that followed, *Peregrine Pickle* (1751) received mixed reviews, while *Ferdinand Count Fathom* (1753) and *Launcelot Greaves* (1761) were even less popular and were generally disparaged by critics. Only *Humphry Clinker*, published just two months before Smollett died in September 1771, stirred the level of interest and acclaim relatively absent since the appearance of his first novel.[3]

By contrast, Smollett's position as editor of the *Critical* from 1756 until 1763 made him one of the most powerful men on the London literary scene. He was courted or attacked by some of the most important writers of the period, and he made the final decisions about both the books that were assigned to his staff of reviewers, and those that would be featured in each month's issue of his journal.[4] I contend that, almost immediately after founding the *Critical* in 1756, Smollett ceased to think of himself as primarily an author and began instead to think of himself as the editor of a major Review. In the aftermath of this transition, from being one of many writers hoping for public notice, to being one of two Review editors capable of bestowing it, his standing as a professional writer was radically redefined, and he in turn completely refigured his representation of the dynamics of literary society, developing an understanding of author-ship more appropriate to his new position of power. That refigura-tion is the subject of this chapter.

I wish to explore the relationship between Smollett's involvement with the *Critical* and the novel writing with which he is now iden-tified. In particular, I will argue that Smollett wrote what are, in ef-fect, two successive narratives of professional success, one that de-scribes his career as an aspiring author, and the other that accounts for his very different life as editor of the *Critical*. I see Smollett's early novels as an attempt to encode plans for survival amid the vicissi-tudes of the literary market as it existed at midcentury. They describe a set of strategies that enables deserving initiates—Roderick Ran-dom, Peregrine Pickle, and Ferdinand Count Fathom—to ascend the professional ladder and gain recognition from the corrupt hierarchies that govern their social environment. This process, though, could en-tail crippling sacrifices of personal integrity. The increasing readiness of these young gentlemen to resort to dissimulation in order to get by reaches a climax in *Fathom*; three years after writing that novel, Smollett attempted to make an ideological break with the writing trade by founding the *Critical*.

My decision to concentrate on the way in which Smollett repre-sents problems inherent in literary relationships is something of a de-parture from my treatments of Sterne and Goldsmith, both of whom responded in some tangible way to the Reviews—changing their sub-sequent work, or explicitly answering the reviewers' charges. For sev-eral reasons, Smollett could not have had that kind of transactive re-lationship with popular critics. First, he began writing before the Re-views were solidly established. *Roderick Random* (1748) appeared a year before the *Monthly* was founded. That journal was, moreover, initially very cautious about venturing evaluations of literary works and thus offered little more than plot summaries of *Peregrine Pickle* and *Ferdinand Count Fathom*. Not until the founding of the *Critical* did the *Monthly* become interested in reforming current reading tastes. Thus Sterne and Goldsmith's work was examined by different criteria than was Smollett's.

Second, Smollett's relationships with the editors of the *Monthly*, both before and after he founded the *Critical*, strongly biased the reviews of his work. John Cleland reviewed the published version of Smollett's tragedy, *The Regicide*, enthusiastically in the very first issue of the *Monthly* (*Monthly* 1 [May 1749]: 72), became friends with Smollett shortly thereafter, and two years later favorably reviewed *Peregrine Pickle* (*Monthly* 4 [March 1751]: 362). Through his association with Cleland, Smollett himself came to write occasionally for the *Monthly*. His first contribution was, appropriately enough, a review of Cleland's *Memoirs of a Coxcomb* (*Monthly* 5 [October 1751]: 386–87), which appeared five months after Cleland's review of *Peregrine Pickle*. Smollett continued to write occasionally for the *Monthly* during the early 1750s, and the one novel he wrote during that period, *The Adventures of Ferdinand Count Fathom*, was thus for all practical purposes exempt from hostile criticism (*Monthly* 8 [March 1753]: 203–14). Even though Smollett entertained a "cordial dislike" for the *Monthly*'s editor, Ralph Griffiths (Knapp, 121), Griffiths could not realistically demean one of his own contributors, and so kept quiet.

After he founded the *Critical*, the treatment Smollett received from the *Monthly* was powerfully influenced by his status as Griffiths's rival. Owen Ruffhead's long review of *The Complete History of England* (*Monthly* 18 [April 1758]: 289–305) is mostly negative. *Sir Launcelot Greaves* is dismissed in one sentence in the Monthly Catalogue (*Monthly* 26 [May 1762]: 391). *Humphry Clinker* is also treated indifferently in a very brief notice, in which Smollett, by then no longer affiliated with the *Critical*, is assessed as follows: "The present Writer . . . has humour and wit, as well as grossness and ill-nature.—But we need not enlarge on his literary character, which is well known to the public" (*Monthly* 45 [August 1771]: 152). The *Monthly*'s inclination after the founding of the *Critical* seems to be to contain and diminish Smollett's reputation in order perhaps that his Review be taken less seriously. Thus, whereas Sterne and Goldsmith made the reviews of their work into polemical documents, Smollett found them that way.

The decision to found the Review (as part of a learned academy) constitutes a reaction against that market, indeed an attempt to replace it altogether with an institutional literary system in which merit is not bound to interest. His hope, in other words, was to provide an institutional setting in which any author's works would be assessed impartially, a setting that would mitigate against the various forces that had kept him, a young, unconnected Scot, from succeeding more easily. The cultural credibility that he helped lend to reviewing paradoxically diminished the conventional notions of authorship that he entertained at the start of his life as a writer. The success of the *Critical* worked to erode the belief that merit in writing, like "quality" in social distinction, was self-evident and could manifest itself without aid. Instead, the *Critical* implicitly asserted that quality in a literary work had to be institutionally determined and ratified. Thus, while the Review deplored the commercialization of writing and appealed to the sensibility of the refined gentleman, its place as an influential institution effectually replaced the model of author as gentleman with that of author as professional. Both Smollett's work for the *Critical* and much of the writing he wrote after founding it reflect a continuing interest in neutralizing or controlling the literary market. His later books are informed by his new perspective and his new concerns as an authoritative judge of other people's literary productions and a self-appointed reformer of the English public's reading tastes. *Launcelot Greaves*, *Travels Through France and Italy*, and *The Expedition of Humphry Clinker* are all, broadly stated, comprehensive social critiques delivered from positions of authority that were unavailable to Smollett's earlier protagonists.

Smollett's attraction to these two kinds of narratives can be explained in part as a desire to make sense of the crucial issues of his own life as a writer. But they open the door to further speculation about the relationship between fictional narrative and professional life story. Smollett drew the narratives that he replayed in his fiction from two novelistic traditions, the picaresque and the quixotic, that had fascinated him since the late 1740s, when he translated Lesage's *Gil Blas* and began translating *Don Quixote*. In *Gil Blas* Smollett found the prototype of the pragmatic, picaresque survivor, in *Don Quixote*, that of the idealistic reformer. The one adopts a variety of professional guises as expediency dictates: as Walter Reed has observed, the basic situation of the picaresque hero is "the marginal man's career of deception."[5] The other, the quixotic figure, tacitly repudiates all professions and attempts to enforce, however naively, an all-encompassing chivalric code on society. To put my claim simply, Smollett adopts the practices of the picaro during the first part of his career, and represents them in *Roderick Random*, *Peregrine Pickle*, and *Ferdinand Count Fathom*; then he adopts the stance of the quixote upon founding the *Critical*, representing that position most completely in *Launcelot Greaves*.

Although I do not wish to rest my argument on assumptions about these borrowings, I think the uses to which Smollett puts *Gil Blas* and *Don Quixote* offer fascinating insight into the ways that careers, particularly literary careers, come into being. Smollett in effect uses, in sequence, two received fictional narratives to construct the narrative of his own career—at a time when no ready-made narrative was available to describe exactly what it was that a novelist does. Smollett's affinity for panoptic representations of society, such as *Gil Blas* and *Don Quixote*, is most appropriate, since a literary career is, as Jerome Christensen has observed, a means of "social composition."[6]

Despite the importance of parallels such as these to the backdrop of my argument, I wish to distance myself from the narrow assertion that the novels are autobiographical. Reducing Smollett's fiction in this way has long been the tendency among his readers, and that tendency even prompted a warning, an "apologue" from Smollett himself in the fourth edition of *Roderick Random*. Instead I want to emphasize that Smollett's critique of the profession of letters is articulated in the same terms in his letters and in his Review, and that the novels simply provide one (albeit voluminous) place from which to recover that critique.

I

Smollett's initial literary ambitions lay entirely in the theater, but his efforts to become a successful playwright were unequivocally disastrous. His first play, a tragedy called *The Regicide*, was passed around the London theatrical establishment for eight years (beginning in 1739) but never produced. It is clear from Lewis Knapp's careful reconstruction of the play manuscript's history that the chief obstacle to Smollett's hopes was the monopolistic nature of play production at midcentury.[7] Covent Garden and Drury Lane, as the only two patented theaters, offered Smollett a very restricted choice, and indeed the story of his efforts on behalf of the play can be reduced to a series of attempts to win the approval of one theater manager or the other, first James Lacy of Drury Lane, then John Rich of Covent Garden. Smollett twice recounted the entire episode: in *Roderick Random*, the failed playwright, Melopoyn, relates the story of his frustrations at the hands of the perfidious "Brayer" (Lacy) and "Vandal" (Rich). In 1749 Smollett printed the play by subscription, confessing in his proposal that "the singular way in which the play has been excluded from both theatres (as will appear in the Preface) obliges the Author to publish it in a way otherwise not agreeable to his inclination."[8] That "Preface" presents Smollett's straightforward account of his disappointments.

In both these recapitulations, as well as in the letters in which he discusses *The Regicide*, Smollett implicitly attempts to locate both himself and, more generally, authorship in the spectrum of professions emerging in English society.[9] The conventional midcentury metaphors for the struggling writer are economic; contemporary writers, however, used these metaphors in contrary ways. As Linda Zionkowski has persuasively argued, writers such as Fielding, Johnson, and Bonnell Thornton feared that writing was in danger of degenerating into a mechanical trade practiced by "Pen and Ink Laborer[s]."[10] Yet while these writers sought to differentiate mental labor (associated with polite letters) from manual labor (associated with hackwork)—and categorized their peers either as authors suitable for the literary market or "drudges of the pen"[11]—others, like James Ralph, argued that writers could succeed in this market only by acting like tradesmen. Insisting that literature is a commodity like any other, Ralph urged his fellow writers to combine together and protect their interests, just as other "Manufacturers" do.[12] But regardless of how differently writers like Johnson and Ralph defined their labor and the kind of conduct suitable for their profession, they constructed a model of authorship that assumes participation in a competitive commerce in letters.

Smollett also justifies his playwriting on the basis of merit, drawing his vocabulary from national politics, and making a case in many ways akin to that articulated by Sterne. In his most detailed private comment on his plight, he writes to Francis Hayman in May 1750:

I have been frustrated in all my attempts to Succeed on the Stage—not by the Publick, which I have always found favourable and propitious; but by the Power of two or three Persons who (I cannot help saying) have accepted and patronized the works of others, with whom, in point of Merit, I think myself, at least, upon a par—this I speak not from Vanity, but Resentment for the hard usage I have met with. I own, I feel very severely, when I reflect upon my (I was going to say) unjust Exclusion from the Theatre—but I begin to grow warm, and therefore will conclude.[13]

The letter alludes to a story full of what Smollett refers to elsewhere as "Pitifull Intrigues" (*Letters*, 4), in which those few who inexplicably occupy positions of power frustrate others like himself who deserve to be recognized. It is vaguely Tory in its line of attack, reminiscent of opposition to Walpole in the 1730s.[14] Most importantly, it is an argument from personal qualifications, those characteristics that make up the "sameness that any profession confers upon its members."[15] Smollett, unlike Ralph, wished not merely to realign the balance of power in the literary market by uniting with other authors against those who are in control, but rather to declare his independence with the help of an idealized (and idealistically unmediated) relationship with the public.

Smollett did not hesitate to generalize: searching for a fitting analogy for his situation, he writes to Alexander Carlyle in October 1749: "I may with great Justice say of the managers, as my Predecessor Michl. Drayton the water poet says of Booksellers—'they are a pack of base Knaves whom I both despise and kick at'" (*Letters*, 12). Though he could conceivably have drawn from expressions of hostility toward the booksellers of his own day, Smollett instead recalls Drayton's comment (from a letter written in 1619) to describe his anger. Drayton, though a professional writer, epitomizes the pristine Elizabethan age before literary production came to be dominated by corrupt oligarchies, a time when authorship (of poetry) entailed an aristocratic perspective from which booksellers appeared as no more than "base knaves."

Why would Smollett reject the typical stance of the contemporary struggling writer in favor of a resentment based in a sense of personal competence? Part of the reason is certainly that he, like Sterne, was firmly established in a traditional profession before he began to flourish as an author. True, he did arrive in London at nineteen with great hopes for *The Regicide*. But his disappointments in promoting the tragedy were matched by accomplishments as a surgeon,[16] and an accompanying sense of professional place—as when Smollett writes almost proudly to a friend in 1744: "I have moved into the house where the late John Douglas, surgeon, died, and you may henceforth direct for Mr. Smollett, surgeon, in Downing Street" (*Letters*, 2).

Smollett's conception of himself from this early stage as a professional (even if a professional surgeon rather than author) lead him to rehearse, in his first three novels, narratives of frustrated merit that are more extensive, radical, and precisely focused than *Joseph Andrews* or *Tom Jones*. Stripped of the idealized love relationships, a feature of romance that figures centrally in Fielding's work, *Roderick Random*, *Peregrine Pickle*, and *Ferdinand Count Fathom* relentlessly examine the nepotistic social biases that threaten to keep deserving young gentlemen from succeeding materially. The indignation that energizes these novels was perceived as sufficiently atypical that it strongly colors representations of Smollett by his contemporaries: Smelfungus in *A Sentimental Journey* and the most obstreperous passenger in the fame machine in Goldsmith's *The Bee*.[17] Smollett is, one senses, a distinctive figure in part because, even when forced into the circumstances of a hired writer, he refused to think of himself as one. I will argue that his refusal to accept the literary market as it was led ultimately to a rejection of the very premise of such a market. He envisioned the *Critical Review* as the agency that would make such a radical move possible.

Society in Smollett's first three novels is characterized, as John Barrell has observed, by a bewildering array of types, each with a different occupation that employs its own professional conventions and vocabulary.[18] The relative prestige of each profession and the obscurity of professional languages offer a seemingly infinite possibility for abuses of power and serve only to camouflage the evil deeds of the imposters who rule. In this cynically depicted environment, Smollett's young heroes must find their way. The early novels raise a difficult dilemma: can one succeed in the world without being absorbed into one or another of these deceitful professional coteries? Smollett's answer to that question, I contend, becomes increasingly pessimistic. He goes from idealizing Roderick Random's integrity (1748), to chronicling Peregrine Pickle's compromises with virtue (1751), to presenting Ferdinand Count Fathom as a consummate assimilator and confidence man (1753).

Roderick is the disinherited grandson of a "gentleman of considerable fortune and influence,"[19] and these beginnings ensure that he is himself at all times "determined to appear to be as much of a gentleman as his means will allow, and as little attached as possible to the occupation he happens at one time or another to be following." But the great difficulty in maintaining this distinction between self-image and social place is that he must learn "how a gentleman should behave, and how he should appear."[20] The narrative that results from this conflict balances Roderick's angry, and usually undercorroborated, claim to entitlement against an ironic distance that characterizes his perspective on social hierarchy.

His socialization is an extensive and difficult course in learning to recognize imposters and to react to them correctly: the first is a question of acquiring practical knowledge; the second involves a more complex ethical choice. Roderick's difficulties, through roughly the first three-quarters of his adventures, fall into the former category as he attempts to learn the etiquette of gentility, a process that is broadly symbolized by his initial stay in London. There, his naïveté quickly leads to overwhelming victimization, as his servant, Strap, laments: "We have not been in London eight-and-forty hours, and I believe we have met with eight-and-forty thousand misfortunes. We have been jeered, reproached, buffeted, pissed upon, and at last stripped of our money; and I suppose by and by we shall be stripped of our skins. . . . Ah! God help us, an ounce of prudence is worth a pound of gold" (*Roderick Random*, 72).

"Prudence," as Strap uses the word, is divorced from any religious connotations: it signifies precisely the kind of sophistication that Roderick needs to gain. Prudence, indeed, is a variant of what Barrell describes as the gentlemanly perspective that Roderick strives to achieve. Much of the first stages of his narrative describe Roderick's progress toward "the acquisition of that comprehensive view . . . from which society can be grasped in terms of relation and not simply of difference."[21] That perspective is essential in order for the initiate to thrive in society, by acting on the relations he discerns, and if he is to write his adventures (by narrating the events of his life in relation to one another).

The ensuing episodes indeed detail the difficulties Roderick has in acquiring prudence, as he tries to obtain a commission as a surgeon's mate in the Navy. He is told by a landlord exactly how to go about bribing Mr. Cringer, the member of parliament from whom he hopes to obtain this favor (73). He is thrown upon his skill in physiognomy as a means of identifying reliable bureaucrats, though in practice this means distinguishing Scotsmen from Englishmen—a somewhat desperate index (78). He is instructed in the bizarre exchanges by which beaus keep each other financially solvent (83–84). Finally, in the most elaborate instance of Roderick's frustration at the hands of powerful and corrupt institutions, he is examined by the Board of Surgeons in a travesty of an interview, and "afterwards obliged to give three shillings and sixpence to the beadles, and a shilling to an old woman who swept the hall" (86–88). Despite his extraordinary labors, he is ultimately denied his commission for lack of influence in the Navy Office, and serves at sea only after he is impressed. These events replicate a host of earlier frustrations by the agents of institutions, beginning with his grandfather, a judge, who disinherits him, to the schoolmaster who binds his hand so that he cannot write.

Roderick's ethical choices—those that affect how he responds to the imposters he meets—come mostly during the high-life period of his last stay in London, in the last quarter of the novel. Only by that point has he become sophisticated enough to thrive in an urban, genteel setting. He must decide, in several crucial episodes, how closely to emulate those people who had excluded him in his earlier naive state. In an enlightening misstep, he becomes a fortune hunter, a sham gentleman, lying awake at night pleasing himself "with the hopes of possessing a fine woman with ten thousand pounds" (282). But he is quickly able to recognize the superficiality of his qualifications. After opportunistically courting the heiress Melinda Goose-trap and proposing marriage, he is deflated by her mother's sugges-tion that "if it pleased, her lawyer should confer with mine upon the matter, and in the meantime, she desired, I would favour her with the perusal of my rent-roll. Not withstanding the vexation I was under, I could scarce forbear laughing in her face at the mention of my rent-roll, which was, indeed, a severe piece of satire upon my pretentions" (295). It is noteworthy that Roderick himself makes the satiric con-nection, since that ability is consistent with his sense of himself as a gentleman, which, undocumented as it may be, is so powerful that he can even laugh at being *mistaken* for a gentleman.

The nightmare of Roderick's encounter with the naval bureau-cracy, and his dilemmas as a fortune hunter, are linked with Smol-lett's own difficulties as an author by the story of the unfortunate Melopoyn, an aspiring playwright who has suffered at the hands of the London theater establishment as Roderick has before the Board of Surgeons. Roderick meets Melopoyn while the two are imprisoned in Marshalsea for debt. Melopoyn immediately demonstrates that his true qualifications, like Roderick's and Smollett's, bear no rela-tion to his present condition: "He advanced into the middle of the congregation [of prisoners], which crowded around him, and hem-ming three times, to my utter astonishment, pronounced with great significance of voice and gesture, a very elegant and ingenious dis-course upon the difference between genius and taste, illustrating the assertions with apt quotations from the best authors, ancient as well as modern" (375).

None of the spectators but Roderick understands so much as "a sentence of what he uttered" in a speech that is appropriately about the difference, in aesthetics, between an internal sense of self-worth (genius) and the external register (taste) on which both Roderick and Melopoyn rank very low. Roderick immediately befriends the play-wright and is the only one able to judge the tragedy he has written. Melopoyn's long and detailed account of his frustrations with the London theater managers and assorted patrons, and his consequent life as a translator and hack writer, is, of course, a thinly fictionalized account of Smollett's own first years as a writer. Melopoyn's most difficult ethical choice parallels Roderick's own: he must either adapt to the requirements of his profession or starve. After years of frustration, he reluctantly adopts the former course:

I studied the Grub-street manner with great diligence, and at length became a proficient. . . . What then? I was a most miserable slave to my employers, who expected to be furnished at a minute's warning with prose and verse, just as they thought the circumstances of the times required, whether the *inclination was absent or present.* Upon my sincerity, Mr. Random, I have been so much pestered and besieged by these children of clamour, that my life became a burden to me. (385)

Immediately after hearing Melopoyn's story, Roderick despairs of his own condition in debtor's prison and becomes a "sloven," refusing to wash or shave for a month. The decline is a resignation, an admission that he has failed to restore himself as a gentleman. The hard choices put to him have thwarted his efforts at socialization, giving him, like Melopoyn, the impossible choice of being a figurative slave to the powerful or a literal prisoner. Even Tom Bowling, who reappears just at this point to rescue Roderick, does not recognize his nephew, but mistakes him for one of the "crazy prisoners broke from his lashings" (398). Roderick has, in effect, lost all outward signs of the identity which he strived to realize in the world. The romance-like intervention by Bowling resolves the debate about personal integrity versus assimilation in the least satisfying way: Roderick is rescued rather than vindicated.

Peregrine Pickle, unlike Smollett's first hero, begins his life under optimal financial conditions that afford him a university education and the Grand Tour. But his growing economic independence, which culminates when he comes into his estate, paradoxically coincides with his voluntary concession of social independence to an assortment of corrupt elite circles. Accordingly, Smollett emphasizes the ethical dimension of his hero's trial and treats it in far greater detail than he had in *Roderick Random*. Specifically, he critiques the young man's readiness to compromise his autonomy by identifying himself with charlatans—a sacrifice that Roderick almost always resists. The indignant anger that dominated Roderick's account of his adventures gives way to a third-person narrator's frequent expression of disappointment at Peregrine's tendency to drift so easily into hypocrisy.

It has been observed that the novel chronicles in three stages Peregrine's moral degeneration, which results from his vanity (a superficial version of Roderick's sense of his essential gentility) and unfocused ambition (the lack of Roderick's ability to discriminate among various social categories or occupations and thereby remain above them all). In the first stage, the Grand Tour (chapters 35–65), Peregrine "concentrates all his talents upon love and wit";[22] in the second (chapters 66–86), he returns to England "dilated with the proud recollection of his own improvement"; the final stage (chapters 87–100) describes Peregrine's complete alienation. Specifically, Peregrine alienates himself, as Ian Campbell Ross has argued, from the moral and social responsibilities attendant on his rank as gentleman, ideals that he comes to recognize as vital only in the closing pages of his story.

Ross's thesis is that, in its final stages, Peregrine's career "takes on an overt social dimension which emphasizes the intimate and reciprocal connection between individual and national corruption."[23] In other words, Smollett uses this novel to draw broader, more polemical conclusions about gentility. Gentility stood as an unexamined ideal that Roderick struggled to achieve, but Peregrine, already in possession of the means of living as a gentleman, inexplicably allows it to slip away, and becomes absorbed into a series of corrupt social orders. His is clearly the more alarming case, and Smollett generalizes his concern to connect Peregrine's failures with those of national politics.

The social world of *Peregrine Pickle*, though kinder to the novel's central figure, is nevertheless pervaded by professional conventions and practices that are more hermetic and strange than those in *Roderick Random*. Commodore Trunnion, Peregrine's guardian, is so thoroughly a sailor that he refers to his residence as a garrison, sends his servants outside around the clock to keep watch, speaks an almost indecipherable nautical dialect, and, riding across country to his wedding, encounters strong headwinds and instinctively "tacks" on horseback toward the church. Peregrine's Grand Tour reveals a far more disturbing version of this alienation between various social stations, for in France even the noblest professions are under the arbitrary tyranny of an absolutist state. A Mousquetaire taunts a "common man" without fear of retribution (because of his rank in the state) and then sneers that an altercation with the man would be beneath him: "Egad! I believe he is a physician" (*Peregrine Pickle*, 212). A barber, giving a shave to an ecuyer, accidentally cuts a pimple on the man's face and is peremptorily stabbed to death by his customer. Peregrine witnesses these flagrant abuses of power and (as he is not yet corrupted himself) is astounded that the French people accept such incidents as routine.

Peregrine's own concessions to corrupt social hierarchies occur chiefly in the final stages of his adventures, when he becomes first a politician and then an author. Peregrine's induction into the "college of authors" is a highly ritualized professional initiation, including "the customary oath obliging him to consult the honor and advantage of the society," and the bestowal of a laurel wreath, "which was kept sacred for such inaugurations" (640). The college has the ostensible aim of "concerting measures to humble the presumption of booksellers, who had, from time immemorial, taken all opportunities to oppress and enslave their authors" (645), but the members engage in so many absurd controversies among themselves that they are ineffectual. Their confusion leaves all the traditional forms of patronage intact: to get a play produced on stage, one must either plead for the "interposition of the great" or ingratiate oneself with the theater manager (644). To win the support of a benefactor, one must play up to the "vanity" and "simplicity" of wealthy fools such as Gosling Scrag, Esq. (a caricature of Lyttleton), "the best milch-cow that any author ever stroaked" (659).

By the time he joins the college of authors, however, Peregrine has already reached the full extent of his willingness to sacrifice all of his own predispositions for the sake of public success. The nadir is his decision to stand for parliament at the behest of a rich patron. Peregrine's campaign strategy entails shamelessly mirroring the tastes of his electors, a practice that erases any notion of his own private identity: "He made balls for the ladies, visited the matrons of the corporation, adapted himself to their various humours with surprising facility, drank with those who loved a cherishing cup in private, made love to the amorous, prayed with the religious, gossiped with those who delighted in scandal, and with great sagacity contrived agreeable presents to them all" (615). The election is forestalled at the last moment by a deal between the incumbent (Peregrine's opponent) and Peregrine's own patron, a resolution that demonstrates the hollowness and corruptibility of the accomplishments the young man pursues.

Peregrine's complicity in his own victimization by members of the professions through which he hopes to identify himself compares unfavorably, in Smollett's perspective, to Roderick's resistance. But at the same time Smollett also seems at least ambivalent about the short-term successes which that complicity can sometimes bring. One episode from the central thread of Peregrine's adventures, his courtship of Emilia, captures the development of Smollett's attitude. After an early misunderstanding, Peregrine and Emilia are reconciled and, despite her excessive reserve, part on good terms when he leaves for his Grand Tour. In Europe he polishes the social arts for which he already has shown considerable aptitude, and he comes home seventeen months later to practice them on Emilia. Upon finding her "surrounded by two or three admirers," he "practiced his Parisian improvements on the art of conversation, and uttered a thousand prettinesses in the way of compliment, with such incredible rotation of the tongue, that his rivals were struck dumb with astonishment." His rhetoric banishes his competition, and he turns his attention to Emilia, but "instead of that awful veneration which her presence used to inspire, that chastity of sentiment and delicacy of expression, he now gazed upon her with the eye of a libertine, he glowed with the impatience of desire, talked in a strain that barely kept within the bounds of decency, and attempted to snatch such favours as she, in the tenderness of mutual acknowledgements, had once vouchsafed to bestow" (361).

Peregrine's newly acquired Parisian libertine manners change his very perception of Emilia, transforming her from an individual into a potential acquisition, and dictating his subsequent behavior toward her. When Parisian conversation fails, he attempts to seduce her at a masquerade with the help of aphrodisiacs (405), and finally tries to abduct her (413). Emilia's repeated rejections drive him to despair, from which he emerges only when he discovers that she might accept him in a reformed state.

The failure of Peregrine's dissimulating tactics is presented in a more ambiguous light than similar events in Roderick's amours, and Smollett's tone is curiously ambivalent: though disapproving of Peregrine's libertinism, he clearly takes delight, in the passage above, in his skill at vanquishing his rivals. Moreover, whereas Roderick's beloved Narcissa was a one-dimensional figure of virtue, Emilia has "a spice of the coquette in her disposition" (122). She does not oppose Peregrine's assaults with innocent platitudes, but with stratagems usually superior to his own, the most ingenious of which is to frustrate his scheme of abduction by setting him on the trail of an imposter of herself. This shift is quite significant: Roderick had trusted his fate to "true Merit," but just three years later, Smollett reassesses true merit in *Peregrine Pickle*, and finds it incapable of standing unaided. Stranger still is merit's source of support. Emilia escapes seduction or rape, and ultimately instigates Peregrine's reform, only because she is skilled in the very kinds of worldly dissimulation that he uses against her. In this second novel, then, the machinations that characterized the "selfishness, envy, malice, and base indifference of mankind" (*Roderick Random*, xxxv), against which Roderick pitted himself, can now be employed by the virtuous as the need arises.

A step beyond *Peregrine Pickle* is the last novel that Smollett wrote before the focus of his career shifted from fiction writing to reviewing. *Ferdinand Count Fathom* (1753) presents a hero for whom there are no ideals and no taboos, and from whom Smollett distances himself in an opening disclaimer far stronger than the expressions of disappointment voiced at Peregrine's behavior: "From this want of inclination or capacity to write, in our hero himself, the undertaking is now left to me, of transmitting to posterity, the remarkable adventures of Ferdinand Count Fathom; and by that time the reader shall have glanced over the subsequent sheets, I doubt not but he will bless God, that the adventurer was not his own historian" (*Ferdinand Count Fathom*, 8).

Fathom is "a perfect genius" in the acquisition of the "profitable arts" (26), first gaming, then seducing women, then more elaborate confidence schemes, all of which depend to some extent on his extraordinary mastery of languages, his ability both literally and figuratively to move from one rhetorical world to another. Upon his arrival in Paris, for example, he speaks several languages so fluently that men from France, Italy, Germany, Holland, and England each mistake him for their compatriot (90). Though Ronald Paulson has declared that Fathom is "the traditional figure of the English picaresque," his aptitude so easily and quickly ensures his repeated successes that he is actually a far more dangerous, subversive type.[24]

Though Fathom is not an author, many of his talents and schemes are described in specifically literary terms, a paradox that reveals, I believe, Smollett's deepening ambivalence about the literary market at midcentury. He seems to imply that though Fathom is too evil to be an author, his behavior most closely resembles that of the most successful authors. In his first love affairs, for example, in which he has to juggle commitments to two women (the Count de Melvil's daughter and her maid), he is compared to an author playing two enemy patrons off against one another to obtain a subscription for work that, in fact, neither admires. Smollett reports, "This common consolation, to which all baffled authors have recourse, was productive of very happy consequences to our bard [Fathom]" (35). Smollett finds the reason for Fathom's successes, both amorous and professional, in his gift for "a sort of elocution, much more specious than solid," that enables him "to speak on every subject that occur[s] in conversation, with that familiarity and ease, which, one would think, could only be acquired by long study and application" (147). Smollett concludes about this gift: "The most superficial tincture of the arts and sciences in such a juggler, is sufficient to dazzle the understanding of half mankind; and if managed with circumspection, will enable him to spend his life among the literati, without once forfeiting the character of a connoisseur" (148). Fathom is precisely the kind of successful imposter who dominated the desirable social circles that excluded Roderick Random. His desire to become a connoisseur and to be welcomed among the literati is, moreover, the antithesis of Roderick's ambition, and something that Peregrine only gradually comes to desire.

Furthermore, Fathom takes no pleasure in acts of dissimulation which had constituted adventure for its own sake for Peregrine. Most of his schemes are designed to establish himself financially. He and his partner, Ratchkali, pass off discarded musical instruments and defective gems as priceless articles (149–50). Ferdinand also contrives a substantial demand for his services as a physician (161). Largely by means of fraudulent emergency requests for his aid, he creates the illusion that he is already an expert, treating a huge following of patients: the plan actually makes him a sought-after doctor (162). But his successes are meager and ephemeral, and he must keep succeeding in order merely to survive. His frauds are thus always dictated by necessity, not only financial but also psychological. An increasingly desperate state of restlessness colors his view of society, and repeatedly compels him to action.

Smollett's first three novels express an increasing pessimism in their valuation of what is presented as a very narrow route to professional advancement. While Roderick had scorned the strategies that would have helped him ascend the social hierarchy (holding fast instead to his conviction that his gentility would ultimately be self-evident), Fathom thinks only of upward mobility and has no scruples about assuming whatever identity will enable him to achieve it. Indeed, from the beginning of his adventures, he abandons the notion of merit derived from an essential gentlemanly self and adopts in its place a cynical view of both professional systems and the qualifications that sustain them. The three novels taken together represent a grudging concession to a Hobbesian view of social order, one in which all behavior is measured on the register of politics, and, as Carol Kay has explained, "No other feature of social life—whether family, economics, language, or science—can provide self-regulating order."[25]

The remarkable shift in the hero's relationship to the social order in Smollett's first novels is, as I have suggested, his most extensive attempt to find a rationale for the trajectory of his own emergent career as an author. Though *Roderick Random* had succeeded, it had not quite lifted him out of obscurity. Several people, Lady Mary Wortley Montagu among them, attributed the book to Fielding. Smollett still bore a grudge against London's theater managers (attacks on Garrick in *Peregrine Pickle* were discreetly excised years later when Smollett, as editor of the *Critical*, asked Garrick to act in his new play, *The Reprisal*).[26] In the early 1750s, he began to drift into a series of hack projects: an anthology of travels in seven volumes, for which he was paid by the sheet, Alexander Drummond's *Travels*, a translation of a French collection of essays on economics. All of these projects were published anonymously, and they marked what Smollett himself diagnosed as "a sudden Transition from an active to a Sedentary Life of hard study and application," which he felt caused an acute physical decline. In March 1754, Smollett confessed to John Moore that he was "so jaded" that he wrote with "infinite reluctance."[27] The novels do not, in some naive mimetic way, reflect this descent into cynicism, but they are acutely relevant to an understanding of Smollett's attempt to reform the literary market comprehensively by establishing an academy of learning. Before he could conceive of such a project, which would include the *Critical* as its journal, he first reached a point of despair over the predicament of the professional writer at midcentury. *Roderick Random*, *Peregrine Pickle*, and *Ferdinand Count Fathom* are the most important vehicles in which Smollett both explores and chronicles that realization.

II

The first notice of Smollett's plans for the *Critical Review* appeared on the front page of the *Public Advertiser* for December 30, 1755. It is fairly easy to supply a practical explanation for why he would draft such a proposal: there were, as I note in Chapter 1, several literary reviews being planned or announced during that year alone, so the idea would have been readily available to Smollett. Moreover, he was then living through his period of greatest financial distress, so a potentially marketable writing project would have had an obvious appeal. But the ideological lure of a move from authorship to reviewing is also understandable, given the kinds of concerns Smollett expressed about his life as a writer up to that point. The Review's "favourite Aim," as the "Proposals" defines it, "is to befriend Merit, dignify the Liberal Arts, and contribute towards the Formation of a public Taste, which is the best Patron of Genius and Science."[28] The Review offered Smollett the dream of reforming the profession of let-

ters as a meritocracy founded on the consensus judgments of an educated public. At least in the preliminary stage it afforded him the
fantasy that proper recognition of writing talent could be guaranteed
by an institution rather than thwarted by it.

Smollett's ideas for forming an "Academy of the belles Lettres"
(*Letters*, 46) have a long and illustrious set of precedents. Basker, in
the most detailed account of Smollett's proposal, observes: "Since the
time of the Restoration, prominent literary figures had been calling
for some sort of English academy. Sprat, Dryden, and Roscommon
in the 1660s, Prior and Defoe at the turn of the century, Addison and
Swift in the 1710s, and even Voltaire in the 1730s had all remarked
on the need for such a body in England."[29] Basker summarizes as follows the main points of Sprat's 1667 proposal, with which Smollett
had been favorably impressed (*Critical* 1 [January/February 1756]:
41): "It was to imitate and rival the French Academy; it was to
be government-sponsored and composed of 'sober and judicious'
gentlemen of letters; it would have authority to improve and regulate
the English language; it would establish a board of critics 'according
to whose Censure, all Books or Authors, should either stand or fall';
it would finance and organize major projects of scholarship, particularly works of history."[30]

But Smollett was aware as well that the promise of an impartial
institution for patronage did not materialize in the Royal Society.
G. S. Rousseau relates that "when it became evident by the first quarter of the eighteenth century that certain promises of science—not
solutions to concrete problems but a change in the total quality of
life itself—would not be fulfilled, envy and malice set in."[31] Thus,
Smollett looked instead for a more promising model to the Society of Arts, which had been founded in December 1755, the same
month that Smollett's proposal for the *Critical* appeared. Rousseau
notes that Smollett is unusually optimistic and enthusiastic each time
he mentions the Society. In the most detailed of these references,
in *The History of England*, he reiterates his confidence in the alert
public that he felt would sustain his own academy of belles lettres by
taking the place of noble patronage: "In other countries, Smollett
observes, 'the liberality of princes' actually patronizes and financially supports the *applied* arts, while in England advancement is

owing to 'the generosity of a public endued with taste and sensibility, eager for improvement, and proud of patronizing extraordinary merit.' "[32]

In practice the *Critical* fell far short of Smollett's hopes. In the same letter (written after just six issues had appeared) in which he describes the Review as "a small Branch of an extensive Plan which I last year projected for a sort of Academy of the Belles Lettres, a Scheme which will one day, I hope, be put in Execution to its utmost Extent," Smollett also claims that it "meets with a very favourable Reception" (*Letters*, 46). The best evidence, though, shows that the *Critical* sold well enough to continue in print, but apparently did not begin to make a profit until 1762 (*Letters*, 108). The plan for an Academy never materialized.

Most importantly, Smollett came to realize after just a few volumes of the Review had come out that his dream of establishing himself as educator of all literate England, curator and cultivator of public taste, and supreme judge in the republic of letters would never be fulfilled. The *Critical* was attacked relentlessly by dissatisfied authors: during the years 1756–63, while Smollett was proprietor, some 45 attacks in print are listed by Claude Jones, and Basker adds many more.[33] In the preface to the eleventh volume in 1761, as I have already described earlier, Smollett seems nearly ready to buckle under the weight of adverse opinion. The most damaging assault came in 1758, in the form of a libel suit won by Admiral Knowles, whom Smollett, in a review of *The Conduct of Admiral Knowles on the Late Expedition Set in a True Light* (1758) (*Critical* 5 [June 1758]: 458–59), had accused of cowardice during the ill-fated Cartegena campaign of the previous year. Smollett served a three-month prison term for the offense.

Aside from the few details emerging from the Knowles suit, Smollett's correspondence during these years does not dwell on his involvement with the Review. This is not surprising, since he was engaged in many other projects at the time. Two reflective letters that he did write, however, agree completely in their description of the reviewer's lot, but differ drastically in how they evaluate it. In a letter written in July 1758, Smollett concludes his discussion of John Shebbeare's scurrilous pamphlet, *The Occasional Critic, or the Decree of the Scotch Tribunal in the Critical Review Rejudged* (1757), with a revealing comment on his new situation: "You cannot conceive the Jealousy that prevails against us. Nevertheless, it is better to be envied than despised" (*Letters*, 65). He seems, in other words, eager to enjoy all aspects of the transition from struggling author to influential reviewer. For Smollett at this optimistic juncture, being singled out for attack constituted a kind of tribute, a recognition of his importance. Though Shebbeare's scathing pamphlet is just as hostile as the slights of Garrick and Rich had been in earlier years, the former is a hostility reserved for someone in a position of power.

When we next find Smollett reflecting on his experience as a reviewer, however, the novelty of being a target has worn off, and he feels trapped by the hostility of the collective of authors. He writes to William Huggins sometime in 1760 (after serving his prison sentence):

For my part, I long eagerly for some quiet, obscure Retreat, where, as from a safe and happy Harbour, I may look back with self gratulation, upon that stormy Sea of Criticism in which my little Bark has been so long and violently tossed and afflicted. I cannot without mortification reflect that it is in the power of the lowest Reptile to asperse my Morals as a man, and impeach my Reputation as a writer. If I neglect the charge, my silence is interpreted into conscious Guilt or Imbecility. If I justify my conduct or character, I am taxed with acting meanly. (*Letters*, 95)

The characterization of the reviewer's vulnerability remains the same, but Smollett has now concluded that the burdens he must bear as a literary justice *are* insupportable. In the midst of this second stage of Smollett's career, then, a new set of problems has arisen. In the face of a deluge of personal and professional attacks, he begins to worry that his judgment might not be grounded in truth, and that his hope of being an impartial, universally respected judge of literary merit is hopelessly unrealistic. On a practical level he begins to search for a way to avoid or manage these challenges to his claims of authority.

The whole array of reviewer's problems are most completely rendered in *Launcelot Greaves*, partly written during Smollett's imprisonment and published over the course of two full years (1760–61) in his own monthly *British Magazine*. Smollett had anatomized in *Ferdinand Count Fathom* the problems of dissimulation as a means of gaining entrance into elite societies, problems central to the writing trade. Beginning with *Launcelot Greaves* he turns to examine the reviewer's twin problems of self-doubt and self-protection.

As the novel begins, Launcelot has already embarked upon a career of knight-errantry, a profession he describes in the same terms Smollett described reviewing in his "Proposals" for the *Critical* and his exchanges with Ralph Griffiths. In addition to exhibiting "the virtues of courage and generosity," a knight-errant must possess a wide-ranging expertise: he ought "to understand the sciences, to be master of ethics and morality, to be well versed in theology, a compleat casuist, and minutely acquainted with the laws of his country" (*Launcelot Greaves*, 61–62). Moreover, Launcelot sees as his chief purpose acting "as a coadjutor of the law" (14), and passing judgment on "the foes of virtue and decorum" (13).

This professional identity is, however, immediately challenged both from without and within. Launcelot's archenemy, Ferret, attacks the weakest aspects of his self-assumed reformist role, and their initial debate establishes the central interpretive dilemma of the novel. Ferret accuses the knight of being an anachronist who sets himself up as "a modern Quixote," a part "equally insipid and absurd, when acted from affectation, at this time a-day, in a country like England" (12). Launcelot claims in response that he pursues his mission with clear sight. In fact, though, he does turn out to be both an affected imitator of Quixote and mentally unstable. Ferret also predicts that Greaves's excursion will end in prison (he later helps make this prediction come true by instigating Greaves's arrest). He questions Launcelot's problematic relationship to the law, raising fundamental doubts about whether his travels are adventures or vagrancy, whether his costume is armor or disguise, and whether Launcelot himself is coadjutor of the law or merely another criminal (14).

Ferret is drawn from Smollett's nemesis, John Shebbeare, author of the most extensive attack on the *Critical, The Occasional Critic*.[34] He opposes Launcelot with a strength that gives him a credibility

which Smollett was reluctant to grant Shebbeare, and he displays
great skill in evading retribution. He is a conjurer (59, 203), able to
make any side of an argument persuasive. In his most characteristic
moment, he appears in the character of a mountebank delivering an
obscure sales pitch for an elixir of long life, making sure to stand just
outside the local constable's jurisdiction (78–86). Ferret's individual
competence and talents sharply distinguish him from the villains or
antagonistic forces that confronted Smollett's earlier heroes. Roderick Random, for example, contends only with insubstantial scoun-
drels whom he easily brushes aside, or bureaucratic juggernauts
which easily brush *him* aside. Ferret typifies the opponents that most
exasperated Smollett in his capacity as a reviewer. His awkward,
puzzling, and inconclusive rhetorical jousts with Greaves suggest, as
does the letter to Higgins cited above, that Smollett despaired of finding a way of managing the kind of challenges that authors such as
Shebbeare posed to him.

Ferret is not the only major figure in *Launcelot Greaves* drawn
from Smollett's reviewing career. Justice Gobble, who presides over
Launcelot's trial, his most pivotal encounter with the law, seems to
be modeled on Ralph Griffiths, the editor of the *Monthly*, and Smollett's most despised professional rival. Both Griffiths and Gobble are
former tradesmen (Griffiths was a watchmaker, Gobble a hosier
[87]), both elevate their wives to positions of coequal professional
authority (at least if one credits Smollett's rumors about Mrs. Griffiths's influence on the *Monthly*), and both are accused respectively
by Smollett and Launcelot of being false or illegitimate judges. This
is a particularly serious charge in light of the consistent concern with
judges and judging that informs the rhetoric of both the Reviews and
their detractors. Indeed, "critic" comes from the Greek *kritikos*,
which means "judge." Gobble wishes to dismiss all charges against
Launcelot in a theatrical display of mercy, but the knight, insisting
that justice be done scrupulously, refuses the pardon, thereby throw-
ing the court (Mr. and Mrs. Gobble) into consternation. By continuing to urge Gobble to do his duty, Launcelot exposes the imposter's
lack of real authority. The episode concludes with Gobble promising
never to act as a magistrate again (101). But this resolution is only
superficial. Though Greaves exposes Gobble's lack of legal power,

their positions are ultimately similar: Greaves is no magistrate either, and his crusade against the foes of virtue and decorum is also an arrogation. Only at the end of his adventures does Launcelot begin to conform to the standards of the judicial system that is already in place. In one of the novel's final episodes, he pursues Sycamore and Dawdle (who have instigated his confinement in a madhouse) through court writs rather than as a knight-errant (202).

In his treatment of Launcelot's relationship to the law, Smollett complicates and qualifies the analogy between judging in a legal court and reviewing that he had drawn many times in the *Critical*. The novel presents a spectrum of legitimate and illegitimate judicial systems, fitting Launcelot among Ferret, Gobble, and Tom Clarke, a companion to the knight who gives voice to the conventional British legal system. Ferret's critique of his quixotism is, as the narrative proves, largely accurate; the similarities between Gobble and Launcelot as illegitimate judges are more subtly implied; and the novel concludes with Launcelot abandoning the self-claimed role of coadjutor of the law and, with Tom's help and encouragement, trusting real magistrates. That Launcelot retires after his adventures end, rather than becoming a magistrate himself, recalls Smollett's letter to Higgins, in which he longs for a retirement from reviewing after conceding that the reforming project he had once idealistically envisioned is impossible.

The attacks that Greaves faces from within his own ranks are of a different nature: both he himself and his closest supporters raise doubts not about his right to assume the prerogatives of the law, but about his sanity. They wonder whether he is a "mirror of wisdom or a monument of folly" (20). Tom Clarke, Launcelot's godson, praises the knight, but still holds as a principle that "madness and knight-errantry are synonymous terms" (104). Even Greaves's ever-loyal squire, Crabshaw, hints at mixed feelings about his master's mental state (64). For a long time, Launcelot seems capable of withstanding these doubts. He admits on several occasions that he may be mad, but insists that "madness and honesty are not incompatible—Indeed I feel it by experience" (60). He acknowledges that Tom's opposition to his behavior is reasonable, but he continues to do battle.

Ultimately it is only by fully testing the practice of knight-errantry

that Launcelot realizes it is absurd. His climactic joust with Sycamore, the rival for his beloved Aurelia, is an extended episode of
pointless, farcical violence. It is the crucial turning point in Launcelot's career, the event that prompts his assimilation into rural English squirearchy. The aftermath of the "battle" finds Launcelot, now
back in his rightful societal niche, cautioning the vanquished Sycamore *against* knight-errantry. Should Sycamore go astray, Launcelot
promises to appear to punish him, "not in the character of a lunatic
knight-errant, but as a plain English gentleman, jealous of his honour, and resolute in his purpose" (159). Certainly a gentleman's crusade cannot be as radically dramatic as that of a knight: in giving up
his armor Launcelot gives up the hope of ever meting out justice
swiftly, in the service of some honorific code, as Smollett had hoped
to do upon founding the *Critical*, and resigns himself to more indirect
and attenuated claims to authority.

Finally, it is significant that Smollett chose to publish *Launcelot
Greaves* in installments, in *The British Magazine*. Robert Mayo, in
The English Novel in the Magazines, makes the point that the book
was the first "long piece of original fiction written expressly for publication in a British magazine."[35] And while Mayo touches on the hero's relation to the book's author, he fails to recognize the thematic
significance of Smollett's choice of the means of publication. At this
moment in his career, as the editor of the *Critical*, Smollett had a
unique perspective on the growing power of periodical literature to
reach large reading audiences. While there is no evidence to suggest
that his decision to serialize *Launcelot Greaves* was anything other
than a pragmatic one, the move has obvious symbolic value as well.
It is an act of deference (however unintended) to the class of publications by which Smollett had recently been elevated to very prominent status as a literary figure.

If *Launcelot Greaves* ends in pessimism about the possibility of independent judgment, *Travels Through France and Italy* (1766) and
Humphry Clinker (1771) represent Smollett's last attempt, in the
aftermath of his editorship of the *Critical*, to decree standards of decorum that would apply across a wide range of topics. The *Travels*
recounts Smollett's extended journey through Europe from June 1763

to July 1765. In leaving for Europe, Smollett ended his tenure as editor of the *Critical* and stepped away from what he described, in the letters I have discussed earlier, as years of frustration he had suffered in his attempt to refine the taste of the English reading public. However, I would suggest that Smollett retained both the sense of responsibility for making a comprehensive account of whatever came before him, as well as the chauvinistic idealism that informed his Review. The *Travels* gave Smollett for the first time the absolute power that he could only have fantasized about wielding as a reviewer.

This power arises out of the book's formal innovations: unlike any of Smollett's earlier works, it is both a travelogue and an epistolary narrative. Both changes have the effect of eliminating the possibility of opposition to Smollett's point of view. There are no villains as there were in *Launcelot Greaves*, and no disputatious correspondents, such as those who plagued the *Critical*. In the absence of any opposition—indeed, in the absence of any real correspondence at all—Smollett was free to review France and Italy, past and present, minutely, rigorously, and with absolute impunity.[36]

Specifically, three significant changes give the *Travels* its distinct character. First, Smollett acts primarily as a letter writer and only incidentally as a participant. He remains a marginal figure in the "plot" of his tour through Europe, and his narrative dwells much more on what he observes than on his own development and personal crises.[37] In contrast to Greaves's inflexible, energetic drive for reform, Smollett is eminently sensible in his dealings with corrupt postilions, innkeepers, and guides. He admits in his concluding letter that the only way to ensure a comfortable journey through Europe "is to allow yourself to become the dupe of imposition, and stimulate [your hosts'] endeavours by extraordinary gratifications" (*Travels*, 328). Though his tone is at times even more indignant than that of his predecessor, Greaves, Smollett sidesteps the risky direct confrontations that Greaves actively sought, and that ultimately made his knight-errantry so dubious a practice. He avoids "adventures" and thus keeps a distance that more closely approximates the reviewer's ideal of impartiality.

Second, everything Smollett describes is unfamiliar to his English audience. This is another strategy that diffuses the confrontational dimension of judgment: never once does Smollett take on the awkward responsibility of judging English architecture, works of art, traveling accommodations, and the like. Instead, the productions, land, and people of England repeatedly serve as foils for their degenerate continental counterparts. Even though the Englishmen he meets are resolutely unfriendly, Smollett is generous and forgiving of their behavior.

Letter 41 serves to illustrate both these characteristics. Smollett begins with a "just comparison of all circumstances" which proves that "posting is much more easy, convenient, and reasonable in England than in France. The English carriages, horses, harness, and roads are much better; and the postilions more obliging and alert" (327). After proceeding to disparage French carriages, horses, harness, roads, and especially postilions at great length, he relates with comparatively little bitterness the story of an English gentleman, "laid up at Auxerre with a broken arm":

I sent my compliments, with offers of service; but his servant told my man that he did not choose to see any company, and had no occasion for my service. This sort of reserve seems peculiar to the English disposition. When two natives of any other country chance to meet abroad, they run into each other's embrace like old friends, even though they have never heard of one another till that moment; whereas two Englishmen in the same situation maintain a mutual reserve and diffidence, and keep without the sphere of each other's attraction, like two bodies endowed with a repulsive power. (330)

What would be a contemptible snub had it come from a Frenchman is here forgiven as English idiosyncrasy.

By placing himself squarely in the British camp and describing differences between England and the rest of Europe in starkly nationalistic terms, Smollett executes a project that had been characteristic of the *Critical Review*. The *Monthly* and the *Critical*, in their many reviews of travel literature during the years 1756–70, split sharply on the issue of the purpose of travel, and therefore held far different expectations of travelogues. The *Monthly* valued travelers for intelligent curiosity and a near-scientific approach to their journeys. They routinely made a fundamental distinction between "the wild excursions of . . . gaping emigrants, and the regular progress of an inquisitive traveller."[38]

The *Critical*, on the other hand, valued a different kind of narrative. Their expectations, as stated in a review of Northall's *Travels* (1766), were often prescriptive in an oddly nationalistic way: "Prepossessed with reading this pompous account, we sat down with great avidity to have our judgment informed, our ideas corrected, and our prejudices removed, to discover the just medium, in a sound English discernment, between the affected hyperboles of the Italians and the whimsical taste of the French; and in short, to see objects represented *as they are*" (*Critical* 21 [April 1766]: 280). Smollett's observations coincide precisely with the *Critical*'s position, suggesting that, though he was no longer officially affiliated with the Review, he still abided by its categories of judgment on the subject of travel.

Finally, Smollett contents himself in the *Travels* with tactfully advising, rather than belligerently attempting to reform his audience. This last change is perhaps Smollett's most significant compromise in the interest of avoiding the kind of confrontation that epitomized his reviewing career. I have suggested earlier that the *Critical* and the *Monthly* put forward contradictory impressions of their intended purpose. They seemed alternately to castigate or to cultivate the taste of the English reading public, without ever establishing a clear relation between the two forms of address. A crucial difference between *Launcelot Greaves* and the *Travels* is that Smollett moves from one form to the other. Greaves had harangued Englishmen who had strayed from his rigorous standards of propriety. His relation to his audience was always literally antagonistic; his only hope of success lay literally in beating it into submission. By choosing to review only foreign countries in the *Travels*, and by drawing on a common nationalistic context, Smollett, instead of standing in quixotic opposition to his countrymen, allies himself with them. All of these changes are motivated not by an abstract desire for "synthesis," to which some have attributed Smollett's adoption of the travelogue form, but by the author's desire to recover, in a setting devoid of real threats, power similar to that which he had possessed as a reviewer.[39]

The formal innovation common to both the *Travels* and *Hum-*

phry Clinker, the use of the epistolary form, as well as the change
from one letter in the *Travels* to several in *Humphry Clinker* is a particularly complex strategy for consolidating this kind of power. Wolfgang Iser distinguishes between the function of letters in Richardson's writing and in Smollett's. For Richardson, the letter is "a means
of self-revelation to be achieved through a variety of situations";
Smollett, by contrast, "takes the situation itself as a theme." Whereas
Richardson is mainly concerned with revealing the moral states of his
characters, Smollett has no such interest: "Precisely on this account
his presentation becomes all the more complex and subtle, since
[reality] is seen through the filter, as it were, of individual observation."[40] The distinction is quite perceptive, but when Iser presses for
a reason that might underlie it, he can only offer the general hypothesis that Matt Bramble and Jery Melford "want to reproduce the
world around them."[41]

The dominant interests of Smollett's career call for a more specific, historically grounded answer, one that is framed in terms of the
power relations I have described so far. In using the letter as he does,
in making the situation itself the theme, Smollett expresses a preference for *un*self-conscious individual observation. By keeping the
individual perspective safe from self-scrutiny, he escapes outside
scrutiny as well: frailties that might become objects of attack or exploitation remain secrets to everyone. Both Smollett in the *Travels*
and Bramble in *Humphry Clinker* present only rigorously integrated
points of view that are resistant to analysis, let alone opposition. The
weaknesses and ambivalence that are the essence of Richardson's
explorations never even emerge in Smollett's and Bramble's letters.
Not only do Smollett's letter writers avoid any Richardsonian self-
reflection, but they also seal out the possibility of outside opposition
by means of one-sided relationships with their correspondents. In
only two letters of the *Travels* does Smollett acknowledge a correspondent's question, and in each case his "reply" is not a real answer,
but a dissertation on a topic of his own choosing (131–38, 224–31).
No rebuttal or continuing argument need be feared. None of the correspondents in *Humphry Clinker* is represented either. Bramble's remark to his correspondent, "You are an excellent genius at hints—

Dr. Arbuthnot was but a type of Dr. Lewis in that respect," is strikingly ironic, since any hints that Lewis might have offered are buried in Bramble's dogmatic ramblings (*Humphry Clinker*, 335).

The absence of actual correspondence and the use of the letter as a vehicle for authoritative survey are common to both the *Travels* and *Humphry Clinker*. The telling distinction between them, of course, is that several letter writers appear in the later book. Once again, Iser correctly notes the oddness of this change: "The possibility of differing impressions . . . is contrary to the purpose of the travel book: namely to convey information about unknown places. . . . Divergent impressions simply draw attention to the extent to which the same thing can look different to different people." But he concludes only that this phenomenon serves "to reveal the subjectivity that colors the perception of the individual."[42] Inspected in light of the view of authority implied in the *Critical* and the *Travels*, however, Smollett's shift to a form allowing a multiple perspective represents a dear concession. He relinquishes, at the beginning of *Humphry Clinker*, the claim that individual judgment or taste can be infallible, a position he had tried very hard to hold from 1756 through *Launcelot Greaves* (the hero of which is forced to confess that his efforts may have been misguided), through the strong statement of the *Travels* in 1766.

Though he admits in *Humphry Clinker* that judgment is not based in fixed principles, Smollett predictably does not give up all hope of standardization. The book is thus multivalent but stops short of anarchy. Smollett continues working toward a solution to the set of problems that had haunted him since the inception of the *Critical*, this time by attempting to resituate judgment in shared experience rather than in absolute value. This new position has much in common with that put forward by Hume in "Of the Standard of Taste"; in particular, "practice" for Hume and travel for Smollett serve similar functions. Jery Melford concludes about the entire expedition: "I am . . . mortified to reflect what flagrant injustice we everyday commit, and what absurd judgment we form, in viewing objects through the falsifying medium of prejudice and passion. . . . Without all doubt, the greatest advantage acquired in travelling and perusing mankind in the original, is that of dispelling those shameful clouds that darken the faculties of the mind, preventing it from judging with candour and precision" (304).

When he wrote for the *Critical*, Smollett rarely emphasized the importance of travel or any other process of education as a possible road to erudition. Instead he presented taste as a faculty inherent in the sensibilities of a few, whose obligation it was to judge on behalf of the many. In *Humphry Clinker* the path to candid judgment is made available, at least hypothetically, to all. Travel serves the inculcating function idealized by the *Monthly*, rather than the *Critical*'s excluding function of endearing England to Englishmen.

But Jery Melford's letter must be located in the larger perspective that the book presents. In fact, taste is not thoroughly democratized. At most, one can claim that Jery's, Matt Bramble's, and Lismahago's opinions have been homogenized, a process made possible chiefly because Jery changes in order to accommodate the two older men's point of view.[43] As P. G. Boucé has pointed out, Winifred Jenkins and Tabitha Bramble return from the expedition neither better nor worse.[44] It is thus impossible to characterize Smollett's "final position" on the nature and extent of the reviewer's authority in the face of disagreement and opposing judgments. We cannot say with certainty, as some critics would wish, that Smollett seems finally resigned to the lasting presence of cultural differences, varied interpretations of virtue, and a plurality of decorums.[45] And we can only speculate on the meaning of Matt Bramble's decision, after an extensive discussion of contemporary Britain, to "renounce all sedentary amusements, particularly that of writing long letters" (336).

Smollett carried this essentialist conception of judgment with him when he began the *Critical Review*. He saw the transition from author to reviewer, at first, in simple terms. By occupying a position of power in literary society, he gained for himself the right to judge, to apply indisputable standards to whatever came before him. The crucial difference between this and Smollett's original view of the literary world is that by virtue of becoming editor of a Review, Smollett is admitting that these standards depend on professional leverage for their successful application. Smollett had tacitly acknowledged this necessary interdependence between merit and interest as early as *Roderick Random*. Roderick judges Melopoyn's tragedy "by the laws of Aristotle and Horace" and finds it excellent, but Melopoyn still lacks the professional influence necessary to ensure that the play gets its critical due. Melopoyn's solution to this problem, however, includes only the choices of continuing to write (in the hope that true merit will eventually be evident to the right people) or giving up altogether. Only in 1756 does seizing control of the apparatus of judgment become a possibility for Smollett himself.

Smollett's optimism during the first few years of the *Critical* about the project of reforming the tastes of the English public indicates that while he recognized the practical advantages of the Review's authority, he remained an essentialist. He hoped eventually to be able to lead a great number of readers to discover moral and aesthetic standards that he believed were indisputable. Only when the *Critical* began to come under siege from authors and other readers who disagreed with its judgments was Smollett forced to reconsider his position. Now it seemed that, even under the aegis of the Review's authority, the cultural standards that he believed self-evident were vulnerable to all sorts of challenges. Smollett reacted (in his fiction rather than in the Review, which he left in 1763) by searching for new, more powerful strategies to bolster his claims to authority. He abandoned his essentialist position and grudgingly came to conclude that correct or refined judgment originates not in immutable truths, nor even in truths supported by professional authority, but in professional authority alone.

Smollett's movement toward this final position demonstrates how powerful were the material conditions of late eighteenth-century literary production. For Smollett's career reveals the extent to which both popular criticism and authorship are dominated by concern for acquiring authority (or at least ensuring economic survival) in a burgeoning and increasingly pluralistic literary society. Smollett's case also pushes at the boundaries of this study, the aim of which has been to examine the pressure exerted by reviewers, as self-proclaimed representatives of all desirable readers, on authors who sought a higher degree of fame than the sales of their work would reflect. Smollett's fictional reactions to the failure of his hopes for the

Critical hint at even stronger forces experienced by all participants in the literary economy.

A final note: It may seem that in the course of these readings I have in a sense used the novels as an extended allegory of Smollett's career. But in fact it is Smollett himself who frequently resorts to allegory. Two moments in *Humphry Clinker*, in particular, culminate a series of episodes (which include the Melopoyn story and the rivalry between Greaves and Ferret) in which Smollett self-consciously supplies a tropology of his professional life. The more famous of the two is the point in the novel at which Jery Melford meets Smollett himself. The scene is a weekly dinner that Smollett supposedly really hosted, "open to all unfortunate brothers of the quill" (123). The hack writers are, for the most part, socially maladjusted and conspicuously ungrateful, even privately contemptuous of their host. Yet Smollett nevertheless treats them to "beef, pudding, and potatoes, port, punch, and Calvert's entire butt beer" (123), and after dinner gives "a short separate audience to every individual" (126). Smollett pointedly dates the episode by having Jery's companion, Dick Ivy, inform him that Smollett is the editor of the *Critical* (no longer the case when *Humphry Clinker* was published) and talks of the scorn and envy to which that position exposes him. The image of Smollett as magnanimous benefactor surrounded by envious, petty, untalented writers is a masterful weave of fact and symbol that recasts the pivotal phase in his career in the most flattering terms.

Another, odder episode looks at precisely the transitional period from author to reviewer that, I have argued, defines Smollett's career. Shortly after the authors' dinner, the Bramble party encounters Ferdinand Count Fathom. In order to escape his well-deserved notoriety, he has changed his name to Grieve and now works as a surgeon. The change is fascinating—it is as if Fathom has transformed simultaneously into the character who marks the transition point in Smollett's career (Greaves) and into Smollett himself (a surgeon). The brief moment is barely relevant to the novel's plot, but reveals, as does the authors' dinner, Smollett's intense interest in looking back and reconstructing himself in his novels.

"Our last expedient"

Female Literary Careers

The aim of this study has been to describe not exhaustively, but rather through three representative cases, possible kinds of literary careers in an era of quickly maturing print culture. I have tried to justify excluding some prominent authors from this brief history. Samuel Johnson and Thomas Gray, to name perhaps the two examples most clearly distinct from each other, led professional lives so different from those authors I have treated that it would have distorted my argument to include them. By midcentury, Johnson no longer needed the institutional endorsement of the Reviews. In a sense self-made as an author, he did not need to be remade along more conventional lines by the *Monthly* and the *Critical*. Gray, by contrast, held the entire literary marketplace in contempt, refusing to authorize an edition of his collected poems until 1768. He scorned even token state patronage as well by declining an offer to become poet laureate in 1757. He envisioned an audience for his poetry unrealistically learned even by the standards of the Reviews. Authorship, as these men understood it, would require very different stories than the ones I have told.

Women, however, represent another consideration. Restricted from professional achievement of any kind, they faced special difficulties in the field of literature.[1] These restrictions pressured the typical woman author to publish anonymously or to excuse her book in ways that were, in fact, different from the apologies that male authors sometimes made. While a man had only to strike a properly humble pose with regard to his book (for example, anticipating the discovery of countless faults), a woman had to justify the very act of writing for publication, which required what was presumed to be an unfeminine temerity. Long after Henry Fielding and others had helped establish the convention of placing the author's name on the title page of a novel, many female authors continued to omit theirs. Frances Brooke and Clara Reeve, to name just two examples, refused to acknowledge their publications until late in their writing lives.

The most common excuse for publishing used by women writers was that financial distress (typically occasioned by the absence of a husband and a stable home life) had forced them to earn their own money. One of the only means by which an educated woman could do this was writing. In several cases the distress was far more poignant than the prefaces admit: both Charlotte Lennox and Charlotte Smith supported themselves (and in Smith's case eight children) in the aftermath of broken marriages to spendthrift husbands. But the practice of anonymous publication and assertions of financial hardship effectually prevented women from taking an active role, as Sterne, Goldsmith, and Smollett did, in publicly presenting their literary productions.

Just as women could only produce literature under marginalizing conditions, so too was the reception of their writing uniformly compromised. The central problem was that Reviews evaluated women's writing according to sharply different standards than those that they applied to writing by men. The most common formulation of these differences, often found in the brief Monthly Catalogue notices in both Reviews, was an extension of mercy to what the reviewers took to be generically inferior writing. Two examples will suffice to illustrate the problems. A reviewer for the *Monthly* says of *The Indifferent Marriage; or Henry and Sophia Somerville*, by Miss Nugent and Miss Taylor, "A novel which appears before the Public under the sanction of two female names, seems entitled, if not to favour, at least to lenity" (*Monthly* 80 [June 1779]: 480). The typical apologies for writing offered by women writers only compounded the dilemma, as a reviewer of *Theodora, a Novel*, by the Right Honorable Lady Dorothea Dubois, readily admits: "An advertisement prefixed to these Memoirs, effectually precludes all criticism and censure. 'As I am impelled,' says the unhappy Writer, 'by *more pressing motives* than a vain desire of applause, to subject these volumes to public inspection, I trust I shall meet with that indulgence to which my sex, and unhappy circumstances, may unambitiously entitle me'" (*Monthly* 43 [July 1770]: 65).

Time and time again, the common assumption about what women writers were "entitled" to, and what they were not—critical lenity but not more enthusiastic praise—informed reviews of fiction. It helped entrench a double standard that all but disabled the hopes any woman author might have of achieving a level of success comparable to that enjoyed by the best male writers. Indeed, the appeal of escaping severe criticism from the Reviews was apparently so strong that some male hack writers chose to write as women.[2] But for women writers who held ambitions to literary celebrity, the gender bias of the Reviews was a nearly insurmountable impediment. The most influential institution in which literature was received indiscriminately rendered all women's writing, regardless of specific merits or weaknesses, as second-rate.

This programmatic condescension was relatively short-lived. By the late 1780s and 1790s, prominent women, in particular Mary Wollstonecraft, distinguished themselves as reviewers, and in general the common understanding of the critical principle of impartiality was sharpened in a way that ensured that men and women authors would be treated on more equal terms. My concern, however, is to explore some of the strategies that women writers employed to try to circumvent the institutional handicaps under which they labored. My conclusion is that all their efforts were destined to fail. In the early stages, described here, the literary career was an exclusively male form of social practice. Chiefly because reviewers did not take their writing seriously, women were denied a means of participating in the dialectic that generated narratives of professional accomplishment.

There are, nevertheless, several cases of women writers who tried, often in rhetorically ingenious ways, to negotiate these obstacles, and to establish career narratives on terms equivalent to those of men. In every instance, I would argue, these authors were somehow attempting to find a substitute for the legitimate reception that the two major

Reviews denied them. Two strategies predominated in the prefaces to novels written by major women authors during this period, and in the prologues to their plays. A woman could present her writing to the general reading public as work endorsed and mediated by a male literary sponsor, thus aiming to share in the legitimacy that the man might command. Or, more radically, a woman could address an exclusively female audience, one that could most fully identify with her concerns and completely appreciate her writing. Neither of these strategies could compensate for the absence of institutional ratification that the Reviews provided, a dilemma that might explain why some women authors resorted, at one time or another, to both. Only Frances Burney, by dedicating her first novel, *Evelina*, to the reviewers, directly addressed the presence of the *Monthly* and the *Critical* and used their position of dominance to her advantage.

Women authors would occasionally represent their decision to publish, or even to write, as having been prompted by a male acquaintance. One of Charlotte Smith's first works, for example, was *The Romance of Real Life* (1787), her adaptation of a "voluminous and ill-written French work." She credits "a Literary friend, whose opinion I greatly value," with directing her to the original and suggesting that she rework it.[3] More common was for a prominent male author to write the preface or prologue to a work by a less known or unknown female writer. Samuel Johnson wrote the dedication to Charlotte Lennox's first novel, *The Female Quixote* (1752), in which he describes the author as dreading "censure" or "neglect," expressing an "eager Wish for Support and Protection," and ridden with self-doubt, the "Consciousness of Imbecility."[4] These kinds of claims are no different than are commonly found in prefaces written by women themselves. But by enlisting Johnson to write the preface, Lennox is able to retain the posture of exaggerated humility, while at the same time allowing the celebrated man of letters to confer a certain prestige on her book.

Yet male-authored prefaces could perhaps more easily undermine rather than legitimate the female-authored works that they introduced, as Sarah Fielding's first novel, *The Adventures of David Simple*, clearly illustrates. It appeared on May 4, 1744, prefaced by a "brief advertisement to the reader." Fielding, writing anonymously (the title page reads "by a Lady"), admits to being a woman writing her first novel, and her chief aim in the advertisement is to offer the standard female apology for publishing, which in her case, as in Smith's and Lennox's, was true: "Perhaps the best Excuse that can be made for a Woman's venturing to write, is that which really produced this book: Distress in her Circumstances: which she could not so well remove by any other Means in her Power."[5]

The book no sooner appeared, however, than it was widely attributed to Sarah's brother, Henry Fielding. Henry then wrote the preface to the second edition (which appeared on July 13 of the same year) to disclaim these rumors, but in addition gave the book an endorsement that could only diminish it. He refers to his sister as "the real and sole Author of this little book." And after disavowing any role in the book's composition, he admits with what seems almost a reluctant scrupulousness: "But in reality, two or three Hints which arose on the reading it, and some little Direction as to the Conduct of the second Volume . . . were all the Aid she received from me."[6] Moreover, Henry subsumed the book into his own paradigm for fiction, first articulated in the preface to *Joseph Andrews*, in which the novel is ideally a comic-epic in prose. Finally, the title page of the second edition, in which Sarah retains her anonymity, prominently displays the name of Henry Fielding as author of the preface. The cumulative effect of Henry Fielding's "help," then, is to undermine all of Sarah's ambitions for her first novel, including the fundamental assumption that she was its sole, albeit anonymous author. If the preface to the second edition convinced its audience that Henry Fielding did not write *David Simple*, it also would have convinced them that he could have written it better.

The convention of using a prologue written by another writer was more firmly established in the theater at midcentury than in prose fiction and was therefore less unstable, less likely to backfire on the female playwright enlisting the support of a male prologue writer. Two prologues to plays by Elizabeth Griffith are particularly complex negotiations of the advantages and disadvantages of male-authored frames to female-authored texts. The prologue to *The Double Mistake* (1766), written by "a Friend," begins with a male persona (the character of Sir Charles Somerville) engaging the female playwright in a conversation about the ambitiousness of the play. After praising "the attempt how bold! The labour how severe!" he turns to the author:

> Thus I addressed our bard; who quick reply'd—
> With honest diffidence, and modest pride:
> "If I should fail, I should not think it shame
> To miss what few have gain'd, the wreath of fame.
>
> . . .
>
> Hence 'tis the Poet's duty to dispense . . .
> Not miser-like . . .
> But to the muse his grateful tribute pay,
> And in the common mint his grateful tribute lay."[7]

The device of a conversation preempts any possible charges that the female author is presumptuous. Only because she is asked to describe herself as a playwright can her honesty remain diffident, her pride modest. She preserves the feminine character ideals of diffidence and modesty by being supplied with a question that licenses her otherwise masculine pride and straightforwardness and keeps the two kinds of qualities from being oxymoronic.

By the same means, her play is given the chance for institutional ratification without her having to ask for it. The male friend concludes the prologue by inviting, on her behalf, the theater audience to judge the play:

> If any worth it bears, assayed to you,
> His private talent is the public due;
> And should it not disgrace your brilliant mass,
> Give it your stamp, and let the metal pass.

Here the kind of praise that the audience is being invited to give is revealing. Prologues typically stratify theater audiences (into pit, box, and gallery, to name the most common example). This one turns the audience into an impersonal government agency. Significantly, the mint is the agency empowered to produce official currency. The poet's bullion delivered to this mint is, through the audience's approval, turned into uniformly legitimate coinage. The metaphor carries a powerful resonance for female literary ambition. That ambition is emphatically figured exactly the same as its male counterpart, no different than one coin from another.

Even more sophisticated is the prologue to Griffith's *The School for Rakes* (1769), also ostensibly "written by a Friend." The "plot" of this prologue is that the female playwright makes her way in the guise of a man into a literary society dominated by male critics, then triumphantly reveals her real gender and makes a direct appeal to the theater audience present before her. The prologue is spoken by a male character, Captain Lloyd, who first describes, in the first person, the trials of the woman writer:

> The Scribbling gentry, ever frank and free,
> To sweep the stage with prologues, fix on *Me*
> A *female* representative I come,
> And with a prologue, which I call a broom,
> To brush the critic cobwebs, from the room.
> Critics, like spiders, into corners creep,
> And at new plays their bloody revels keep;
> With some small venom, close in ambush lie,
> Ready to seize the poor dramatic *Fly*.[8]

This female playwright's means of averting the venom of the critics is to disguise herself as a man, Captain Lloyd. Like the metaphor of the mint, which Griffith had used three years earlier, the image of the transvestite authoress is an ingenious device that demonstrates the overwhelming difficulties facing women who hoped for literary success. Once again, the chief impediment is that women's writing per se is not granted the same legitimacy as men's. Griffith's drastic recourse in this case is to pass as a man in the cultural circle where male literary fame is manufactured.

But she does not wish to be forever unknown. Once she makes her way before the audience, she steps forward and claims her true gender:

> Whate'er I have, I'll try my winning ways,
> Low'ring my voice, and rising from my stays;
> Warm with anxiety, this hat my fan,
> I'm now an *Auth'ress*, and no longer man.

The second half of the prologue carefully segments that audience and attempts to secure the support of those elements in it most likely to look favorably on an authoress. She begins by representing herself to the women present as a married woman herself, with a young child (the play), and by excepting herself from the traditional suspicion that women involved in the theater were prostitutes:

> The Ladies, I am sure, my brat will spare,
> For I'm not young, nor am I over fair;
> Assemblies, balls, dek'd out I ne'er appear at,
> My husband is the only man I leer at.

She then appeals more broadly to the pit and the gallery (named in the margins of the prologue) as the "more patient folks" whom she opposes to the Beaux in the gallery (also named in the margins) "who scorn all writing." She recognizes that the tastes of these two groups are incompatible, and states plainly to the pit and gallery that those in the boxes "will, as well as you, both laugh and sigh, / Sigh, when you laugh, and laugh, where'er you cry."

She then turns, quite bizarrely, to members of the military in the audience for protection:

> Ye *Soldiers*, *Sailors*, valiant as you're free,
> O lend your aid, protect my babe, and me!
> Cowards spare none; but you, the truly brave,
> Women, and children, will for ever save!

The gesture is wildly ironic: rank-and-file military figures were typically among the rowdiest element in theater crowds, the most notoriously dangerous to women. Her prologue idealizes them and implores their protection for herself and her baby. But the words are spoken by the still-costumed character of Captain Lloyd, as if they constituted not only a mother's supplication but also, in some odd way, an officer's direct order. Griffith concludes by underscoring rather than resolving the gender ambiguities of her professional station, curtseying like a lady, then bowing like a man:

> Here ends my talk—and for our last expedient—
> The auth'ress makes you this (curtsies)—
> And this (Bows), Your most obedient.

The prologue to *The Double Mistake* and even more so that to *The School for Rakes* powerfully illustrate the nature and severity of the frustrations facing women writers who wished to succeed professionally in the same way that men could. Male intermediaries and transvestism were indeed their "last expedient," desperate attempts to keep femininity and authorship from compromising each other.

A far more radical strategy was to posit a separate, exclusively female audience, redefining authorship accordingly. The epilogue to Griffith's *The Times* (1780) concludes with a critique, addressed only to women, of the relevancy of male exemplars in modern times (in part the subject of the play):

> Our sex—but shall I charge the weaker kind?
> Or can those fail to stray, whose guides are blind!
> Let men reform themselves, they're our examples—
> And goods prove seldom better than their samples.
> . . .
> But now, alas! I speak without jest,
> Women are not inspired—they're but possest.
> Men are our pilots! They should mark the shelves;
> For when they blame us, they reproach themselves.[9]

The epilogue challenges the core of assumptions about gender relations in literary texts, which often represent exemplary behavior in one form or another. Chiefly, Griffith undermines all expressions of misogyny as tacit indictments of the kinds of bad examples women have found in men. More than simply excusing the shortcomings of women by attributing them to men, Griffith takes issue with the notion, formalized in Pope's "To a Lady," that a woman is meant to be a "softer man." Instead she points the way toward a distinction between the sexes that precludes the exemplar-imitation relationship so dominant during the period.

What is largely tacit in Griffith's prologue is far more assertively stated in Frances Sheridan's prologue to her play *The Discovery* (1763). Sheridan redraws the commonplace prologue conceit of the author/prisoner before an audience / court of law. But this particular "female culprit" presents a special case who appears unlikely to receive a fair trial. She sees her "utmost crime" as:

> A simple trespass—neither more nor less;
> For truant-like, she rambled out of bounds,
> And dared to venture on poetic grounds.

But the men who act as judges at this tribunal read the crime in a much harsher light:

> The fault is deem'd high-treason by the men,
> Those lordly tyrants who usurp the pen!
> Then try the vile monopoly to hide
> With flattering arts, "You, ladies, have beside
> So many ways to conquer—sure 'tis fit
> You leave to us that dangerous weapon, wit!"

The determination of whether the crime in question is the minor offense of trespassing or the capital crime of high treason—using one's weapons against the state—is a life and death matter for the female playwright. Her attorney thus ingeniously demands a trial by the woman's peers:

> Our author, who disclaims such partial laws,
> To her own sex appeals to judge her cause.
> She pleads old magna charta on her side,
> That British subjects by their peers be try'd.

She then concludes with a resounding challenge:

> Ladies, to you she dedicates her lays,
> Assert your right to censure or to praise:
> Nor doubt a sentence by such lips decreed,
> Firm as the laws of Persian or of Mede:
> Boldly your will in open court declare,
> And let the men dispute it if they dare.[10]

The ramifications of the prologue's legal distinctions are far-reaching: the attorney defines the "peers" by whom the author would be tried, unconventionally, not according to social status, but rather, exclusively, according to gender. The prologue thus participates in a broader process of social definition, one which emphasizes absolute differences between the sexes.[11] But this change in no way helps legitimate female participation in print culture. The idealistic separatism of a woman author writing only for an audience of women renders all the more remote the possibility that they might attain the kind of literary celebrity available to men. Taken together with the other prefaces and prologues that I have discussed, Sheridan's prologue to *The Discovery* suggests that the obstacles to female literary careers were apparent early—indeed, before the beginning of institutional criticism—and that they did not change for more than a generation. Like the hope of male mediation, or the fantasy of transvestism, the idea of a separatist literary community of women is an unworkable solution, one that did not help realize the possibility of literary careers for women.

The circumstances under which Frances Burney's first novel, *Evelina*, was brought to market, so to speak, make it a highly unusual, if not unique, instance of female literary production. The details are supplied most completely in Margaret Doody's biography, but some key points are especially important to my attempt to frame questions about women writers and literary careers.[12] The daughter of England's foremost music historian, Burney enjoyed a more socially prominent and culturally enriched early life than did any of the women I have discussed so far. There was no urgent financial pressure that compelled her to turn to writing. Nevertheless, she began writing fiction at a remarkably young age: she claims in the dedication to *The Wanderer* that she destroyed all of her writings, including a full-length novel manuscript, *The History of Caroline Evelyn*, on her fifteenth birthday in 1767; she published *Evelina* ten years later at age 25. In her generation of eighteenth-century fiction writers, male and female, this makes her something of a prodigy: Sterne was 46 when he published the first installment of *Tristram Shandy*, while Charlotte Smith was 39 and Sarah Fielding 34 when their first novels were published.[13]

The high visibility of her family, together with her obvious desire to be a novelist, virtually deprived Burney of any successful recourse to anonymous publication and would have compromised any excuse she might have made for publishing. With her brother Charles, himself in disguise, acting as her agent, she managed to have the book published by Thomas Lowndes in January 1778. It did appear anonymously, but Burney's identity as its author became common knowledge within six months.

Just as Burney's novel appeared amid very complicated circumstances, the text itself is preceded by an arrangement of preliminary documents that present both *Evelina* and its author to a variety of audiences. A poem to Burney's father (from whom the publication of *Evelina* was nevertheless kept secret), "Author of my Being," urges him to "accept the tribute—but forget the lay," and more importantly figures Frances Burney as a text first, an author second. A preface introduces the book to the general reading audience, significantly novelists in general, and the author of *Evelina* in particular into a gallery of writers "to whom this species of writing is indebted for being saved from contempt, and rescued from depravity."[14] The list includes Rousseau, Johnson (a footnote reminds readers that *Eloise* and *Rasselas* qualify these first two as novelists), Marivaux, Fielding, Richardson, and Smollett. The list is ingenious in its careful, almost casuistic elevation of the genre. But membership in this select group all but requires the author of *Evelina* to be male, and indeed, Burney clearly implies that this is the case, referring to "*his* brethren of the quill" and "*his* fate in the world at large."

By far the most remarkable feature of the prefatory material, however, is its dedication to the "Authors of the *Monthly* and *Critical Review*." Burney is the first author to dedicate a novel to the editors of the *Monthly* and the *Critical*. In doing so she became, in a sense, the first author to acknowledge openly and seriously that Reviews occupy a legitimate place of power in the field of literature. That Burney chose to address the Reviewers in a dedication is itself fascinating. As noble patronage ceased to be capable of supporting a rapidly increasing pool of authors, dedications became a site of anxiety. They had, of course, traditionally been the place where an author genuflected to his or her elite benefactor, but as such benefactors became scarce, dedications (to novels especially) often either disappeared or degenerated into parody: Sterne waits several chapters in *A Sentimental Journey* before representing the composition of a comic preface as an afterthought; Smollett dedicates *Ferdinand Count Fathom* to himself. Burney restores the dignity of the genre in a peculiarly modern way by naming the Reviewer as the successor to the traditional noble patron. This means, significantly, that she saw the Reviews as something more than a conduit to readers, even to elite readers. Rather, she ascribes to them powers that transcend even their own sense of themselves as mediators in the literary marketplace.

The dedication of *Evelina* is a tour de force: Burney systematically recapitulates all the essential characteristics and functions of the Reviews (as the *Critical* and the *Monthly* had themselves defined them) and shows how they must inevitably work in her favor. In her view, the reviewers, seemingly operating independently of readers, confer identities upon authors. She justifies her dedication by asking rhetorically: "Without name, without recommendation, and unknown alike to success and disgrace, to whom can I so properly apply for patronage, as to those who publicly profess themselves Inspectors of all literary performances?" (*Evelina*, 3).

While the recognition of an unknown author by a noble patron had been a matter perhaps of idiosyncratic preference, such notice is built into the *Critical*'s and the *Monthly*'s agendas. Burney shrewdly assumes of them that "the extensive plan of [your] critical observations . . . entitles me to your annotations. To resent, therefore, this offering, however insignificant, would ill become the universality of your undertaking" (3). The claim is an archly logical, thoroughly self-conscious exploitation of the Reviews' commitment to consider every publication. That promise "entitles" Burney to at least a modicum of "patronage," and she contents herself with that small victory. As I have described earlier, the editors of the *Critical*, at least, soon felt haunted by the "universality" of their undertaking. But while the authors of the political pamphlets and sentimental novels that exhausted the patience of the reviewers in the early 1760s gained their notoriety unwittingly, Burney exacts hers as though the reviewers were legally bound to bestow it.

Burney next reminds the reviewers, whom she refers to as "Magistrates of the Press" and "Censors for the Public," that they are also "bound by the sacred ties of integrity to exert the most spirited impartiality" (3), and that she is therefore also "entitled" to their justice. She uses the guarantee of impartiality not only to help ensure that *Evelina* will receive an unbiased reading, but also, ingeniously, to differentiate herself from those classes of authors who are likely to write a bad novel. She observes that most authors do *not* want impartial reviews: "No hackneyed writer, inured to abuse, and callous to criticism here braves your severity;—neither does a half-starved garretteer . . . implore your lenity; your examination will be alike unbiassed by partiality and prejudice; no refractory murmuring will follow your censure, no private interest be gratified by your praise" (4). Only Burney herself has the "temerity" required to invite the reviewers to judge her novel. That temerity, here figured as the rightful confidence of a genteel amateur, sets her apart from those widely disparaged types, the hack (successful writer for hire) and the garretteer (aspiring writer for hire).

Finally, having refused to appeal directly to the mercy of the reviewers, she does so indirectly by stepping away from her rehearsal of the tenets of professional criticism and collapsing the distinction between reviewer and author: "Remember, Gentlemen, you were all young writers once, and the most experienced veterans of your corps, may, by recollecting his first publication, renovate his first terrors, and learn to allow for mine" (4). The reminder is extremely subtle. The notion that the reviewers were "all young writers once" is potentially offensive, as it echoes the stereotype that reviewing was the last recourse for failed or frustrated writers. But any negative connotations are quickly counterbalanced by the more flattering metaphor which places writers and critics in the same army. The notion that "the most experienced veterans" might sympathetically identify with (and possibly feel obliged to support) a fledgling soldier entering combat for the first time recasts authorship in terms that the Reviews could only approve: male, military, nationalistic.

The dedication concludes with a reminder that, for all her ingenuity, Burney is not able to resolve the complications that her gender introduces into her aspirations as an author. She coyly preserves her anonymity by signing the dedication:

> I have the honour to be,
> GENTLEMEN,
> Your most obedient
> humble servant,
> * * * * * * *
>
> (5)

The seven asterisks can plausibly be replaced either with "Evelina" or with "Frances." That Burney imagined her heroine as a version of herself is a thematic point ably discussed by several of her scholars.[15]

Like Evelina's intensive introduction to all the customs and conventions of urban society, Burney's debut as an author is a "young lady's entrance into the world." If we set aside the central romantic strand of the novel, the courtship and marriage of Evelina and Orville, the conditions that determine how young women are socialized are quite pessimistically presented. Evelina seems restricted from candid expression at every turn. As Mrs. Selwyn bluntly generalizes, "Young ladies . . . are *no where*" (275).

Only writing offers any hope of actualizing Evelina's hopes, but even then, the most important readers are powerful men. The paternal Villars is the recipient of most of her letters. And in the novel's pivotal scene, Evelina's father, Sir John Belmont, reads a letter from her mother, Caroline Evelyn, that implores him to receive their daughter. The letter, kept sealed for years, is a powerful rhetorical instrument, but Evelina's future depends entirely on how her father reads and judges it. Like Burney before the reviewers, Evelina appears before her father "without name, without recommendation, and unknown alike to success and disgrace," and only he can confer legitimacy on her.

The reception of *Evelina* and its consequences for Burney's future as an author are as complex as the intricate strategies by which she presented it to its critics. The ingenious dedication simply did not have its desired effect: *Evelina* received positive, though perfunctory, notices in the Monthly Catalogues of both Reviews. Burney's celebrity as its author came only after her father was let in on the secret. Only then, as Doody records, was she introduced to the "Streatham circle," where she was befriended by Samuel Johnson, and made the acquaintance of London's literary elite.[16] But the price of this celebrity was Charles Burney's aggressive intervention in her subsequent writings. Her next project, a comedy entitled *The Witlings*, was completed in 1780. However, claiming that he was anxious that the play's harshly satiric edge might reflect badly on his and his daughter's reputations, Charles refused to allow her to have it produced. He then pushed his daughter to return to "the Novel Way" of writing and hurried her to the somewhat premature completion and publication of *Cecilia* in 1782.[17]

The publication of *Cecilia* was, as Doody and Peter Sabor have described, the most eagerly awaited literary event since the appearance of *Humphry Clinker* in 1771.[18] It *was* received with tremendous enthusiasm (as *Evelina* had not initially been)—praised in extensive reviews in both the *Monthly* and the *Critical*, which permanently secured Burney's fame. But the success of *Cecilia* is in some sense compromised by the recognition that, during this phase of Burney's writing life, the management of her career had, in effect, been wrested from her. In an introduction to *Cecilia*, which she struck from the published version of the novel, Burney wonders aloud about the inevitability of vanity in a life of writing and expresses her anxieties about writing for publication in terms far less optimistic and intrepid than she had in *Evelina*.[19] Just four years of public literary practice, so dominated by her father's interventions, seem to have resurrected in a different form the barriers to a literary career that had inhibited her predecessors.

The efforts of the women authors to carve a place for themselves as literary professionals are both ingenious and heroic in ways that the careers of Goldsmith and Smollett are not, and that are perhaps only rivaled by Sterne's strategy for contacting Garrick. Perhaps because of these qualities, though, these cases bring to light the strength of the institutional constraints I have sought to describe. The conventions of the career-long battles and negotiations between male professional authors and their reviewers have the effect of obscuring the power of the *Monthly* and the *Critical*. Rather than standing as an exception, then, Burney's strategic acts of deference afford us a more accurate perspective on author-reviewer relations than do the careers of many of her male counterparts.

Reference Matter

Notes

Introduction

1. Lindenbaum, "John Milton and the Republican Mode," 121. The other possibilities are summarized by Lindenbaum. I wish to acknowledge rather than specify the complex prehistory of the period I treat. That complexity is largely a function of the survival of aristocratic patronage throughout the century. Several major authors, including Sterne, received money from noblemen, and the symbolic value of patronage during this time, a token of affiliation between author and aristocracy, cannot be underestimated. But I think it is fair to assume, as is commonly done, that the task of sponsoring literature was drifting during this period away from aristocratic patrons toward a market subject to more anarchic forces of supply and demand. In general I follow Paul Korshin's argument in "Types of Eighteenth-Century Literary Patronage." As Korshin puts it, "Royal and noble patronage of literature, in the form of direct support or appointment to government posts, was not much greater in the eighteenth century than it had been in the Renaissance. It became relatively insignificant because the writing population grew so enormously while Court and Crown influence remained relatively stable" (463). Dustin Griffin complicates the traditional notion that the decline of patronage was a simple process, examining attitudes toward the sponsorship of letters in "Johnson's *Lives of the Poets* and the Patronage System," and "Swift and Patronage."

2. Leo Braudy discusses this problem in the context of the transition from patronage to the market: "Until the eighteenth century, the poet's assertion has been, 'I create works that last through time,' and the patron's response had been, 'Make me your subject, or at least an important bystander.' But with the eighteenth century the artist himself becomes the re-

cipient of that lasting fame, and the search for it becomes one of his prime subjects and vexations" (*Frenzy of Renown*, 363).

3. See Crane and Kaye, *A Census of British Newspapers*, and Sullivan, *British Literary Magazines*.

4. I borrow the phrase from Arjun Appadurai, *The Social Life of Things*. In his introductory essay, "Commodities and the Politics of Value," Appadurai "justifies the conceit that commodities, like persons, have social lives" (3).

5. Karl Mannheim describes the stages of a career as "specified in advance," in *Man and Society*, 56. So too do Eliot Freidson, *Professional Powers*, and Harold Wilensky, "Work, Careers, and Social Integration," 554. I take my lead from Magali S. Larson, *The Rise of Professionalism*, who describes the career as a "pattern of organization of the self" (229); Stanley Fish, *Doing What Comes Naturally*, who captures the concept's paradoxical nature when he states that "the self of the professional is constituted and legitimized by the very structures—social and institutional—from which it is supposedly aloof" (244); and Samuel Weber, *Institution and Interpretation*, who observes that "having donned the habits of the profession, its practitioner can hope to be protected against the rigors of social struggle" (31).

6. The obstacle of anti-Scottish prejudice that faced Smollett and others (Boswell, Lord Kames, Hugh Blair among them) is treated by Robert Crawford, *Devolving English Literature*. For his suggestive treatment of Smollett, see 55–75.

7. Williams, 139–40. For a more extensive meditation on the subject, see Hohendahl, *The Institution of Criticism*, 11–85. For the sake of clarity, I will use uppercase when referring to book-reviewing journals and lowercase when referring to review articles.

8. Nancy Armstrong, *Desire and Domestic Fiction: A Political History of the Novel*; Terry Lovell, *Consuming Fiction*; and Kathryn Shevelow, *Women and Print Culture: The Construction of Femininity in the Early Periodical*. For treatment of these issues in the nineteenth century, see Mary Jean Corbett, *Representing Femininity: Middle-Class Subjectivity in Victorian and Edwardian Women's Autobiographies*, especially 17–82.

9. For an account of the period following the one that my study covers, see John Gross, *The Rise and Fall of the Man of Letters*.

10. The Oxford English Dictionary defines "career" as "a person's course or passage through life" and cites it as first used in this sense in 1803.

11. The most complete account of the emergence of new kinds of reading material and reading habits is J. Paul Hunter, *Before Novels*, especially 61–88.

12. *Examiner*, no. 15, quoted in Sutherland, *Defoe*, 185. Defoe's rivalry with Swift is described in Backscheider, *Daniel Defoe*, 294–98.

13. *The Dunciad Variorum*, 2: 139, in *The Poems of Alexander Pope*, 384.

14. *The Letters of the Republic*, 5. See also Henry Knight Miller, "The 'Whig Interpretation' of Literary History," 60–84. Two recent studies that naively privilege the medium of print over cultural circumstances in an extremely implausible way are Alvin B. Kernan, *Printing Technology, Letters and Samuel Johnson*, and Julie Stone Peters, *Congreve, the Drama, and the Printed Word*.

15. An anonymous article, "The Reviewer as Executioner," originally published in *The Monthly Anthology and Boston Review* 4 (February 1807): 84–85, reprinted in Simpson, 177.

16. The most valuable recent study is William Epstein, *Recognizing Biography*, supplemented by Epstein's collection of essays, *Contesting the Subject*. Ira Bruce Nadel's *Biography: Fiction, Fact and Form* offers a well-informed history of biography from the nineteenth century to the present, though Nadel clings to a naive empiricism that views biographies as always necessarily "incomplete." He seems to imagine human lives as standing independent of language and interpretation, and sees the biographer's (always impossible) task as one of striving to present as complete a picture of his or her subject as possible. Epstein, who draws heavily on the work of Derrida, in particular on "The Law of Genre," is much more sophisticated in his discussion of the relationship between life and biography. Hayden White's objection that "historical theorists for the past twenty-five years have . . . tried to clear up the epistemological status of historical representations and to establish their authority as explanations, rather than to study various types of interpretations met with in historiography" applies as well to most theorists of biography (*Tropics of Discourse*, 51–52).

17. Boswell, 3: 64–66.

18. This point is made by Malcolm Bradbury, "The Telling Life: Some Thoughts on Biography," 136. Bradbury quotes Wellek and Warren: "No biographical evidence can change or influence critical evaluation" (*Theory of Literature*, 80).

19. Christensen, xi. The book's severest reviewer is Kevin L. Cope. Though he admits that *Practicing Enlightenment* "sets an important precedent," his tone is dismissive: he claims that "names like Gramsci, Jameson, and Derrida clatter and bang through this text like misplaced cymbal-crashes," and complains that Christensen's "tiresome use of sensational language" is "usually . . . a cover for incoherent thinking." He concludes that "Christensen's study . . . has cracked under the weight of its own rhetoric" (2: 503–10). David Womersley is also distressed by what he perceives as Christensen's "desire to re-create in English the slow dazzle of French intellectual writing" (450). The common denominator of these two negative re-

views is a resistance to poststructuralist theory in general. But even critics not so easily upset by Christensen's vocabulary seem not to know what to make of the book. John Richetti praises it as "entirely, strikingly original, an often dazzling, fiendishly inventive commentary," but speculates that "perhaps too much of this book is . . . needlessly difficult" and confesses, "I still find certain passages baffling" (405). W. B. Carnochan, while stating that the argument of the book is "exciting and persuasive," nevertheless wonders if Christensen's skepticism about the foundations of identity make his biographical project impossible.

20. Larson, 229.

Chapter 1

1. Frederick A. Pottle, *Boswell's London Journal*, 271; *The Works of Thomas Gray*, 4: 57; Joseph Craddock, *Literary and Miscellaneous Memoirs*, 43.

2. Fielding, 37. See also 566–71.

3. Boswell, *Life of Johnson*, 2: 39–40.

4. Leslie Marchand, *Byron's Letters and Journals*, 3: 209.

5. Renaissance studies in the last decade have addressed questions of the power of cultural forms with great resourcefulness, and both my methods and vocabulary are indebted to this body of scholarship, especially to Arthur Marotti's *John Donne* and Richard Helgerson's *Self-Crowned Laureates*, which persuasively account for sixteenth- and seventeenth-century literary careers.

6. Brewer, McKendrick, and Plumb, *The Birth of a Consumer Society*.

7. See Thomas McFarland, *Originality and Imagination*.

8. Antonia Forster discusses the use of notices from the Reviews in advertisements in *Index to Book Reviews in England, 1749–1774*. Her introduction provides the best available short overview of book-reviewing practices during the period.

9. The most comprehensive example of attribution studies of review criticism is B. C. Nangle's *The 'Monthly Review,' First Series, 1749–1789: Indexes of Contributors and Articles*, largely based on the records of the journal's first editor, Ralph Griffiths. Derek Roper uses an annotated file copy of the first two volumes of the *Critical* owned by Archibald Hamilton (its editor after Tobias Smollett's departure) as the basis for his "Smollett's 'Four Gentlemen.'" James Basker, in *Tobias Smollett, Critic and Journalist*, discusses the authority and reliability of Hamilton's copy (39–40), and offers his own list of Smollett's contributions to the journal (220–78). Attempts to define the critical principles of the Reviews include Edward A. Bloom, "'Labors of the Learned,'" and William Park, "Change in the Criticism of the

Novel after 1760." Most recently, Joseph F. Bartolomeo examines the construction of a valorized notion of the novel in periodical criticism. See *A New Species of Criticism*, esp. pp. 112–60.

10. The most influential of the abstract journals was the *Journal des Sçavans*, established in 1665 by Dennis de Sallo, Counsellor of the Parliament of Paris. The *Journal* was a twelve-page weekly paper whose format, widely imitated first in France and later in England, was a collection of abstracts of important books. It made no critical assessments, but simply offered itself as a shortcut for the benefit of a certain elite class of busy readers. It clearly anticipates at least part of the function of later Reviews. Edmund Gibbon, cited in Walter Graham, *The Beginnings of English Literary Periodicals* (2), refers to it as "the father of the rest [of the journals]." In particular, the *Journal*, the *Monthly*, and the *Critical* share the hope of a comprehensive account of recent publications and a definition of literature that included scientific and mathematical discoveries. The key differences are a shift in the Reviews from synopsis to commentary and a willingness to discuss popular literature. Addison and Steele's essays were, of course, not reviews, and in no way did they attempt a comprehensive account of contemporary writing. But when they did turn to poetry or drama, they never offered an abstract, but always evaluated, and urged their praise or disapproval upon their readers, and thereby helped establish registers of popular taste. For an account of how the *Spectator* papers delineate and address their audiences, see Michael Ketcham, *Transparent Designs*. Donald F. Bond's editions of *The Tatler* and *The Spectator* supply important contexts. As Bond makes clear, the contemporary success and lasting influence of these essays is beyond dispute.

11. Walter Graham, *Early English Periodicals*, 200–201.

12. C. Lennart Carlson, "Edward Cave's Club." See also Carlson's *The First Magazine*, 110–50.

13. Basker, in *Tobias Smollett*, 170–71, notes the rise and fall of the *Gentlemen's Magazine*'s commitment to book reviewing. In 1754 the journal expanded its list of recently published books (with comments) to two or three pages per issue. Immediately following the debut of the *Critical*, the March, April, and May issues in 1756 each devoted eight pages to reviews. This decreased to four pages in June 1756, and finally shrank to a single page throughout the 1760s. Basker argues, correctly, I think, that these changes reflect the magazine's initial attempts to compete with the *Monthly* and the *Critical*, followed by a quick retreat from the field of reviewing once those journals established their supremacy. For useful brief profiles of the *Literary Magazine, Gentleman's Magazine*, and *London Magazine*, as well as the *Monthly* and the *Critical*, see Alvin Sullivan, *British Literary Magazines*, 1: xvi–xxxi, 72–77, 136–40, 198–201, and 202–6.

14. Forster, *Index*, 3.

15. The early versions of this theory claim a transparent cause and effect relationship between the booming trade in letters and the emergence of Reviews. Collins argues that the success of the *Monthly* "meant that the small section of the reading public, which it is convenient to call the literary public, had sufficiently increased to be able to support a magazine devoted to literature and science" (201), while Walter Graham states that the Reviews' success was entirely dependent on "the appeal of the works selected" for review (*Early English Periodicals*, 209).

16. Boswell, *Life of Johnson*, 1: 285.

17. Miller, "The 'Whig Interpretation' of Literary History." Two recent studies that fetishize the medium of print and yield an implausible account of eighteenth-century letters are Alvin B. Kernan, *Printing Technology, Letters and Samuel Johnson*, and Julie Stone Peters, *Congreve, the Drama, and the Printed Word*.

18. Kernan, 59. See Ian Maxted, *The London Book Trade*.

19. Kernan, 61. See C. J. Mitchell, "The Spread and Fluctuation of Eighteenth-Century Printing."

20. Bertelsen, *The Nonsense Club*.

21. As Michael Warner has argued, the fundamental premise of this progressive account—that print technology "has an ontological status prior to culture"—is impossible and must be set aside before we can examine the relationship of print to enlightenment culture. See *The Letters of the Republic*, 7.

22. Samuel Johnson's frequently cited pronoucements about the differences between the *Monthly* and the *Critical* are oversimplified and give the mistaken impression that the ideological distinctions between them are obvious and politically overt. For the record, Johnson said: "The Monthly Reviewers . . . are not Deists; but they are Christians with as little christianity as may be; and are for pulling down all establishments. The Critical Reviewers are for supporting the constitution, both in church and state" (*Life of Johnson*, 3: 32).

23. Forster, *Index*, 3.

24. Nangle, *Indexes*, xi.

25. Keeble, *The Literary Culture of Nonconformity*, 128.

26. Ibid., 157.

27. Ibid., 161.

28. Richard Altick, *The English Common Reader*, 57.

29. *Memoirs of James Lackington*, 231–32. John Wesley himself "abridged" several books, including *Paradise Lost, Pilgrim's Progress*, and Brooke's *Fool of Quality* in a pioneering effort to popularize literature and bring more people into the reading public (Altick, 37).

30. Basker, *Tobias Smollett, Critic and Journalist*, 37. Basker's account of the day-to-day operations of the *Critical* (29–87) is definitive.

31. The phrase is from Tony Bennett, "Texts in History," 7.

32. These phrases occur over and over in reviews during the early years of the *Monthly*. The notion that "a short extract may, perhaps, enable the reader to conclude with tolerable certainty" about the quality of a work (*Monthly* 1 [August 1749]: 270) and its corollary, "As to the merit of the piece, we can say but little" (*Monthly* 14 [June 1756]: 583) are foregrounded as critical principles. A review of Smollett's translation of *Don Quixote*, for example, offers without commentary an excerpt of Smollett's translation side by side with that of his predecessor, Charles Jarvis (*Monthly* 13 [September 1755]: 198.

33. Larson, *The Rise of Professionalism*, 32. Traditional, functionalist approaches to the sociology of professions include most notably Talcott Parsons, "The Professions and Social Structure," in *Essays in Sociological Theory*, 34–49, and Wilbert E. Moore, *The Professions: Roles and Rules*. Geoffrey Holmes applies functionalist methods to the early eighteenth century in *Augustan England*.

34. Forster, *Life and Adventures of Oliver Goldsmith*, 2: 79–80; Boswell, *Life of Johnson*, 3: 32 n.; Roper, *Reviewing Before the Edinburgh*, 29. Forster does not supply a specific reference for the quotations. Antonia Forster points out, however, that the *Critical* initiated most of the attacks (*Index*, 8).

35. See James Ralph, *The Case of Authors*, and Richard C. Taylor, *Goldsmith as Journalist*, 17–27.

36. For a discussion of this vocabulary as professional credentials, see JoAnne Brown, "Professional Language."

37. Jean-Paul Sartre, *What Is Literature?* 91–92.

38. Johnson, *Dictionary of the English Language*, 37.

39. Fielding, 396.

40. Basker, in *Tobias Smollett*, cites Philip J. Klukoff, "A Smollett Attribution in the *Critical Review*," *Notes and Queries*, n.s., 14 (1967): 418–19, as presenting "convincing evidence" that the first preface was written by Smollett (261). The 1765 preface remains unattributed.

41. The most complete lists of attacks on the *Critical* by various authors appear in Basker, 279–83, and in Claude E. Jones, *Smollett Studies*, 107–10.

42. Sartre, *What Is Literature?* 81. Sartre, discussing the situation of writing in France in the seventeenth and eighteenth centuries, goes on to speculate that the division between author and reader is a function of romanticism's positing a mass audience: "A revolution analogous to romanticism is not conceivable in this period [the seventeenth century] because

there would have to have been the concurrence of an indecisive mass, which one surprises, overwhelms, and suddenly animates by revealing to it ideas or feelings, of which it was ignorant, and which, lacking firm convictions, constantly requires being ravished and fecundated" (82).

43. There are occasional exceptions. The reviewer of *The Adventures of Miss Beverly* refrains from wholly blaming the author for writing a bad novel, and instead steps back to take the more generous, if patronizing, view that "this publication is evidently fabricated in the cave of Poverty," for "nothing but the necessity of the author's writing *something* could have produced it" (*Critical* 26 [September 1768]: 209). As I describe in Chapter 5, women authors were invariably exempted from rigorous criticism.

44. Sterne, *Tristram Shandy*, 1: 447.

45. The allusion is to Priam's "weak and helpless spear" in the *Aeneid*, Book 2, 544. The analogy seems an odd one to draw, since Pyrrhus, the villain in this episode, kills the aged Priam in cold blood.

46. Terry Eagleton observes that this is a characteristic irony of Enlightenment criticism: "While its appeal to standards of universal reason signifies a resistance to absolutism, the critical gesture itself is typically conservative and corrective, revising and adjusting particular phenomena to its implacable model of discourse." *The Function of Criticism*, 12.

47. Familiar examples can be found throughout Pope's "Essay on Criticism" and *Dunciad*, and in Swift's "The Progress of Poetry," "Advice to Grub-Street Verse Writers," "Directions for a Birth-Day Song," and "On Poetry: A Rhapsody."

48. Douglas, *How Institutions Think*, 48.

49. The *Critical's* response to the pamphlets I discuss later was consistent with this metaphor. *Critical* 16 [September 1763]: 184, 231, 234; [October 1763]: 267; [January 1764]: 17, 63, are all programmatically in favor of government policy. The most extraordinary example is an October 1763 review of the collected papers of *The North Briton*. A polemical tour de force, the article first places the *North Briton* in a long tradition of opposition papers (*Mist's Journal, Fog's Journal, Common Sense, The True Briton, The Craftsman*, and *Old England*), condemning each in turn, then justifies the entire list by an appeal to neutrality that typifies the new professional rhetoric I have been describing: "Upon the whole, we hope we shall be acquitted by every candid and judicious reader, in the account we have given of those celebrated papers, from every imputation of rancour or party, but above all of resentment. What we mean is, to present to the public, in a cool hour of recollection, a Review of those objects, which, when they first made their appearance, presented themselves to many through the mediums of party and presupposition" (17 [April 1764]: 285). Even as early as June 1764, however, the *Critical* began to show a sensitivity to the complexities

of imperial government. Reviewing *The Administration of the Colonies* (the thesis of which was that if the Crown could not establish its right to govern, the American colonists should be allowed to govern themselves), the writer for the *Critical* disagrees very respectfully, conceding several points in the pamphlet's argument (*Critical* 17 [April 1764]: 281–84). The editors' identification with the difficulties of the colonial governor is all the more poignant in light of a notice such as this.

50. Gipson, *The Triumphant Empire*, 9: 17–18.

51. Forster (*Index*, 7) notes that, initially at least, the *Critical* acknowledged contributions from readers.

52. Sekora, *Luxury*, 66, 75. Sekora lists the following examples: *Critical* 2 (August 1756): 451–52; 4 (September 1757): 219–20; 5 (April 1758): 290; 9 (April 1760): 263; 10 (July 1760): 42; and 14 (May 1765): 395.

53. Sekora, 93.

54. Louis Althusser, *Lenin and Philosophy*, 173–75.

55. The term "innocent amusement" is from *Critical* 8 (December 1759): 458. One example of an apology for a negative review is *Critical* 2 (September 1756): 140. The treatment of novels by the Reviews was explored quite thoroughly in the 1940s, so I shall not repeat that inquiry here. See W. F. Galloway, "The Conservative Attitude Toward Fiction"; John Tinnon Taylor, *Early Opposition to the English Novel*, 21–86; and Claude E. Jones, "The English Novel."

56. The "common herd of novelists" are disparaged in *Critical* 21 (March 1766): 257, which describes one novel as circulating library "furniture"; also *Critical* 29 (January 1770): 43, 29 (April 1770): 294, and 34 (December 1772): 472.

57. Campbell, *The Romantic Ethic*, 155.

58. Taylor, *Goldsmith as Journalist*, 42.

59. Shevelow, 32.

60. The Reviews continued to thrive in their second and third decades. Basker cites an increase in the *Monthly*'s circulation, from 2,500 in 1758 to 3,000 in 1768 to 3,500 in 1776. The *Critical* most likely kept pace (*Tobias Smollett*, 172–73).

61. Campbell, *The Romantic Ethic*, 90.

62. Brewer, McKendrick, and Plumb, *The Birth of a Consumer Society*, 268.

63. Charles Grivel, "The Society of Texts," 160.

64. Michel deCerteau, *The Practice of Everyday Life*, 168.

65. *Political Register* 1 (1767): 181; Lovett, *Electrical Philosopher*, 247, both cited in Forster, *Index*.

66. *Gentleman's Magazine* 26 (March 1756): 141.

67. Churchill, 39, lines 94–101. All subsequent citations to this text refer to Grant's edition by line numbers only.

68. See Thomas Lockwood, *Post-Augustan Satire*, 152–66, for a discussion of the author-audience relationship as Churchill conceived of it. Lockwood has some interesting observations about the genre of satires on reviewers, which flourished in the latter half of the century. These include Peter Pindar's *A Poetical, Supplicating, Modest, and Affecting Epistle to Those Literary Colossuses, the Reviewers* (1778), and John Hall-Stevenson's *Two Lyric Epistles: or, Margery the Cook Maid to the Critical Reviewers* (1762).

69. The allusion is to the court's supposed sponsorship of the *Critical*. Walter Graham is one of many to make this claim (*English Literary Periodicals*, 213), though he offers no evidence for this conclusion. The origin of this legend seems to be Samuel Johnson's claim that "the Critical Reviewers are for supporting the constitution both in church and state" (*Life of Johnson*, 3: 32).

70. T. Underwood, *A Word to the Wise*. Further references will be to page numbers in this text. Attacks on the *Critical* are often polemics against the Scottish, and as such, they are part of a more widespread bias in English literary culture. See Crawford, *Devolving English Literature*.

71. *The Plays of Samuel Foote*, 2: 5–6 (plays are facsimiles paginated individually).

Chapter 2

1. *Letters of Laurence Sterne*, 105, hereafter cited in the text as *Letters*. I have supplied the dates of particular letters, where available.

2. John Traugott's *Tristram Shandy's World*, which reads *Tristram Shandy* as a philosophically sophisticated critique of rationalism, set the tone for the bulk of Sterne criticism that followed. In one way or another, William V. Holtz, *Image and Immortality*; Richard Lanham, *"Tristram Shandy" and the Games of Pleasure*; Helene Moglen, *Philosophical Irony of Laurence Sterne*; James Swearingen, *"Tristram Shandy": An Essay in Phenomenological Criticism*; and most recently, Jonathan Lamb, *Sterne's Fiction and the Double Principle*, all explore the thematic and philosophical complexities of Sterne's work. Others, most significantly Melvyn New, *Laurence Sterne as Satirist*, attempt to place *Tristram Shandy* within the more traditional literary boundaries of satire. The "Introduction Polemical" to New's *New Casebooks*, 1–16, provides an extremely thorough, if hyperactively opinionated, survey of the criticism. I have tried in this chapter to read Sterne's work along far more exclusively materialist lines. My argument throughout is influenced by Brian Spooner's fascinating account of the power of consumer demand to alienate the labor of weavers of oriental carpets in "Weavers and Dealers."

3. The notion that *Tristram Shandy* can be grasped from either a comic or a sentimental "handle" is from one of Sterne's last letters, written to Dr. John Eustace, February 9, 1768 (*Letters*, 411).

4. Although several scholars have observed a stylistic continuity between Laurence Sterne's early writings and his two novels, the relationship between his sequential careers as clergyman and writer of fiction remains a problem. Some choose simply to ignore his entanglement in Anglican party politics; others view his difficulties advancing in the Church hierarchy as a kind of fortunate fall. Indeed, Wilbur Cross, in a 1925 biography, sees Sterne's whole life in these naive terms, going so far as to claim about his attempts to farm an estate he purchased in 1744: "Fortunately for literature, his land projects . . . issued in miserable failure" (*Life and Times of Laurence Sterne*, 163). Even Arthur Cash, in what will remain the standard biography of Sterne for many years to come, does not directly address this relationship, but instead cites approvingly an anonymous letter of 1759 that claims that it was to the failure of *A Political Romance* (Sterne's last clerical polemic) "that the World is indebted for Tristram Shandy" (*Laurence Sterne: The Early and Middle Years*, 277). The relationship between *A Political Romance* and *Tristram Shandy* is discussed by Alan B. Howes in "Laurence Sterne, Rabelais, and Cervantes," 46, and by Melvin New, *Laurence Sterne as Satirist*, 96.

5. Holmes, *Augustan England*, 106. Holmes includes an invaluable bibliographical note (297–302) that surveys the scholarship on the clergy as a profession. The most useful entries for my purposes are Sykes, cited below, Rosemary O'Day, *The English Clergy*, and John H. Pruett, "Career Patterns Among the Clergy of Lincoln Cathedral."

6. Addison, *The Spectator*, 1: 89. Bond explains, "The meaning is, that if the clergy followed the example of landowners and cut up their glebes and tithes into forty-shilling freeholds (the requirement for voting) they could control most of the elections" (n. 3).

7. Norman Sykes, *Church and State in England*, cited in Holmes, 95.

8. Holmes, *Augustan England*, 90.

9. Ibid., 101.

10. Ibid., 108.

11. See Cash, *Early and Middle Years*, 137–50.

12. Ibid., 261.

13. Ibid., 262–77.

14. For discussions of Garrick as a patron and stage manager, see Percy Fitzgerald, *Life of David Garrick*, 1: 327–437; Alan Kendall, *David Garrick*, 49–72; and George Winchester Stone and George Kahrl, *David Garrick: A Critical Biography*. See also Ronald Hafter, "Garrick and *Tristram Shandy*." Most recently, Peter M. Briggs, in "Laurence Sterne and Literary

Celebrity in 1760," glosses much of the same primary material I do in this section. He offers two additional insights: (1) that Sterne derived as much from Colley Cibber's style of self-presentation, and even writing style, as he did from Garrick's, and (2) that, by eschewing literary circles and seeking out Garrick, Sterne sought a more immediate and distinctly theatrical kind of celebrity. But Briggs fails to answer his opening question—"Who, if anyone, legislates the codes of behavior and the underlying values that seem to accompany celebrity?" (254)—because, as his title suggests, he stops his inquiry at 1760, just as the moment when the processes by which fame was conferred upon Sterne were beginning to change.

15. For an account of the revisions, see Cash, *Early and Middle Years*, 278–97.

16. *Letters*, 99–100. Sterne employed the same strategy while striking a slightly different pose in his dedication of *Tristram Shandy* to William Pitt. In the dedication, which appears for the first time in the second, London edition of volumes one and two, Sterne presents himself as a simple, humble clergyman, who has written his book "in a bye corner of the kingdom, and in a retired thatch' house," with none of the pretentions to urbane wit that he advertises for his London audience. See Melvyn New and Joan New, eds., *The Life and Opinions of Tristram Shandy*. All further references will be to this edition, and will be cited in the text.

17. Frederick W. Hilles, *Portraits by Sir Joshua Reynolds*, 97.

18. Boswell, *Life of Johnson*, 3:386. Johnson continues, "He found people always ready to applaud him, and that always for the same thing."

19. *Portraits by Sir Joshua Reynolds*, 98.

20. Ibid., 99.

21. Cash, *Later Years*, 8.

22. *Early and Middle Years*, 127.

23. Dr. John Hill, "A Letter to the Ladies Magazine," *Royal Female Magazine* (April 1760), reprinted in Wilbur L. Cross, *Works and Life of Laurence Sterne*, 6:33.

24. This development is only now beginning to receive a great deal of critical attention. Allardyce Nicoll, *The Garrick Stage*, 1–19, is a useful starting point. Important recent studies include Leigh Woods, *Garrick Claims the Stage: Acting as Social Emblem*, 29–53, 127–52; Shearer West, *The Image of the Actor*; and Kristina Straub, *Sexual Suspects*.

25. George Taylor, "'The Just Delineation of the Passions,'" 55.

26. Richard Sennett, *Fall of Public Man*, 152.

27. Cited in Alan B. Howes, *Laurence Sterne*, 64.

28. Cash, *Later Years*, 33–37. Extracts from several of these pamphlets appear in Howes, *The Critical Heritage; The Clockmaker's Outcry, Explanatory Remarks*, and *The Life and Opinions of Jeremiah Kunastrokius*, as

received the critical acclaim it deserves. He offers the best recent treatment, though Friedman's introduction (1: 245–50) is excellent.

4. Hopkins, *True Genius*, 34.

5. For contemporary reaction to the incident, see Robert D. Spector, *English Literary Periodicals*, 16–34. Byng was in all likelihood the scapegoat of the Bute administration.

6. Ricardo Quintana describes it in these terms in *Oliver Goldsmith*, 29.

7. David Hume, "Of the Standard of Taste," 227.

8. John Bender, "Prison Reform and the Sentence of Narration," 168. The major critical treatments of *The Vicar of Wakefield* follow very different paths than I do here. The chief contrast is between Martin Battestin's association of the novel with the myth of Job in *The Providence of Wit*, 193–214, and Robert Hopkins's insistence on the book's ironies in *The True Genius of Oliver Goldsmith*. Most recently, see Marshall Brown, *Preromanticism*, 141–80.

9. See Paul Langford, *Public Life and the Propertied Englishman*.

10. Pierre Bourdieu, *Distinction*, 77. See also Bryan S. Turner, *Status*, a monograph that combines the approaches of Weber and Marx toward issues of class stratification.

11. Campbell, *Romantic Ethic*, 159.

12. Habermas, *Structural Transformation of the Public Sphere*. See also Peter Uwe Hohendahl, *The Institution of Criticism*, 44–82, 242–80.

13. Wardle, 73. Goldsmith hoped Samuel Richardson would publish this tragedy (now lost) for him in 1756.

14. For many years, critics represented Oliver Goldsmith's plays and criticism as satiric reaction against a dominant mode of sentimental playwriting. Since Arthur Sherbo's *English Sentimental Drama*, however, this cliché has increasingly come under scrutiny from scholars who point out that sentimental comedy was in fact not dominant at all, but rather accounted for only a small percentage of the plays produced for the Georgian stage. The most voluminously documented of these attacks is an essay by Robert D. Hume centered on Goldsmith's "Comparison Between Laughing and Sentimental Comedy" (1773). Hume successfully challenges Goldsmith's representation of contemporary theater as a sentimental morass, and he correctly observes that "an uncritical acceptance of the terms of Goldsmith's essay" has helped perpetuate the myth about the role Goldsmith played in opposing that kind of comedy. See Hume, "Goldsmith and Sheridan," 313. More recently, George Haggerty rehearses Sherbo's argument in "Satire and Sentiment."

15. There were, of course, earlier controversies similar to the one that Goldsmith instigated: attacks on the immorality of the stage and defenses of

well as many others, are reprinted in the Garland Press series *Ste* (New York, 1974–76).

29. Quoted in Cash, *Later Years*, 37.

30. Ibid., 87.

31. This interpretation was largely derived from Diderot's "Eloge de Richardson," originally published in the *Journal Etranger* uary 1762. It is reprinted in Denis Diderot, *Œuvres Complètes*, 1 208.

32. Putney, "Evolution of *A Sentimental Journey*."

33. Stout, Introduction to *A Sentimental Journey*. See also Stout ick's *Sentimental Journey*," as well as Henri Fluchère, *Laurence Ster* James Aiken Work's widely used classroom edition of *Tristram Shan* a sentimental interpretation of Sterne's entire canon. Ernest Dilwort *Unsentimental Journey of Laurence Sterne*, John Stedmond, *The Co* *of Laurence Sterne*, and Melvyn New, *Laurence Sterne as Satirist*, see as satirizing the techniques of sentimental fiction.

Chapter 3

1. Goldsmith's known reviews for the *Monthly* and the *Critical* printed in Arthur Friedman, *Collected Works*, vol. 1. All references to smith's works are to Friedman's edition and are cited parenthetically text by volume and page number. He wrote many notices for the M Catalogues of both Reviews, but also began working out his understa of major literary issues and genres by doing feature reviews of such wo Home's tragedy, *Douglas*, Burke's *Enquiry into the Origin of Our Id the Sublime and the Beautiful*, Smollett's *Complete History of En* Marriott's *Female Conduct*, and Ward's *A System of Oratory*.

2. This image has been perpetuated by Goldsmith's biographer since. The major biographies, from James Prior, *The Life of Oliver smith* (1837), and John Forster, *The Life and Times of Oliver Gold* (1848), to what is still the standard today, Ralph M. Wardle, *Oliver smith*, seem unable to reconcile Goldsmith's social awkwardness and e tricity (so thoroughly documented in Boswell's *Life of Johnson*) with l riousness as a writer. They tend toward excessive rationalization of his v nesses, and their apologetic tone shifts the emphasis of their accounts from Goldsmith's writings. Samuel H. Woods, Jr., voices his concern a this tendency in "Boswell's Presentation of Goldsmith." Morris Gol "corrective" review essay, "Goldsmith's Reputation in His Day," also to balance the account.

3. Robert Hopkins describes the context of the *Enquiry* in *The Tru nius of Oliver Goldsmith*, 28–29. As Hopkins notes, the *Enquiry* has r

the right of comic dramatists to pursue humor "into the recesses of the mean," as Goldsmith put it. The laughing-sentimental debate bears a striking resemblance to the Steele-Dennis controversy of the early 1720s, with which Goldsmith would certainly have been familiar. Though the roles in this earlier controversy were reversed—Steele was trying to introduce a *new* moral comedy, Dennis opposed it—the theoretical strategies used by both sides approximate those of the laughing-sentimental debate.

16. The phrase is from the *Monthly* 24 (March 1761): 181. Although the *Critical* and the *Monthly* set the standard for reviewing in the 1750s, the important theater critics of the 1760s and 1770s were not confined to these prominent journals. Notices of plays in newspapers were largely a mixture of plot summary and gossip about actors, but monthly magazines such as *Town and Country*, *Gentleman's Magazine*, and *London Magazine* consistently offered sophisticated reviews. These magazines were aimed at a broader range of readers than the two major Reviews and were therefore more appropriate forums for the discussion of theater. Theater audiences, to be sure, contained book readers and Review readers, but on the whole they were far more heterogeneous groups and included many members (servants, for example) who were not candidates for the Reviews' tutelage. While the Reviews addressed the reader of sensibility, the magazines were almanacs that appealed to everyone curious about his or her society. They contained "essays and disputes," political poems, current news, births, deaths, and stock market information. All the same, the magazines did imitate the conventions of reviewing made standard by the *Monthly* and the *Critical*.

17. William Freeman, *Oliver Goldsmith*, 210; Wardle, *Oliver Goldsmith*, 182.

18. *The London Chronicle*, January 28–30, 1768, cited in John Forster, *Life and Times of Oliver Goldsmith*, 2: 98.

19. *Monthly Review* 38 (February 1768): 160; *Critical Review* 25 (February 1768): 148 (the phrase "into the recesses of the mean" is Goldsmith's [5: 13]); *London Magazine* 37 (February 1768): 60; *St. James's Chronicle* (January 30–February 2, 1768); *Gentleman's Magazine* 38 (February 1768): 78–82.

20. An early review of *She Stoops to Conquer* (*Morning Chronicle*, March 16, 1773) pointed out that Goldsmith's play was aided by Foote's recent puppet shows in the Haymarket, which satirized sentimentalism. Cited in Morris Golden, "Goldsmith's Reputation in His Day," 227.

21. *Theatrical Review* 1 (1763), iii.

22. *Critical Review* 30 (December 1770): 445. Cited in Claude E. Jones, "Dramatic Criticism in the *Critical Review*," 135. Jones does not give the name of the play.

23. *London Magazine* 37 (February 1768): 61.

24. My argument at this point is guided by Gerald Newman, *Rise of English Nationalism*, especially 87–158, in which the author describes a conception of nationalism that integrates political and literary developments. His thesis, in short, is that "nationalism is, at the outset, a creation of writers" (87).

25. *Monthly Review* 48 (March 1773): 309. The list is quite an odd mix: probably Cibber and certainly Steele do not belong in this grouping. The reviewer may be trying to excuse his praise for the first three by placing them in the company of Steele, and praising all five for their ability to represent the manners of their time.

26. Cited in *Poems and Plays of Oliver Goldsmith*, 313.

Chapter 4

1. Basker's *Tobias Smollett, Critic and Journalist* is, of course, a recent and welcome exception, although Claude E. Jones's *Smollett Studies* and Lewis Knapp's *Tobias Smollett: Doctor of Men and Manners* also emphasize Smollett's versatility as a writer. Perhaps more than that of any other eighteenth-century man of letters, Smollett's reputation suffered at the hands of scholars during the 1950s and 1960s who wished to account for the rise of the novel and to codify the eighteenth-century fictional canon. Smollett's place in that canon was a matter of debate: Alan Dugald McKillop, in *Early Masters of English Fiction*, included him (along with Defoe, Richardson, Fielding, and Sterne); Ian Watt's far more influential *The Rise of the Novel* did not. Those choices have to a large extent directed the critical history of Smollett's work, in that his supporters have chiefly sought to rehabilitate him as a writer of fiction. During the period from 1960 to 1985, although G. S. Rousseau consistently urged a broader perspective, all the book-length studies of Smollett presented him *as a novelist*. D. J. Bruce's important study, *Radical Doctor Smollett*, for example, does not even mention the *Critical*.

2. *Roderick Random* sold 6,500 copies from January 1748 through November 1749, a remarkable accomplishment considering Smollett's relative obscurity at the time of its publication. After *Peregrine Pickle*, Smollett's title pages bore the phrase "By the author of *Roderick Random*" (Knapp, 94–95).

3. Four editions of *Peregrine Pickle* appeared during Smollett's lifetime, the last in 1769; a second edition of *Ferdinand Count Fathom* was issued in November 1771, chiefly, it seems, to capitalize on the popularity of *Humphry Clinker*; *Launcelot Greaves* was reprinted only in Ireland.

4. Basker notes that Smollett allowed much more journalistic freedom to his reviewers than did Ralph Griffiths (*Smollett: Critic and Journalist*,

151). Nevertheless, his administrative power as editor could not but have been extensive.

5. *An Exemplary History of the Novel*, 71. Michael Rosenblum, in "Smollett as Conservative Satirist," 560–61, describes Smollett's first two heroes in exactly these terms: "In *Roderick Random* and *Peregrine Pickle* the hero is a young man petitioning for his proper place in society. . . . But the society in which Random and Pickle move neither recognizes nor rewards [traditional] criteria, and the order of the professions and social classes is subverted by the imposters who dominate them."

6. Christensen, *Practicing Enlightenment*, 21.

7. *Smollett*, 52–53.

8. Ibid., 106. Publication of a play before its production virtually indicated that the play had been rejected by both theaters. See Pope's "Epistle to Arbuthnot" (lines 55–65).

9. Roy Porter touches briefly on the relatively unformed state of the professions at midcentury in *English Society in the Eighteenth Century*.

10. "Territorial Disputes in the Republic of Letters," 17.

11. Samuel Johnson, *The Rambler*, no. 145, *Yale Edition*, 5: 10.

12. Zionkowski, 15.

13. *Letters of Tobias Smollett*, 13–14. Hereafter this collection will be referred to in the text as *Letters*.

14. In *The History of England*, Smollett appreciates Walpole's talents for political maneuvering (2: 464), but takes a decidedly critical view of the nepotistic character of his administration.

15. Observing that "institutions bestow sameness," Mary Douglas claims that in forming and defining an institution (or a profession, I would add) individuals are "constituting a machine for thinking and decision-making on their own behalf." *How Institutions Think*, 63.

16. See especially Knapp, 44–73.

17. *The Bee*, November 3, 1759, in *Collected Works*, 1: 449.

18. *English Literature in History, 1730–1780*, 181.

19. *Roderick Random*, 1. As I write this, the University of Georgia Press edition of Smollett's works has not yet been completed. I will refer to Smollett's writings in the text by page number, citing the editions listed in the Works Cited.

20. Barrell, 193.

21. Ibid., 183.

22. M. A. Goldberg, *Smollett and the Scottish School*, 68. Goldberg discusses the structure of *Peregrine Pickle* (68–75). See also Rufus Putney, "The Plan of *Peregrine Pickle*."

23. "'With Dignity and Importance,'" 158.

24. *Satire and the Novel*, 188. For an attempt to place *Fathom* in relation to other eighteenth-century fictional forms such as the sentimental novel and the novel of education, see Thomas R. Preston, "Disenchanting the Man of Feeling."

25. *Political Constructions*, 4.

26. Knapp, 126.

27. Ibid., 163–64.

28. The "Proposals" is reprinted in both Knapp, 171–72, and Basker, 31–32.

29. Basker cites the following: Thomas Sprat, *History of the Royal Society* (1667), ed. Jackson I. Cope and Harold Whitmore Jones (St. Louis: Washington University Press, 1958), 39–45; Samuel Johnson, "Life of Roscommon," *Lives of the English Poets*, ed. George Birkbeck Hill (Oxford: Clarendon Press, 1905), 1: 232–34; Matthew Prior, *Carmen Seculare for the Year 1700* (1701), stanza 34; Daniel Defoe, *An Essay upon Projects* (1697), 227–51; Joseph Addison, *The Spectator*, no. 135 (August 4, 1711); Jonathan Swift, *A Proposal for Correcting, Improving, and Ascertaining the English Tongue* (1712); Voltaire, *Lettres sur les Anglais* (1733), no. 24, translated in Smollett's *Works of Voltaire*, vol. 13 (1762), "On the Royal Society and Academies," 176–83.

30. Basker, 18.

31. "Smollett and the Society of Arts of London," 27. Rousseau cites, in particular, *Gulliver's Travels* and parts of *Essay on Man* as evidence of this disappointment.

32. Rousseau, 26–27.

33. Jones, *Smollett Studies*, 107–10; Basker, 279–83.

34. See James R. Foster, "Smollett's Pamphleteering Foe Shebbeare."

35. Mayo, 277.

36. Apparently, though, this was only a limited impunity. David Hume wrote in 1767 that Smollett was a bad candidate for a consulship in Nice, since it was certain that if he were to reappear there, "people would rise upon him and stone him in the streets." *New Letters of David Hume*, 173.

37. This tendency is constantly at odds with an equally powerful impulse to make concern for his well-being the dominant subject of the narrative (Smollett went to Europe chiefly for his health). See John F. Sena, "Smollett's Persona and the Melancholy Traveller."

38. *Monthly Review* 30 (January 1764): 42. See also 34 (December 1766): 420.

39. Louis Martz, *Later Career of Tobias Smollett*, 1.

40. *The Implied Reader*, 62–3.

41. Ibid., 63.

42. Ibid., 67.

43. John Sekora makes this point in *Luxury*, 243.

44. *Les Romans de Smollett*, 297.

45. For example, Robert Folkenflik, "Self and Society," 204.

Chapter 5

1. See Elaine Showalter, *A Literature of Their Own*, 47.

2. Q. D. Leavis, 120.

3. Smith, vi. Since there are as yet no standard editions of the works I discuss in this chapter, I have tried, as much as possible, to cite from readily available modern editions. When no modern edition is available, I have tried to cite from first editions.

4. Lennox, 3.

5. Fielding, *Adventures of David Simple* (1744), iii.

6. *Adventures of David Simple* (1987), 5. Oxford's decision to reproduce the second edition (corrected by Henry Fielding) is puzzling. Stranger still is Kelsall's decision not to reprint Sarah Fielding's original "advertisement to the reader."

7. *The Double Mistake*, no page numbers.

8. *School for Rakes*, v.

9. *The Times* (London, 1780). Griffith published the play under her own name, something she had not done in the case of *The Double Mistake* or *The School for Rakes*.

10. *Plays of Frances Sheridan*, 41.

11. See Ruth Bloch, "Untangling the Roots of Modern Sex Roles." The argument of Kathryn Shevelow's *Women and Print Culture* is also bound up with the theory that "increasingly throughout the eighteenth century, the interrelated categories of masculine and feminine, public and private, home and 'world,' assumed the shape of binary oppositions in which the meaning of one category was produced in terms of the other" (10). The texts that I examine here are transgressive in that they represent appeals by women authors to audiences of women, all in a completely public realm.

12. Doody, *Frances Burney*, 35–65.

13. Elaine Showalter makes this point in *A Literature of Their Own*, 53.

14. *Evelina*, 7. All further references are to this Oxford edition, which will be cited by page number in the text.

15. Two important book-length studies are Julia Epstein, *The Iron Pen*, 93–122, and Kristina Straub, *Divided Fictions*, which focuses primarily on *Evelina* and *Cecilia*. Gina Campbell, "How to Read like a Gentleman," is a fascinating account of reading in *Evelina* that takes as its starting point the same dedication that I examine here. Campbell does not see Burney as making so radical a break with earlier women authors as I argue. Instead, she

emphasizes about the dedication that "the extraordinary convolutions of her prose here testify to Burney's embarrassment at her own daring." Campbell goes on to argue persuasively that "Burney includes a model of reading within *Evelina* that resembles conduct literature in its emphasis on propriety and that is meant to serve Burney's literary ambitions by teaching critics how they *ought* to read her work" (557).

16. Doody, 68–70. For an account of Charles Burney's suppression of *The Witlings* and intrusions into the composition of *Cecilia*, see Doody, 95–98.

17. Ibid., 99.

18. See Doody and Peter Sabor's introduction to the World Classics edition of *Cecilia*, xi.

19. This introduction is published in the World Classics edition, 943–45.

Works Cited

Addison, Joseph. *The Spectator*. Ed. Donald F. Bond. Oxford: Clarendon Press, 1965.
———. *The Tatler*. Ed. Donald F. Bond. Oxford: Clarendon Press, 1987.
Althusser, Louis. *Lenin and Philosophy and Other Essays*. Trans. Ben Brewster. New York: Monthly Review Press, 1971.
Altick, Richard. *The English Common Reader: A Social History of the Mass Reading Public, 1800–1900*. Chicago: University of Chicago Press, 1957.
Appadurai, Arjun, ed. *The Social Life of Things: Commodities in Cultural Perspective*. New York: Cambridge University Press, 1986.
Armstrong, Nancy. *Desire and Domestic Fiction: A Political History of the Novel*. New York: Oxford University Press, 1987.
Backscheider, Paula. *Daniel Defoe: His Life*. Baltimore: Johns Hopkins University Press, 1989.
Barrell, John. *English Literature in History, 1730–1780: An Equal Wide Survey*. London: Hutchinson, 1983.
Bartolomeo, Joseph F. *A New Species of Criticism: Eighteenth-Century Discourse on the Novel*. Newark, Del.: University of Delaware Press, 1994.
Basker, James. *Tobias Smollett, Critic and Journalist*. Newark, Del.: University of Delaware Press, 1988.
Battestin, Martin. *Henry Fielding: A Life*. New York: Routledge, 1989.
———. *The Providence of Wit: Aspects of Form in Augustan Literature and the Arts*. New York: Oxford University Press, 1974.
Bender, John. "Prison Reform and the Sentence of Narration in *The Vicar of Wakefield*." In Laura Brown and Felicity Nussbaum, eds., *The New Eighteenth Century*, 168–88. New York: Methuen, 1987.

Bennett, Tony. "Texts in History: The Determination of Readings and Their Texts." *MMLA* 18 (1985): 1–16.

Bertelsen, Lance. *The Nonsense Club: Literature and Popular Culture, 1749–1764*. New York: Oxford University Press, 1986.

Bloch, Ruth. "Untangling the Roots of Modern Sex Roles: A Survey of Four Centuries of Change." *Signs* 4 (1978): 237–52.

Bloom, Edward A. "'Labors of the Learned': Neoclassical Book Reviewing Aims and Techniques." *Studies in Philology* 54 (1957): 537–63.

Boswell, James. *The Life of Samuel Johnson*. Ed. G. B. Hill, rev. L. F. Powell. 6 vols. Oxford: Clarendon Press, 1934–50.

Boucé, Paul-Gabriel. *Les Romans de Smollett*. Paris: Didier, 1971.

Bourdieu, Pierre. *Distinction: A Social Critique of the Judgment of Taste*. Trans. Richard Nice. Cambridge, Mass.: Harvard University Press, 1984.

Bradbury, Malcolm. "The Telling Life: Some Thoughts on Biography." In Eric Homberger and John Charmley, eds., *The Troubled Face of Biography*. New York: Macmillan, 1988.

Braudy, Leo. *The Frenzy of Renown: Fame and Its History*. London: Oxford University Press, 1986.

Brewer, John, Neil McKendrick, and J. H. Plumb. *The Birth of a Consumer Society: The Commercialization of Eighteenth-Century England*. Bloomington: Indiana University Press, 1982.

Briggs, Peter M. "Laurence Sterne and Literary Celebrity in 1760." In Paul Korshin, ed., *The Age of Johnson* 4, 251–80. New York: AMS Press, 1991.

Brown, JoAnne. "Professional Language: Words That Succeed." *Radical History Review* 34 (1986): 33–51.

Brown, Marshall. *Preromanticism*. Stanford, Calif.: Stanford University Press, 1991.

Bruce, D. J. *Radical Doctor Smollett*. London: Victor Gollancz, 1964.

Burney, Frances. *Cecilia*. New York: Oxford University Press, 1988.

———. *Evelina, or the History of a Young Lady's Entrance into the World*. New York: Oxford University Press, 1982.

Campbell, Colin. *The Romantic Ethic and the Spirit of Modern Consumerism*. New York: Basil Blackwell, 1987.

Campbell, Gina. "How to Read like a Gentleman: Burney's Instructions to Her Critics in *Evelina*." *ELH* 57 (1990): 557–84.

Carlson, C. Lennart. "Edward Cave's Club, and Its Project for a Literary Review." *Philological Quarterly* 17 (1938): 115–20.

———. *The First Magazine: A History of the "Gentleman's Magazine."* Providence: Brown University Press, 1938.

Carnochan, W. B. Review of Jerome Christensen, *Practicing Enlightenment*. *Modern Language Review* 84 (1989): 449–50.

Cash, Arthur. *Laurence Sterne: The Early and Middle Years*. London: Methuen, 1975.

————. *Laurence Sterne: The Later Years*. London: Methuen, 1986.

Charmley, John, and Eric Homberger, eds. *The Troubled Face of Biography*. New York: Macmillan, 1988.

Christensen, Jerome. *Practicing Enlightenment: Hume and the Formation of a Literary Career*. Madison: University of Wisconsin Press, 1987.

Churchill, Charles. *Poetical Works of Charles Churchill*. Ed. Douglas Grant. Oxford: Clarendon Press, 1956.

Collins, A. S. *Authorship in the Days of Doctor Johnson*. London: Robert Holden, 1927.

Cope, Kevin L. Review of Jerome Christensen, *Practicing Enlightenment*. In Paul Korshin, ed., *The Age of Johnson*, 2: 503–10. New York: AMS Press, 1989.

Corbett, Mary Jean. *Representing Femininity: Middle-Class Subjectivity in Victorian and Edwardian Women's Autobiographies*. New York: Oxford University Press, 1992.

Craddock, Joseph. *Literary and Miscellaneous Memoirs*. London: J. B. Nichols, 1828.

Crane, R. S., and F. B. Kaye. *A Census of British Newspapers and Periodicals, 1620–1800*. Chapel Hill: University of North Carolina Press, 1927.

Crawford, Robert. *Devolving English Literature*. Oxford: Clarendon Press, 1992.

Cross, Wilbur. *The Life and Times of Laurence Sterne*. New York: Russell and Russell, 1925.

————, ed. *The Works and Life of Laurence Sterne*. New York: J. F. Taylor, 1904.

deCerteau, Michel. *The Practice of Everyday Life*. Trans. Stephen Randall. Berkeley: University of California Press, 1984.

Derrida, Jacques. "The Law of Genre." Trans. Avital Ronell. *Glyph* 7 (1980): 202–29.

Diderot, Denis. *Œuvres Complètes*. Ed. Jean Varloot et al. Paris: Hermann, 1975–present.

Dilworth, Ernest. *The Unsentimental Journey of Laurence Sterne*. New York: King's Crown Press, 1948.

Doody, Margaret Ann. *Frances Burney: The Life in the Works*. New Brunswick, N.J.: Rutgers University Press, 1988.

Douglas, Mary. *How Institutions Think*. Syracuse, N.Y.: Syracuse University Press, 1986.

Eagleton, Terry. *The Function of Criticism from "The Spectator" to Post-Structuralism*. London: Verso, 1984.

Epstein, Julia. *The Iron Pen: Frances Burney and the Politics of Women's Writing*. Madison: University of Wisconsin Press, 1989.

Epstein, William H. *Recognizing Biography*. Philadelphia: University of Pennsylvania Press, 1987.

——, ed. *Contesting the Subject: Essays in the Postmodern Theory and Practice of Biography*. West Lafayette, Ind.: Purdue University Press, 1991.

Fielding, Henry. *The History of Tom Jones, A Foundling*. Middleton, Conn.: Wesleyan University Press, 1975.

Fielding, Sarah. *The Adventures of David Simple*. London: A. Millar, 1744.

——. *The Adventures of David Simple*. New York: Oxford University Press, 1987.

Fish, Stanley. *Doing What Comes Naturally: Change, Rhetoric, and the Practice of Theory in Critical and Legal Studies*. Durham, N.C.: Duke University Press, 1989.

Fitzgerald, Percy. *The Life of David Garrick*. London: Tinsley Brothers, 1868.

Fluchère, Henri. *Laurence Sterne: From Tristram to Yorick*. Trans. and abridged by Barbara Wray. New York: Oxford University Press, 1965.

Folkenflik, Robert. "Self and Society: Comic Union in *Humphry Clinker*." *Philological Quarterly* 53 (1974): 195–204.

Foote, Samuel. *The Plays of Samuel Foote*. Ed. Paula Backscheider and Douglas Howard. New York: Garland, 1983.

Forster, Antonia. *Index to Book Reviews in England 1749–1774*. Carbondale: Southern Illinois University Press, 1991.

Forster, John. *The Life and Times of Oliver Goldsmith*. London: Ward, Lock, 1848.

Foster, James R. "Smollett's Pamphleteering Foe Shebbeare." *PMLA* 57 (1942): 1053–1100.

Freeman, William. *Oliver Goldsmith*. London: Herbert and Jenkins, 1951.

Freidson, Eliot. *Professional Powers*. Chicago: University of Chicago Press, 1986.

Galloway, W. F. "The Conservative Opposition Toward Fiction." *PMLA* 55 (1940): 1041–59.

Gipson, Laurence Henry. *The Triumphant Empire: The British Empire Before the American Revolution*. New York: Alfred A. Knopf, 1954.

Goldberg, M. A. *Smollett and the Scottish School*. Albuquerque: University of New Mexico Press, 1959.

Golden, Morris. "Goldsmith's Reputation in His Day." *Papers on Language and Literature* 16 (1980): 213–38.

Goldsmith, Oliver. *Collected Works of Oliver Goldsmith*. Ed. Arthur Friedman. 5 vols. Oxford: Clarendon Press, 1966.

——. *The Poems and Plays of Oliver Goldsmith*. Ed. Austin Dobson. London: Everyman, 1926.

Graham, Walter. *The Beginnings of English Literary Periodicals*. New York: Oxford University Press, 1926.

———. *Early English Periodicals*. New York: T. Nelson, 1930.

Gray, Thomas. *The Works of Thomas Gray*. Ed. Edmund Gosse. New York: Macmillan, 1884. Reprinted, New York: AMS Press, 1968.

Griffin, Dustin. "Johnson's *Lives of the Poets* and the Patronage System." In Paul Korshin, ed., *The Age of Johnson*, 5: 1–34. New York: AMS Press, 1991.

———. "Swift and Patronage." *Studies in Eighteenth-Century Culture* 31 (1991): 197–205.

Griffith, Elizabeth. *The Double Mistake*. London: Allman, Lowndes, Blendon, and Williams, 1766.

———. *The School for Rakes*. London: T. Beckett and P. A. DeHoudt, 1769.

———. *The Times*. London, 1780.

Grivel, Charles. "The Society of Texts: A Meditation on Media in 13 Points." Trans. Michael Jurich. *Sociocriticism* 1 (1985): 153–78.

Gross, John. *The Rise and Fall of the Man of Letters*. New York: Macmillan, 1969.

Habermas, Jürgen. *The Structural Transformation of the Public Sphere*. Trans. Thomas Burger. Cambridge, Mass.: MIT Press, 1989.

Hafter, Ronald. "Garrick and *Tristram Shandy*." *Studies in English Literature* 7 (1967): 475–89.

Haggerty, George. "Satire and Sentiment in *The Vicar of Wakefield*." *The Eighteenth Century: Theory and Interpretation* 32 (1991): 25–38.

Helgerson, Richard. *Self-Crowned Laureates: Spenser, Jonson, Milton, and the Literary System*. Berkeley: University of California Press, 1983.

Hilles, Frederick W., ed. *Portraits by Sir Joshua Reynolds*. New York: McGraw-Hill, 1952.

Hohendahl, Peter Uwe. *The Institution of Criticism*. Ithaca, N.Y.: Cornell University Press, 1982.

Holmes, Geoffrey. *Augustan England: Professions, State and Society, 1680–1730*. London: George Allen & Unwin, 1982.

Holtz, William V. *Image and Immortality*. Providence: Brown University Press, 1970.

Hopkins, Robert. *The True Genius of Oliver Goldsmith*. Baltimore: Johns Hopkins University Press, 1969.

Howes, Alan B. "Laurence Sterne, Rabelais, and Cervantes: The Two Kinds of Laughter in *Tristram Shandy*." In Valerie Grosvenor Myer, ed., *Laurence Sterne: Riddles and Myths*, 39–56. Totowa, N.J.: Barnes and Noble, 1984.

———, ed. *Laurence Sterne: The Critical Heritage*. London: Routledge & Kegan Paul, 1974.

Hume, David. *New Letters of David Hume*. Ed. Raymond Klibansky and Ernest Mossner. London: Oxford University Press, 1954.

———. "Of the Standard of Taste." In Eugene F. Miller, ed., *Essays Moral, Political, and Literary*, 226–48. Indianapolis: Liberty Classics, 1985.

Hume, Robert D. *The Rakish Stage: Studies in English Drama, 1660–1800*. Carbondale: Southern Illinois University Press, 1983.

Hunter, J. Paul. *Before Novels: The Cultural Contexts of Eighteenth-Century Fiction*. New York: W. W. Norton, 1990.

Iser, Wolfgang. *The Implied Reader*. Baltimore: Johns Hopkins University Press, 1974.

Johnson, Samuel. *Dictionary of the English Language*. New York: AMS Reprint, 1967 [1755].

———. *The Rambler*. In *The Yale Edition of the Works of Samuel Johnson*, No. 145. New Haven, Conn.: Yale University Press, 1958.

Jones, Claude E. "Dramatic Criticism in the *Critical Review*, 1756–1785." *Modern Language Quarterly* 20 (1959): 18–28, 118–44.

———. "The English Novel: A *Critical* View, 1756–1785." *Modern Language Quarterly* 9 (1948): 17–36.

———. *Smollett Studies*. Berkeley: University of California Press, 1942.

Kay, Carol. *Political Constructions: Defoe, Richardson, and Sterne in Relation to Hobbes, Hume, and Burke*. Ithaca, N.Y.: Cornell University Press, 1988.

Keeble, N. H. *The Literary Culture of Nonconformity in Later Seventeenth-Century England*. Leicester: Leicester University Press, 1987.

Kelly, Lionel, ed. *Tobias Smollett: The Critical Heritage*. New York: Routledge & Kegan Paul, 1987.

Kendall, Alan. *David Garrick*. New York: St. Martin's Press, 1985.

Kernan, Alvin P. *Printing Technology, Letters and Samuel Johnson*. Princeton, N.J.: Princeton University Press, 1987.

Ketcham, Michael. *Transparent Designs: Reading, Performance, and Form in the Spectator Papers*. Athens: University of Georgia Press, 1985.

Knapp, Lewis. *Tobias Smollett: Doctor of Men and Manners*. Princeton, N.J.: Princeton University Press, 1949.

Korshin, Paul. "Types of Eighteenth-Century Literary Patronage." *Eighteenth-Century Studies* 7 (1973–74): 453–73.

Lackington, James. *Memoirs of the Forty-Five First Years of the Life of James Lackington*. 13th ed. London, 1810.

Lamb, Jonathan. *Sterne's Fiction and the Double Principle*. Cambridge: Cambridge University Press, 1989.

Langford, Paul. *Public Life and the Propertied Englishman, 1689–1798*. Oxford: Clarendon Press, 1991.

Lanham, Richard. *"Tristram Shandy" and the Games of Pleasure*. Berkeley: University of California Press, 1973.

Larson, Magali Sarfatti. *The Rise of Professionalism: A Sociological Analysis*. Berkeley: University of California Press, 1977.

Leavis, Q. D. *Fiction and the Reading Public*. London: Chatto and Windus, 1932.

Lennox, Charlotte. *The Female Quixote, or the Adventures of Arabella*. London: Oxford University Press, 1970.

Lindenbaum, Peter. "John Milton and the Republican Mode of Literary Production." *Yearbook of English Studies* 21 (1989): 121–36.

Lockwood, Thomas. *Post-Augustan Satire: Charles Churchill and Satirical Poetry, 1750–1800*. Seattle: University of Washington Press, 1979.

Lovell, Terry. *Consuming Fiction*. London: Verso, 1987.

Mack, Maynard. *Alexander Pope: A Life*. New York: W. W. Norton, 1986.

Mannheim, Karl. *Man and Society*. Trans. E. A. Shills. New York: Harcourt, Brace, 1940.

Marchand, Leslie, ed. *Byron's Letters and Journals*. Cambridge, Mass.: Bellknap Press, 1974.

Marotti, Arthur. *John Donne, Coterie Poet*. Madison: University of Wisconsin Press, 1987.

Martz, Louis. *The Later Career of Tobias Smollett*. New Haven, Conn.: Yale University Press, 1942.

Maxted, Ian. *The London Book Trade*. Kent: Dawson, Folkenstone, 1977.

Mayo, Robert D. *The English Novel in the Magazines, 1740–1815*. London: Oxford University Press, 1962.

McFarland, Thomas. *Originality and Imagination*. Baltimore: Johns Hopkins University Press, 1985.

McKillop, Alan Dugald. *Early Masters of English Fiction*. Lawrence: University of Kansas Press, 1956.

Miller, Henry Knight. "The 'Whig' Interpretation of Literary History." *Eighteenth-Century Studies* 6 (1972–73): 60–84.

Mitchell, C. J. "The Spread and Fluctuation of Eighteenth-Century Printing." *Studies on Voltaire and the Eighteenth Century* 230 (1985): 305–21.

Moglen, Helen. *The Philosophical Irony of Laurence Sterne*. Gainesville: University of Florida Press, 1975.

Moore, Wilbert E. *The Professions: Roles and Rules*. New York: Russell Sage Foundation, 1970.

Nadel, Ira Bruce. *Biography: Fiction, Fact and Form*. New York: St. Martin's Press, 1984.

Nangle, B. C. *The "Monthly Review," First Series, 1749–1789: Indexes of Contributors and Articles.* Oxford: Clarendon Press, 1934.

New, Melvyn. *Laurence Sterne as Satirist: A Reading of "Tristram Shandy."* Gainesville: University of Florida Press, 1969.

———. *New Casebooks: The Life and Opinions of Tristram Shandy, Gentleman.* New York: St. Martin's Press, 1992.

Newman, Gerald. *The Rise of English Nationalism: A Cultural History.* New York: St. Martin's Press, 1987.

Nicoll, Allardyce. *The Garrick Stage.* Manchester: Manchester University Press, 1980.

O'Day, Rosemary. *The English Clergy: The Emergence and Consolidation of a Profession.* Leicester: Leicester University Press, 1979.

Park, William. "Change in the Criticism of the Novel after 1760." *Philological Quarterly* 46 (1967): 34–41.

Parsons, Talcott. *Essays in Sociological Theory.* New York: Free Press, 1954.

Paulson, Ronald. *Satire and the Novel in Eighteenth-Century England.* New Haven, Conn.: Yale University Press, 1967.

Peters, Julie Stone. *Congreve, the Drama, and the Printed Word.* Stanford, Calif.: Stanford University Press, 1990.

Pope, Alexander. *The Poems of Alexander Pope.* Ed. John Butt. New Haven, Conn.: Yale University Press, 1963.

Porter, Roy. *English Society in the Eighteenth Century.* New York: Penguin, 1982.

Pottle, Frederick A., ed. *Boswell's London Journal, 1762–1763.* New York: McGraw-Hill, 1950.

Preston, Thomas, "Disenchanting the Man of Feeling: Smollett's *Ferdinand Count Fathom.*" In Larry S. Chapman, ed., *Quick Springs of Sense: Studies in the Eighteenth Century,* 223–39. Athens: University of Georgia Press, 1974.

Pruett, John H. "Career Patterns Among the Clergy of Lincoln Cathedral, 1660–1750." *Church History* 44 (1975): 205–16.

Putney, Rufus. "The Evolution of *A Sentimental Journey.*" *Philological Quarterly* 19 (1940): 349–69.

———. "The Plan of Peregrine Pickle." *PMLA* 60 (1945): 1051–65.

Quintana, Ricardo. *Oliver Goldsmith: A Georgian Study.* New York: Macmillan, 1967.

Ralph, James. *The Case of Authors by Trade or Profession.* Reprint, ed. Philip Stevick. Gainesville, Fla.: Scholars' Facsimiles and Reprints, 1966 [1758].

Reed, Walter. *An Exemplary History of the Novel: The Quixotic Versus the Picaresque.* Chicago: University of Chicago Press, 1981.

Richetti, John. Review of Jerome Christensen, *Practicing Enlightenment.* *Eighteenth-Century Studies* 21 (1988): 400–405.

Roper, Derek. "Smollett's 'Four Gentlemen': The First Contributors to the *Critical Review.*" *Review of English Studies.* n.s. 10 (1959): 38–44.

———. *Reviewing Before the Edinburgh: 1788–1802.* Newark, Del.: University of Delaware Press, 1978.

Rosenblum, Michael. "Smollett as Conservative Satirist." *ELH* 42 (1975): 556–79.

Ross, Ian Campbell, "'With Dignity and Importance': Peregrine Pickle as Country Gentleman." In Alan Bold, ed., *Smollett: Author of the First Distinction,* 148–69. London: Vision Press, 1982.

Rousseau, G. S. *Tobias Smollett: Essays of Two Decades.* Edinburgh: T. & T. Clark, 1982.

Sartre, Jean-Paul. *What Is Literature?* Trans. Bernard Frichtman. New York: Harper & Row, 1949.

Sekora, John. *Luxury: The Concept in Western Thought, Eden to Smollett.* Baltimore: Johns Hopkins University Press, 1977.

Sena, John. "Smollett's Persona and the Unfortunate Traveller." *Eighteenth-Century Studies* 1 (1968): 353–69.

Sennett, Richard. *The Fall of Public Man.* New York: Alfred A. Knopf, 1977.

Sherbo, Arthur. *English Sentimental Drama.* East Lansing: Michigan State University Press, 1957.

Sheridan, Frances. *The Plays of Frances Sheridan.* Ed. Robert Hogan and Jerry C. Beasley. Newark, Del.: University of Delaware Press, 1984.

Shevelow, Kathryn. *Women and Print Culture: The Construction of Femininity in the Early Periodical.* New York: Routledge & Kegan Paul, 1989.

Showalter, Elaine. *A Literature of Their Own: British Women Novelists from Brontë to Lessing.* Princeton, N.J.: Princeton University Press, 1977.

Simpson, Louis P., ed. *The Federalist Literary Mind.* Baton Rouge: Louisiana State University Press, 1962.

Smith, Charlotte. *The Romance of Real Life.* London: T. Cadell, 1787.

Smollett, Tobias. *The Adventures of Ferdinand Count Fathom.* Athens: University of Georgia Press, 1988.

———. *The Adventures of Launcelot Greaves.* New York: Oxford University Press, 1973.

———. *The Adventures of Peregrine Pickle.* New York: Oxford University Press, 1964.

———. *The Adventures of Roderick Random.* New York: Oxford University Press, 1979.

———. *The Expedition of Humphry Clinker*. Athens: University of Georgia Press, 1990.

———. *The History of England, From the Revolution to the Death of George the Second*. London, 1757–58. Reprinted, London, C. Baldwin, 1800.

———. *The Letters of Tobias Smollett*. Ed. Lewis Knapp. Oxford: Clarendon Press, 1970.

———. *Travels Through France and Italy*. New York: Oxford University Press, 1979.

Spector, Robert D. *English Literary Periodicals and the Climate of Opinion During the Seven Years War*. The Hague: Mouton, 1966.

Spooner, Brian. "Weavers and Dealers: The Authenticity of an Oriental Carpet." In Arjun Appadurai, ed., *The Social Life of Things: Commodities in Cultural Perspective*, 195–235. Cambridge: Cambridge University Press, 1986.

Stedmond, John. *The Comic Art of Laurence Sterne*. Toronto: University of Toronto Press, 1967.

Sterne, Laurence. *Letters of Laurence Sterne*. Ed. Lewis P. Curtis. London: Oxford University Press, 1955.

———. *The Life and Opinions of Tristram Shandy, Gentleman*. Ed. Melvyn New and Joan New. 2 vols. Gainesville: University of Florida Press, 1978.

———. *A Sentimental Journey Through France and Italy*. Ed. Gardner D. Stout, Jr. Berkeley: University of California Press, 1967.

Stone, George Winchester, and George Kahrl. *David Garrick: A Critical Biography*. Carbondale: Southern Illinois University Press, 1979.

Stout, Gardner D., Jr. "Yorick's *Sentimental Journey*: A Comic 'Pilgrim's Progress' for the Man of Feeling." *ELH* 30 (1963): 395–412.

Straub, Kristina. *Divided Fictions: Fanny Burney and Feminine Strategy*. Lexington: University of Kentucky Press, 1987.

———. *Sexual Suspects: Eighteenth-Century Players and Sexual Ideology*. Princeton, N.J.: Princeton University Press, 1992.

Sullivan, Alvin, ed. *British Literary Magazines*. Westport, Conn.: Greenwood Press, 1983.

Sutherland, James. *Defoe*. Philadelphia: J. P. Lippincott, 1938.

Swearingen, James. *"Tristram Shandy": An Essay in Phenomenological Criticism*. New Haven, Conn.: Yale University Press, 1977.

Sykes, Norman. *Church and State in England in the Eighteenth Century*. London: Cambridge University Press, 1934.

Taylor, George. "'The Just Delineation of the Passions': Theories of Acting in the Age of Garrick." In Kenneth Richards and Peter Thomson, eds., *Essays on the Eighteenth-Century Stage*, 51–72. London: Methuen, 1972.

Taylor, John Tinnon. *Early Opposition to the English Novel: The Popular Reaction from 1760 to 1830.* New York: King's Crown Press, 1943.

Taylor, Richard C. *Goldsmith as Journalist.* Rutherford, N.J.: Fairleigh Dickinson University Press, 1993.

Traugott, John. *Tristram Shandy's World: Sterne's Philosophical Rhetoric.* Berkeley: University of California Press, 1954.

Turner, Bryan S. *Status.* Minneapolis: University of Minnesota Press, 1988.

Underwood, T. *A Word to the Wise. A Poetical Farce, Most Respectfully Addressed to the Critical Reviewers.* London: G. Scott, 1770.

Wardle, Ralph. *Oliver Goldsmith.* Lawrence: University of Kansas Press, 1957.

Warner, Michael. *The Letters of the Republic: Publication and the Public Sphere in Eighteenth-Century America.* Cambridge, Mass.: Harvard University Press, 1990.

Watt, Ian. *The Rise of the Novel.* Berkeley: University of California Press, 1957.

Weber, Samuel. *Institution and Interpretation.* Minneapolis: University of Minnesota Press, 1986.

Wellek, René, and Austin Warren. *Theory of Literature.* New York: Harcourt, Brace, 1949.

West, Shearer. *The Image of the Actor: Verbal and Visual Representation in the Age of Garrick and Kemble.* London: Pinter, 1991.

White, Hayden. *Tropics of Discourse: Essays in Cultural Criticism.* Baltimore: Johns Hopkins University Press, 1978.

Wilensky, Harold. "Work, Careers, and Social Integration." *International Social Science Journal* 12 (1960): 551–68.

Williams, Raymond. *Keywords: A Vocabulary of Culture and Society.* London: Fontana/Croom Helm, 1976.

Winn, James. *John Dryden and His World.* New Haven, Conn.: Yale University Press, 1987.

Womersley, David. Review of Jerome Christensen, *Practicing Enlightenment. Review of English Studies* 39 (1988): 449–50.

Woods, Leigh. *Garrick Claims the Stage: Action as Social Emblem.* Westport, Conn.: Greenwood Press, 1984.

Woods, Samuel, Jr. "Boswell's Presentation of Goldsmith: A Reconsideration." In John A. Vance, ed., *Boswell's "Life of Johnson": New Questions, New Answers,* 228–47. Athens: University of Georgia Press, 1985.

Zionkowski, Linda. "Territorial Disputes in the Republic of Letters: Canon Formation and the Literary Profession." *The Eighteenth Century: Theory and Interpretation* 31 (1990): 3–22.

Index

In this index "f" after a number indicates a separate reference on the next page, and "ff" indicates separate references on the next two pages. A continuous discussion over two or more pages is indicated by a span of numbers. *Passim* is used for a cluster of references in close but not consecutive sequence.

Library of Congress Cataloging-in-Publication Data

Donoghue, Frank
    The fame machine : book reviewing and eighteenth-century literary
careers / Frank Donoghue.
        p.   cm.
    Includes bibliographical references and index.
    ISBN 0-8047-2563-2 (cloth : alk. paper)
        1. English literature—18th century—History and criticism—
Theory, etc.   2. Book reviewing—Great Britain—History—18th
century.   3. Sterne, Laurence, 1713–1768—Criticism and
interpretation—History—18th century.   4. Goldsmith, Oliver,
1730?–1774—Criticism and interpretation—History—18th century.
5. Smollett, Tobias George, 1721–1771—Criticism and interpretation—
History—18th century.   6. Women and literature—Great Britain—
History—18th century.   7. Criticism—Great Britain—History—18th
century.   8. Authorship—History—18th century.   9. Fame—
History—18th century.   10. Canon (Literature).   I. Title.
PR448.B67D66   1996
820.9'005—dc20   95-22803
                                                                      CIP

⊗ This book is printed on acid-free, recycled paper.

Original printing 1996
Last figure below indicates year of this printing:
05   04   03   02   01   00   99   98   97   96